Family Therapy
with
Suicidal Adolescents

Family Therapy

with

Suicidal Adolescents

Anthony P. Jurich

Routledge
Taylor & Francis Group
New York   London

Routledge
Taylor & Francis Group
270 Madison Avenue
New York, NY 10016

Routledge
Taylor & Francis Group
2 Park Square
Milton Park, Abingdon
Oxon OX14 4RN

© 2008 by Taylor & Francis Group, LLC
Routledge is an imprint of Taylor & Francis Group, an Informa business

Printed in the United States of America on acid-free paper
10 9 8 7 6 5 4 3 2 1

International Standard Book Number-13: 978-0-415-96086-1 (Hardcover)

Library of Congress Cataloging-in-Publication Data

Jurich, Anthony P.
    Family therapy with suicidal adolescents / Anthony P. Jurich.
      p. ; cm.
  ISBN-13: 978-0-415-96086-1 (alk. paper)
  ISBN-10: 0-415-96086-X (alk. paper)
   1. Teenagers--Suicidal behavior--Treatment. 2. Adolescent psychotherapy. 3. Family psychotherapy. I. Title.
   [DNLM: 1. Suicide. 2. Adolescent. 3. Family Therapy--methods. WM 165 J95f 2007]

RJ506.S9J87 2007
616.89'140835--dc22
                                                 2007007152

Visit the Taylor & Francis Web site at
http://www.taylorandfrancis.com

and the Routledge Web site at
http://www.routledge.com

To Olivia. You are my strength in the hard times and my joy in the good times.

CONTENTS

FOREWORD

Working with suicidal adolescents is the bane of most therapists. Not only are therapists highly intimidated by these unpredictable and difficult to read challenging youth but mental health professionals often try and avoid having to work with them at all costs. The thought of the big liability issues and potential malpractice suits, and possibly having to field crisis calls late at night or during the wee hours of the early morning, instill fear in the minds of most therapists. However, there is one highly seasoned and compassionate therapist that dares to enter and has worked therapeutic wonders in the unpredictable world of suicidal adolescents and their families, and his name is Anthony P. Jurich. After many years of encouragement and nudging to put in print his clinical wisdom and artistry, Jurich has provided the mental health and family therapy fields with a gift, *Family Therapy with Suicidal Adolescents*.

To my knowledge, *Family Therapy with Suicidal Adolescents* is the first family therapy handbook devoted entirely to the family treatment of suicidal adolescents. Jurich provides us with a comprehensive grand tour of the research on suicidal adolescents, including his cutting edge and scholarly clinical research. In a clear and practitioner-friendly way, he presents in this well-written book his advanced strategic family therapy approach that targets interventions at the adolescent, family, peer group, and larger systems levels. His book is filled with challenging case examples which nicely illustrate his therapeutic approach in action, some of which read like on the edge of your seat suspense mysteries. What comes out the most from reading Jurich's case examples, is his high level of compassion, empathy, and commitment that he provides to these troubled youth and their overwhelmed parents. Jurich shows us that therapeutic flexibility, humor, being able to thrive in chaos, how not to get therapeutically paralyzed by adolescents' self-destructive tendencies, and improvise at any given moment is a must in working with these adolescents and their families. Finally, Jurich clearly drives home the message that despite the intimidating nature of adolescents' suicidal thoughts or previous attempts to take their lives, we as clinicians need to not lose sight of and utilize their multitude of strengths and resources to empower and co-create with them and their families more preferred workable realities.

Matthew D. Selekman, MSW

PREFACE

As he stood at the threshold of the fulfillment of his quest, from the depths below there arose a beast, terrible to behold, who blocked his path and threatened his life. He drew his sword from his belt and prepared to commence battle. The stakes were life or death.

Although the above paragraph is not connected to any specific story or legend, the scene is familiar to anyone who has read a classic heroic tale. From *The Odyssey* to the *Lord of the Rings* to *Star Wars* to *Spider-man*, the hero has had to overcome some beast to accomplish his or her quest. The battle is epic in proportion and the price of failure is death. This is not only a tale which appears in books and movies but is also a story which gets acted out daily by suicidal adolescents. The beast is not external, although there are external manifestations of its presence in the form of abusive parents or harshly critical peers. The beast is internal to the adolescent. It is all of the monsters and demons that can be summoned by the heart and mind to well up inside of the child journeying through the adolescent years.

Therapy with suicidal adolescents embodies that epic struggle with the beast within. The epic hero may face the beast alone in battle. However, he or she most often has the help of the gods or the magic of some special weapon. The therapist is one of the gods from whom he or she seeks help. I would pose that family therapy enlists the aid of other gods who are powerful in the adolescent's life—his or her family. As good as the therapist may be in helping the young hero with his or her fight against the beast, the therapist cannot duplicate the power of the family, summoned to assist and validate the hero who is their child or sibling. The therapist may call up the family to help in this struggle but their validation is theirs to withhold or bestow. Family therapy asks for their help in a way that individual therapy cannot do. It not only asks for the family to help but it also asks the family to journey along the therapeutic path with the adolescent.

In order to battle the beast within, the therapist must employ weapons with special powers. There are many weapons available to the therapist, as there are many methods of therapy that the therapist may employ. This book describes the use of one of these weapons, a blend of insight-oriented, behavioral, and strategic family therapy that I have developed over thirty-four years of doing therapy with suicidal adolescents. It is not put forth to replace other forms of therapy but rather to augment the therapist's own therapeutic style.

In the first chapter I try to explore why suicide is such a Pandora's Box for therapists. I try to analyze how it derails therapy and generates uncomfortable feelings in the therapist, such as helplessness and inadequacy.

Chapter 2 addresses the scope of the problem of adolescent suicide. It also explores an integrated model of how suicidal etiology develops.

Chapter 3 describes the nature of adolescent suicide. It tries to address the question of why adolescents are so vulnerable to the temptations of suicide.

In Chapter 4 the factors which create suicidal ideation and actions in adolescents are explored. The research into these factors is reviewed and presented in order to give the reader a background in both adolescent development and the causes of adolescent suicide. I believe that this foundation in adolescent development is crucial to understanding the nature of suicidal ideation and behavior from the adolescent's perspective. It is from this knowledge base that the therapist will draw the content of many of the interventions which will be explored later in the book. This knowledge base will also allow the therapist to pinpoint interventions so that therapy will be most efficient in its delivery.

Chapter 5 describes the integrated framework for intervention with suicidal adolescents. It describes the origins of my form of strategic therapy. It outlines the integration of insight-oriented behaviors and strategic therapies into a unified style of therapy.

Chapter 6 explores the issues surrounding crisis intervention. I feel that this is important for two reasons: (1) the therapist may have to shift gears from "therapeutic modality" to "crisis modality" if the adolescent becomes actively suicidal, and (2) exploring the "worst case scenario" of crisis intervention will help the therapist ask of each intervention employed, "Does it take me closer to or further away from the suicidal crisis point?"

Chapter 7 discusses the rationale for using family therapy as the treatment of choice. The critical importance of joining with a suicidal adolescent and his or her family is discussed. Patterns for joining are explored.

Chapter 8 focuses on the analysis of the adolescent and his or her family through the lens of strategic therapy. Methods of identifying and analyzing maladaptive recursive cycles are elaborated. An overview of testing, diagnosis, and medication is presented.

Chapter 9 reviews cognitive interventions. Presenting insight-oriented interventions in conjunction with changing cognitive distortions are explored.

Chapter 10 explores behavioral interventions. Safety plans are outlined and behavioral contracting is outlined.

Chapter 11 addresses strategic interventions. Strategic techniques are specifically designed to address suicidal adolescents and their families. Extensive examples are provided to see how the theory of intervention is applied to specific situations.

This mode of therapy will not be able to address all of the problems of every suicidal adolescent. No therapeutic motif can accomplish that. Some therapists might be able to use the therapeutic style described here with little alteration. Others may choose specific aspects of this model to augment or supplement their own style of therapy.

In fighting the beast within, it is helpful to wield a magic sword. This method has worked well for me throughout my career. It has served as my magic sword throughout many years. It has slain dragons and chased away demons. It is my hope that it will be useful to you, the reader, in your quest to tame the beast within.

ACKNOWLEDGMENTS

There are several people I would like to acknowledge for greatly contributing to the preparation of this work. Matthew Selekman asked me, "Why don't you write a book on family therapy with suicidal adolescents?" He then proceeded to encourage me and facilitate that process as only a true friend could do. Simply put, without you, this book would not exist.

I would like to thank Lindsay Shepard, Amie Goldman, and Jane Bieber for their assistance in the preparation of this manuscript. Putting up with my handwriting deserves a purple heart.

I would like to thank my wife, Olivia, for her support and her patience during the writing of this book. You are my cornerstone.

My colleagues, students, and my mother-in-law, Georgie Layne Potter, all sacrificed time with me so that I could work on this book. Thank you for your understanding and support.

Thanks to Charlie and Claire, our cats, who kept me company in the middle of the night when I wrote.

A special thank you is also given to the adolescents who were, are, and will be my clients. You teach me more than you will ever know.

Finally, I would like to thank Kurt Cobain. Although I never met him, he has been my muse throughout the writing of this book. His life and death by his own hand kept me focused as I wrote. I have a portrait of Kurt Cobain, which was always with me when I wrote. I looked at it often to remind me of why this work is so important. You will live on through your music. It is my hope that you will not have died in vain but that your death will help to prevent other young people from choosing death over life.

One

INTRODUCTION
The Journey Begins

There we sit on the deck; my wife Olivia, our cat Munchie, and I, sipping lemonade and solving the problems of the world. It is a great conversation with our cat who is making profound pronunciations about the human condition. It is the kind of dream that is both whimsical and satisfying for the dreamer. It is the kind of dream which only comes to the dreamer in a deep, restful sleep at 2:00 in the morning. This flight of fancy is interrupted by a ringing sound. I hit the alarm clock in order to block out the intrusion but the ring continues. With half open eyes, I look at the table beside the bed and realize that it is not the clock, but the phone that is invading my idyllic fantasy. As I prop up on one elbow, I pick up the receiver and think to myself, "This better be important or I'm going to blow a gasket at the caller." I clear the fog from my vocal chords and force a "Hello?" into the phone.

From the other end of the line there is a moment of silence and then a timid, small voice asks, "Dr. J.? This is Mary." Recognition floods into my growing awareness that this is one of my adolescent clients, calling me at 2:15 in the morning. My mind races and focuses upon the fact that Mary is not the type of client to over-exaggerate a problem or "cry wolf" to get attention. Mary is a serious, sometimes too serious, 16-year-old whose presenting problem is depression. This wave of information has splashed me in the face to wake me from my slumber. She softly speaks into the phone the words, "My life sucks. It would be easier to end it." Now a rush of adrenaline pushes my heart into my throat and reflexively causes me to sit bolt upright. Fighting back the staccato fire of neurons, I reply, "Mary, we need to talk. Where are you?"

This is the moment most feared by a therapist, even the ones who have supreme confidence in their therapeutic abilities. Life and death at 2 a.m. and the responsibility is on my shoulders!

SUICIDE: THE PANDORA'S BOX OF THERAPY

In my more than 30 years of professional practice as I visit and consult with other therapists, therapists-in-training, and teachers of therapy, I have found few things to disturb therapists more than suicidal clients. Regardless of the discipline—psychiatry, psychology, clinical social work, counseling, pastoral counseling, or marriage and family therapy, the mention of the word "suicide" changes the basic nature of therapy immediately (Jurich, 2001). Instead of promoting "growth" and fostering "change" in our client or clients, we feel the need to immediately refocus therapy to insure the survival of the client. The presenting problem of the client's quality of life has been superceded by continuance of the client's existence, regardless of the quality of life. The journey of problem solving has been replaced by an existential crisis.

As therapists, we are used to dealing with crisis and disruptions in therapy. Why is suicide so stress inducing? There are some obvious answers to this question. When a client talks about suicide, his or her life is on the line. Therefore, the consequences of our therapy may literally be life or death. Any word or action might be the factor to tip the balance towards the client's life or death. A very experienced psychologist shared these thoughts with me:

> I am a fairly cheerful guy most of the time. In fact, I believe that I am quite skilled at helping my clients see the silver lining in every cloud. I've taken depressed clients in therapy to the point that they can smile and even laugh before the therapy hour is over. But a suicidal client undoes me. I keep worrying that, if I smile or laugh in our session, the client will take that to mean that I am laughing at him (or her) and belittling the problem. I'm afraid that this will push him (or her) further toward suicide, and it will be my fault.

This therapist exemplifies several problems with dealing with a suicidal client.

DERAILING THERAPY

A client who cries "suicide" throws us out of our normal path of therapy. We begin to feel so self-conscious that we feel we cannot be ourselves in therapy. A therapist who cannot be himself or herself in therapy is trying to do therapy under a tremendous handicap. We begin to "spectate" our own therapy. The sex therapy literature shows us that many sexual partners who place themselves into the spectator role while they are trying to engage in sexual acts find themselves becoming so self-conscious of their every move and sound that they lose their ability to perform and enjoy their sexual encounter. The partner can feel this sense of awkwardness and often ceases to enjoy his or her part in the sexual act. To a degree, therapy is like lovemaking. If the therapist is "spectating" his or her own therapy, awkwardness begins to set in and both the client and the therapist feel ill at ease. The therapist feels as if he or she is letting the client down and, therefore, escalates the stress with increased performance anxiety. This only makes matters worse. However, the client will also feel this build-up of anxiety, even if he or she was at first comfortable in discussing suicidal ideations.

A client may respond to this awkwardness in several ways. The client may become caught in the emotional contagion of escalating anxiety. As the therapist becomes more anxious, the client mirrors that escalation by also becoming more anxious. This triggers more anxiety, resulting in a symmetrical escalation that can immobilize both the therapist and the client.

Clients may use the awkwardness to derail therapy. Many clients who bring up suicidal thoughts in therapy do so as a test. They want to see the therapist's reactions to suicide as a subject for therapy. For some clients, this is a pure manipulation so that they reduce the work that they are expected to do in therapy. For other clients their use of "suicide" as a "resistance strategy" is far more indirect and not in their conscious awareness. They may be afraid of therapeutic change and "drag their feet" in therapy because of that fear. As a strategic therapist, I believe that is very normal and typical for a client. Therefore, I expect to encounter this type of resistance. However, when such a client mentions suicidal ideations and encounters the therapist's anxiety in response, this often becomes too tempting for the client to use in order to avoid what he or she considers to be a dangerous situation, namely therapeutic change. The client feels that they have more control over whether or not they kill themselves than they do over the uncertainty of therapeutic change. To quote an old adage, "Better the devil you know than the one you don't." Therefore, the client may bring up suicidal thoughts every time that the therapy takes a direction that is perceived to be scary. Whether it be conscious or subconscious, the therapy can still be derailed by the topic of suicide.

A client may also react to the awkwardness in therapy by trying to take care of the therapist's anxiety. The client's rationale is that, since the therapist has relieved some of the client's anxieties, it is only fair that the client should reciprocally try to remove some of the therapist's anxiety, in this case the anxiety about suicide. In this situation, the client will proceed to minimize the seriousness of the suicidal ideation and refuse to bring it up again. Typically, the therapist responds in one of the two ways:

1. The therapist becomes more anxious and presses for more information, making the client more anxious. This exacerbates the emotional escalation.
2. The therapist conspires with the client to never bring up suicidal thoughts again. What is created is a "conspiracy of silence" that masks true problems in order to reduce anxiety. To say the least, this is a very dangerous game.

In either case, this is counter-therapeutic.

Whose Responsibility Is It?

If we go back to the quote from the psychologist cited above, there is also a more subtle source of anxiety for the therapist. Notice the last line of the above quote, "...it will be my fault." Responsibility for change is a constant topic among those of us who train therapists and our students. Do we change clients, or do we help clients to change themselves, or do clients change with just a little assistance from us therapists, or do clients change with little or no help from us? These questions form a continuum upon which most schools of therapy fall, typically somewhere in the middle. If clients were capable of change with little or no help from us, why would we do therapy? Do we change clients? If we believe that we do, we sound like we are advocating scenes from *Brave New World, 1984*, or *Clockwork Orange*. In training therapists, we constantly try to remind budding therapists that they cannot make the clients change. They can facilitate change, and even push for change, but they can't force change without the client's taking some responsibility for that change. A typical question in supervision is, "Do you think you are working harder than your client?" We may engage in polemics about the level of responsibility that we, as therapists, should take in therapy but we all can agree that we cannot change for the client.

However, when a client brings up suicidal thoughts, therapists are struck by two things: a) the severity of the issue and b) the "cry for help." The former leads to anxiety. The latter leads to a feeling that we, as therapists, must suddenly shoulder a much higher sense of responsibility than we would typically do with our clients. As a school counselor confided to me:

> He (the client) mentioned suicidal thoughts and stopped talking. I asked if he wanted to say more and he told me that I was the adult and should tell him what to do. I was going to give him my typical line about clients' taking responsibility for their own lives when I realized that, in a real sense, his life was in my hands and, as a counselor, I better be good or he could wind up dead.

As therapists, we feel compelled to overtake responsibility for our clients when they are suicidal.

In the above example, the client seemed to be expecting that the therapist would think for him and tell him what to do. Most therapeutic schools of intervention set some fairly explicit boundaries demarking the therapist's from the client's responsibilities. A client such as this seems to be inviting, or even demanding, that we violate those boundaries or else he or she will die on us. Whether the client really means that or not is not the issue. We, as therapists, feel that responsibility, despite all that we have been taught, and it puts us into a horrible double-bind. We feel the cognitive dissonance of following our "gut instincts" as compassionate people, yet we know clinical research on overtaking responsibility. Therapy is the juxtaposition of science and art. We feel crucified upon the point at which those two intercept. No therapist likes to be put into that position.

HELPLESSNESS

In addition to feeling that our therapy is disrupted, the stakes are high, and we are being asked to do something which we do not want to do, we also feed a terrible helplessness. If we were dealing with a threat of homicide, it is a simpler process. Law enforcement would tell us to "separate the potential victim from the potential perpetrator." We put the potential perpetrator under surveillance or put the potential victim into protective custody. What if the potential victim and potential perpetrator are the same person? How do you separate them? We can hospitalize the suicidal person and put him or her under "suicide watch." What level of suicidal ideation justifies that type of action? Who decides? If we err on the side of caution, do we have enough beds in enough institutions to accommodate the flood of new clients? In today's world of managed care and utilization reviews, who pays for such hospitalizations? These are all questions with no easy answers but they are crucial questions when someone's life may hang in the balance.

Returning to the school counselor cited above, she went on to explain:

After a while, I began to think that, even if I told him the "right thing to do," how would I know he is doing it? I only see him sporadically at school. Even if I had him watched all the time he was at school, who would monitor him when he is at home? How about when he's with his friends. I felt so helpless!

Never more do our limitations come into focus than when we have a client with suicidal thoughts. If the therapist is doing individual therapy, he or she may feel as if he or she is the only game in town. The sad part is that the therapist may be correct. Even if I do family therapy, I may expand my sphere of influence by enlisting the parents' and siblings' help. However, even they cannot be with the suicidal ideation client 24/7. These feelings of helplessness and isolation may also mirror the client's own feelings. This may help us feel empathy with the client but it does not instill confidence in dealing with the problem.

LACK OF TRAINING

When therapists find themselves in difficult therapeutic situations, they often rely on their training to help them decide the correct course of action. In training therapists, my mind is set to not only teach my students sound research and theory but also to give them guidelines when the going gets tough. Egocentrally, as I always discuss suicide with my students and am often consulted when there is a suicidal case at our clinic, I assumed that all therapy training programs did this. As I speak to my colleagues and to students from other therapy training programs, I find that my assumption was incorrect. Although most programs seem to mention suicide and discuss diagnosis, in many programs it is not a major topic of discussion. Many therapists are taught to "hospitalize or refer to inpatient treatment programs." What if the suicidal ideation is not advanced enough to warrant hospitalization? What if, for financial reasons, prophylactic inpatient treatment is not feasible? Who does therapy with the client after hospitalization or inpatient treatment? Many of these crucial issues are not addressed.

When suicidal ideation is discussed, we often rely on what is in the scientific literature. There is a lot of work on prevention programs. In many cases trainees are told to read the prevention programs and adapt them to doing therapy with a client who has suicidal ideations. The problem with this strategy is that many prevention programs are designed to be proactive with the general population and not designed for the client who is already having suicidal thoughts. There is some literature on suicidal crises. How to talk somebody off of a ledge is important but it may have limited viability in the office with a client with suicidal ideation. Even much of the research literature has holes in it. For example, we know more about the etiology of suicide and the factors which contribute to suicide than we do about the decision point of suicide: "The gun is in my hand and I have it to my head. Should I pull the trigger or not?" Unfortunately, there are times when our formal training, our theories, and our research fail us.

In order to explore therapy with clients who are having suicidal thoughts, we must try to understand the nature of suicide and its special fascination for the population of adolescent clients. In the next chapter we will examine the nature of suicide for adolescents and explore a theoretical model for looking at the etiology of adolescent suicide.

Two

FORMULATIONS OF SUICIDE
Examining the Nature of the Beast

THE SCOPE OF THE PROBLEM

Although suicidal ideations cause many problems for therapists and the therapeutic relationship, it is not a phenomenon that can be ignored. Although suicide rates appear to have been relatively constant over the last two decades, the last number is still alarming. In 2000, 29,250 people committed suicide in the United States (Center for Disease Control and Prevention, 2002). In order to put this number into perspective, this means that, in the United States, over 80 people kill themselves every day! This makes suicide the eleventh leading cause of death for Americans and the third leading cause among young people aged 15–24. More people in the United States die from suicide than from homicide. It is ironic that our culture chooses to focus so much of our news and entertainment (e.g., crime shows) on homicides when there are 1.7 times more suicides than homicides. Perhaps there is more "entertainment value" in homicide. Perhaps suicide is too disturbing in our culture to have any "entertainment value." In a culture where medical science treats death as an "enemy" to be conquered, we find it particularly disturbing that so many people, especially young people, choose death, as opposed to life.

What makes these statistics even more alarming is that these estimates of suicide are low compared with the actual number of people who take their own lives. Many suicides go unreported for a variety of reasons (Garland & Zigler, 1993). Many civil and religious authorities are reluctant to report a death as a suicide because of religious implications. Because it is a sin to take one's own life, questions may be raised as to whether the individual died "in the state of grace." This can cause relatives and friends tremendous grief in speculating about their loved one's destination in the afterlife. Many churches and congregations put restrictions on funeral and burial procedures, if the deceased person was thought to have committed suicide. Even if there were no religious implications involved, the surviving family, friends, and loved ones have a great burden to carry concerning their loved one's death. If that death was chosen voluntarily, as in the case of suicide, that burden is tremendously increased. Survivors are likely to feel guilt or anger at the deceased love one who chose suicide. They may blame each other. All of this makes the grieving process much more difficult. There may be financial considerations to consider. Insurance companies greatly restrict benefit payments when a suicide is the cause of death. For all of these reasons, many people in authority (e.g., police, coroners, religious leaders) would much prefer to consider the death to be an "accident" rather than label it as a suicide. Although their human compassion is understandable, it masks how many suicides actually occur.

In addition, many individuals plan their suicides so that they really do look like accidental deaths. The teenager who has driven home to his parents' farmhouse for four years knows the road home. Is it an accident that he does not make the hairpin turn at the edge of the property line and runs into the oak tree on his way back one evening? We have no reason to believe that this was anything but a tragic accident. However, what if he and his girlfriend of two years had just broken up the week before? It still might be an accident. Maybe he was distracted by his thoughts of his girl and maybe he was despondent and didn't see the turn coming up. Possibly, but he may also have tried to end his pain by crashing into the tree on purpose. Another adolescent may get drunk, take out a toy plastic gun that looks very much like the real thing, and threaten to shoot a police officer. It is dim lighting, the gun looks genuine, and the teenager says he is going to shoot. The officer fires in self-defense. Is this a tragic accident? Is it another victim of alcohol? Maybe it is a "death by cop" situation. In this latter scenario, the victim puts his own life in jeopardy on purpose, so that he will force another person (e.g., the police officer, gang member, shop owner) to react in self-defense. I've listened to many adolescents who told me that they could not commit suicide but they would kill themselves by putting themselves into this type of situation in order to orchestrate their own death. I would label this as "suicide by proxy." Their situations will most likely not be recorded as suicides but as accidental deaths or homicides. If we add to these examples the number of adolescents who "put themselves in harm's way" on purpose, by risky behavior such as drug abuse, the potential number of suicides grows at an alarming rate. It may increase the recorded number of suicides to truly epidemic proportions.

As we look at the number of suicides, we see only part of the picture. Individuals may have suicidal thoughts but never act upon those thoughts and feelings in ways that do lead to death. In these situations, the suicidal ideations of the adolescents are often discounted by statisticians as being inconsequential because they did not lead to the adolescent's death (Arensman & Kerkhof, 1996). As a clinician, I believe that nothing could be further from the truth. Thoughts of death and ending one's own life are among the most disturbing and damaging that a person in an existential crisis can have, in which one questions one's own very being and "right to live." The ego damage to the person is substantial. When this occurs in the life of an adolescent, it can damage the young person for life and leave him or her with scars that slowly, if ever, heal.

There is no way of estimating how many people have suicidal ideation because there is no uniform definition of what suicidal ideation specifically means. Do fleeting thoughts of self-destruction count as suicidal ideation? If they do, I would judge that we would have to consider suicidal ideation to be the norm, rather than the exception, among adolescents. In fact, I would guess that it would be only the exceptional adolescent who never had at least a fleeting suicidal thought. Clearly, obsessions with suicide and one's own death would be labeled as suicidal ideation. Where do we draw the line between these two extremes? Regardless of the specificity of our definition of suicidal ideation, I would pose that to do therapy with adolescents is to deal with at least some form of suicidal ideation in a high percentage of cases.

Even if suicidal ideation is not a presenting or secondary problem in a case, suicide is so prevalent in our culture most clients, especially adolescent clients, that one cannot escape being influenced by it. A recent computer search, using Google.com, revealed 7,120,000 items when suicide was entered as a key word. A search of leoslyrics.com, which covers songs and musical lyrics, yielded 46 songs with suicide in the title and 491 songs with suicide in the lyrics. Considering the importance of music to the adolescent and young adult culture, the music reflects the importance of suicide among this segment of the population. As one of my adolescent clients told me:

> Suicide is always there. Sometimes it is in your face. Sometimes it's subtle. But even if you adults don't see it, we know it's there. It's like the theme song of "MASH." My mom always watched that

show and now watches it on reruns. She just knows the melody and calls it "the Mash theme song." We know the title: "Suicide Is Painless." It's always there calling to you if you let it.

For those of you unfamiliar with the television show "MASH" and its theme song, let me elaborate. "MASH" was a movie about the Korean War directed by Robert Altman and released in 1970. It is best described as a very irreverent comedy about the horrors of war. Its theme song is "Suicide Is Painless" and the words were sung over a crucial scene in the movie. This popular film spawned an even more popular television show of the same name that ran from 1972 through 1983. The television show kept the theme song but eliminated lyrics. The chorus of the song exemplifies the theme of the song:

> It states that "Suicide Is Painless." Although it may bring about many changes, it is the individual's choice to "take it or leave it."

To many adults and most parents, it is a harmless little theme song. To many adolescents, it has become a very meaningful anthem. It has been rerecorded by a number of heavy metal and Goth groups, such as Manix Street Preachers and Marilyn Manson and has a special significance to a portion of the adolescent population. Interestingly, the lyrics were written by director Robert Altman's son Michael when he was 14 years old. Many of today's adolescents see it as a troubled teen writing to them about their feelings. Suicide, for many adolescents, is a pervasive theme in the culture and few are unaffected by it.

THE PERSONAL PATH TO SUICIDE

Suicide is a very complicated phenomenon. Although there are some typical kinds of cases and some archetypal patterns that may lead an individual to choose suicide as an option, each client has unique aspects of his or her case that make his or her journey idiosyncratic. This is an excellent example of the systems theory concept of equifinality. Sometimes many different paths lead to the same place. People commit suicide for a variety of reasons. For some, it is a personal struggle with life. For others, there are strong influences from outside social forces, such as friends and family. A physical illness or condition may be involved. There could be problems with work or, in the case of adolescents, with school. To the outside world, there may seem to be nothing amiss or certainly nothing draconian enough to push a person to take his or her own life. This is much like in the folk song about Richard Cory, which is sung by a blue-collar worker who works in the factory that Richard Cory owns. The worker envies the rich and privileged life that Richard Cory seems to live until the last line of the last verse: "Richard Cory went home and put a bullet in his head!" To a great degree, the factors that influence a person to commit suicide are in the eye of the beholder and can only be understood from that person's idiosyncratic perception.

Coming from a psychoanalytic framework, Menninger, Mayman, and Pruyser (1963) constructed a five-stage model, outlining the course of the process that brings a person to suicide. The first stage of the suicidal process was thought to be the impairment of a person's coping abilities. The authors reasoned that, in stressful times, a person could only cope for so long, before his or her coping abilities would begin to wear down and become less effective. The authors also described that, in some people, there may have been a flawed ability to cope before stress levels ever elevated. This flawed coping ability was sufficient under typical or normal circumstances but, with increased levels of stress, may become insufficient to handle the stress. In the second stage, the individual's personality becomes increasingly disorganized and neurotic symptoms begin to appear. In the next stage, the person feels a substantial loss of control and is increasingly unable to cope with the present situation. These three stages may occur slowly over a period of time but the individual feels an acceleration of the process, which contributes to a mounting feeling of being out of control.

At the fourth stage, the person begins to sever himself or herself from this overwhelming reality of both stress and the inability to cope successfully with his or her life. Increasing disorganization fosters more and more overwhelming emotional stress. To escape from this, the person retreats from his or her reality, regressing to a time in his or her life where he or she felt more control over life. The person begins to romanticize about death and its ability to relieve the emotional stress in life. Finally, the person falls into severe depression, intense anxiety, and uncertainty. At that point, death appears to be a reasonable solution to life's problems.

Menninger and his colleagues (1963) have outlined the intrapsychic struggle that takes place in a person who is under stress and is having trouble coping. As the individual goes though these five stages, his or her self-concept becomes a crucial factor in determining the outcome of this journey (Jurich, 1983). If the person's self-esteem and ego strength are high, the person is more likely to develop new coping mechanisms (Cassidy, O'Connor, Howe, & Warden, 2004). The person feels good enough about his or her self to take the chance of trying new strategies for coping. Using new strategies, instead of trying to recycle old coping techniques which haven't been sufficient, is breaking the maladaptive recursive cycle in which the person feels trapped. New strategies for coping increase the person's chance for being successful. Furthermore, this success is a way of triggering a new adaptive cycle that will breed continued success. As each crisis is successfully resolved, the situation produces ego growth and enhances the person's self esteem (Bard, 1972). If the person has a rigid self-concept and low levels of self-esteem, the ego will find itself incapable of defending itself against the overwhelming anxiety (Crocker & Park, 2004; Wekstein, 1979; Wilburn & Smith, 2005). Some authors have hypothesized this as the basis for the "suicidal personality" that would be most vulnerable to committing suicide (Hollinger & Offer, 1981). This model has emphasized the intrapsychic factors that propel a person to consider suicide as a viable option.

INTEGRATIVE THEORETICAL MODEL

Although early models of the genesis of suicide focused on the intrapsychic struggles of the individual, later models tried to broaden the scope of the study of suicide to include other spheres of influence. Intrapsychic conflict, self-esteem, and coping mechanisms were important but told only part of the story. Other theoreticians began to look to other factors which play a part in the path to suicide.

Some scientists have hypothesized that suicidal tendencies have a biophysical dimension in their genesis and development. Hollinger and Offer (1981) put forth the idea that suicide is generated by means of psychiatric disorders that have their foundations in the biological realm of life. They pointed out that some psychiatric disorders such as clinical depression or bipolar disorder have strong biophysical origins and respond well to medication. As people with both of these diagnoses are more prone to suicidal ideation, suicide attempts, and completed suicides, than the typical population members, the authors raise the issue of the biophysical aspects of suicide as being an important factor. Other scientists have studied the biological transmission of suicidal precursors (Hawton, 1986). Still others have studied the biochemical changes and fluctuations which increase suicidal vulnerability (Shaughnessy & Nystul, 1985). This would be especially important for looking at adolescents who are ravaged by puberty and hormonal changes. Such explorations into the biophysical components of suicide do not provide a complete answer to the genesis of suicide for each client but they do focus on an important component (Hendin, Brent, Cornelius, Coyne-Beasley, Greenburg, Gould, Hass, Harkavy-Friedman, Harrington, Henriques, Jacobs, Kalafat, Kern, King, Ramsey, Shaffer, Spirlto, Sudek, & Thompson, 2005).

Sociologists such as Durkheim (1951) have postulated that broad societal and cultural factors may foster suicide in both the general population and among adolescents. Suicide potential may vary with the degree of integration into social institutions. Those people, especially adolescents, who feel less involved and integrated into the community, may have little loyalty to the community's values and rules. This may isolate them, thereby cutting off resources that could be used in times of crisis and high stress. In addition, people who are alienated from society's institutions are those who feel little loyalty to society's regulations or taboos. Killing oneself, a major societal taboo, may have little power over a person who feels alienated and isolated. Therefore, that person would be more likely to see suicide as a viable option. Other aspects of today's world can contribute to suicidal ideation. Increasingly, many people feel isolated from their family and friends by frequent geographical moves and by an emphasis on technology, rather than people, in today's world. Many people today view the world as being more malevolent and dangerous than did previous generations. Their awareness of global terrorism has confirmed that belief. Mass media contributes to this feeling in a number of ways. The news is filled with tragedy. Reality shows often have a nasty streak in them. Radio "shock jocks" are perpetually confrontive with anyone who disagrees with them. When a public figure, especially a teenage idol (like Kurt Cobain, the lead singer of the rock-grunge group Nirvana) commits suicide, the death is sensationalized. Clearly, the society plays a key role in the genesis and proliferation of suicide as an answer to a hostile world.

Scientists from the field of social psychology have focused on situational factors rising out of a person's social environment (Jurich & Collins, 1996). For the adolescent population, the main structures in their social environment would be their family, their peers, and their community (Henry, Stephenson, Hanson & Hargott, 1993).

Ruben Hill, in 1949, put forth his classic ABC → X Model of Crisis. In this model he proposed that three factors would interact to produce a crisis such as a suicide. Those factors were:

A. The stressor event or events that precipitated the onset of the crisis.
B. The resources, both personal and social, that the person could garner in an effort to cope with the stressor events.
C. The perception and meaning that the individual (and his or her family) attach to both the stressor events and the resources.

The interaction of these three factors will serve either to push the individual into crisis or will dampen the individual's escalation into crisis.

Stressor events may come in many forms. Some may be cataclysmic, like death, divorce, or the loss of a job. The loss of a job depletes an individual's monetary resources and cuts off that person from his or her social connections, which were job related. There may also be a social stigma to "losing one's job." In addition, because a person's identity is so closely linked to one's job, when one loses one's job, part of that person's ego and identity is also lost. This can cause a true existential crisis.

Death is the five-letter "four-letter word." Most people in the American culture would feel more comfortable listening to a diatribe of foul language than to be confronted with a serious discussion about death. We treat death as an enemy to be conquered, rather than a normal and natural close to a life well lived. Death may be looked upon as the punctuation at the end of life's sentence. For some it is a period. Others end their life with a question mark. Still others, especially those who believe in an afterlife, will see death as a comma as they transform from this life to the next. However, if death is the enemy who must be conquered, to succumb to death is to fail and suffer some unknowable fate. Even though we may believe in an afterlife, it is a belief born of our faith and not our knowledge. Therefore, it is sill scary. As Albert Camus, the French philosopher mused, as death is both universal, inevitable, and we don't know what's on the other side of death, humankind has simply decided not to think about it (1961). If Camus' observation is valid, not only does the death of a loved one cause pain and the loss of the resources of a loved one, it also almost always comes as a surprise for which we are unprepared.

Likewise, divorce signifies the pain of separation and the loss of the resources brought into the relationship by the departing spouse. However, there is a higher probability of parting on good terms when a person dies than there is of parting on good terms in a divorce. There is a greater likelihood of the animosity of the relationship will carry over to the divorce process and its aftermath. In addition, our culture has ceremonies which aid the survivors of a death. Rituals, such as wakes, funerals, and graveside services, help the survivors cope with death. Divorce has no such rituals. Therefore, the ceremonies which helped survivors of death to cope are absent as resources to those going through a divorce. In all three cases, the cataclysmic stressors cause upheaval in an individual's life and may throw him or her into the pit of crisis.

Stressors may also be chronic erosions of a person's resources. Mental illnesses, such as bipolar syndrome or chronic depression, may progress, gradually wearing away the individual's abilities to cope with the illness. For example, people may find themselves alone when they do not wish to be. It is not voluntary aloneness but involuntary loneliness. Over time such individuals may feel more helpless to change the situation, and they may begin to feel hopeless. As they look for reasons for their situation, they may begin to blame themselves. Freud (1955) hypothesized that, at its root, depression is anger turned inwards. This anger at oneself causes a great deal of pain in a person. Because the individual knows all of his or her weak spots, any self anger will be able to be more efficient at causing pain than would an attack from the outside of the self, because another person would not have the knowledge of one's own vulnerabilities that one's self has. In addition, if one is attacked by another, one way to cope with the situation is to retreat away from the attacker. However, when one is attacking oneself, the attack and, therefore, the pain is incessant. As one can't run away from oneself, that very efficient source of pain is never-ending. Because there is no escape from such pain and because such self-anger is such an energy-draining mechanism, a depressed person may spend large amounts of time sleeping. Before long, death may seem like a reasonable alternative to such a life of unending pain. Death may cease to be the Grim Reaper and, instead, become a seducer or seductress, tempting the person to end the pain by embracing death. In a song by Blue Oyster Cult in 1976, Death asks a young woman to join him:

> The singer of the song, the Reaper, says that things of nature, "the wind, snow, and rain" don't fear the Reaper. The Reaper then asks the young woman to "take his hand" so that they "will be able to fly". He ends the chorus by saying that "I'm your man".

This is not a song of terror. It is a song of seduction.

The resources that a person has may come from several sources. Good health and the physical abilities to complete certain tasks is a crucial resource. As pointed out above, ego strength and self-esteem can be important in coping with stress. Family stability and support is another factor which can help. People who commit suicide often die painfully alone (Arensman & Kerkhof, 1996; Rutter & Behrendt, 2004). For adolescents especially, friends and peers are critical allies for coping successfully with stressors. Community resources may also be very helpful in times of crises. Spiritual resources may come into play. The individual's ability to draw upon any of those resources is crucial in determining whether he or she will be swept away in the undertow of stress or will be able to successfully cope with the stressors and adapt to the stressful situation (Eisenberg & Morris, 2004).

The last of the three factors is the perception and meaning that the individual gives to both the stressors and the resources. Drawing upon the Sociological Theory of Symbolic Interaction, Hill hypothesized the individual's perception and understanding of both the stressors and the resources were crucial determinants as to whether he or she would escalate into crisis. A resource is not really a resource if the person doesn't know that it is available to him or her. A person may recognize a potential resource but feel that he or she doesn't have a right to utilize it. An individual may judge the price of using a resource as too costly. For example, the female college student would ask her parents for money but she will feel further in debt to them and is afraid that they will feel as if they have more power over her. The individual's role in determining which resources, if any, can be used is determined by his or her perception of their resources.

Likewise, the perception of the stressors will determine the degree of stress produced. A male adolescent from an inner city environment may view violence as an expected part of life. Although he would not like to be put in a physical confrontation, if one occurred, he would cope with the situation. As a male in our society, he has been taught to respond physically when attacked. Therefore, he feels somewhat competent in his abilities to defend himself. In addition, his peers and community have taught him to expect some violence in life. He isn't asking to be hit but, if a blow is struck, this young man will treat it as an event within the realm of reality. Let us compare this teenager with a rural adolescent female who hails from a sleepy little old Kansas town where the most violent thing that happens is two squirrels fighting over a nut. If that woman gets struck or assaulted, her definition of the incident will be very different than the urban male's perception of the same incident. In her effective environment, both her gender and her community have protected her from any exposure to physical violence. Being hit is simply not in her definition of "normal" interpersonal interaction. Therefore, being hit would result in an existential crisis. The impact would be far more devastating than it would be for her male, urban counterpart. The degree of malevolence rests in the eye of the beholder. It cannot be objectively rationalized. It must be subjectively felt.

In summary of Hill's model, let us revisit the equation. If a stressor of significant proportion or perceived to be of significant proportion befalls an individual and if the resources are low or thought to be low, a crisis will occur. This gives the therapist three strategies to utilize. The therapist can lessen or eliminate the stressors. He or she may build up the resources. Finally, he or she can work towards changing the client's perceptions of both the stressors and the resources. The understanding of the genesis of the problem gives rise to potential therapeutic interventions.

THE DOUBLE ABC → X MODEL

McCubbin and Patterson (1982) sought to improve upon Hill's ABC → X Model by looking at crisis over time. They proposed that, if enough crises were created; due to the interaction of the family's existing stressors (A), resources (B), and perceptions (C); this would result in "pile-up" (Aa). Even when minor stressful events occur and people feel competent in dealing with them, those same people may feel overwhelmed if those stressors occur at the same time or in close temporal proximity of each other. This situation exemplifies the concept of pile-up. For example, a baby's crying is a stressor event that is difficult but can be handled by most parents. Likewise, a grocery store checker who puts your eggs and other breakables in the bottom of your grocery sack and canned goods on top of them is irritating but you can cope with it reasonably. If a person backs into your car in the parking lot, leaving a small dent, you might get angry but your rage will be tempered with reason. However, what if your baby is crying, the grocery store clerk smashes your eggs with your canned goods, and someone dents your car (while your baby still cries on), all within five minutes? I would propose such a pile-up situation would cause a "melt-down" in most people and might leave you ranting (with choked voice, red face, and fire in your eyes) at the person who hit your car. Often, major crisis situations evolve from a pile-up of smaller crisis events. As paraphrased in the motto for Morton Salt, "When it rains; it pours." This pile-up of stressful life events has been strongly linked to suicidal ideation and behavior (Arensman & Kerkhof, 1996; Lester, 1996; Paykel, Prusoff, & Meyer, 1975; Wilburn & Smith, 2005).

This new major crises of pile-up (Aa) will, as in Hill's original model (1949), be influenced by the resources (both existing and new) available (Bb) and the perceptions of the triggering crisis (X), the pile-up (Aa), and the resources available to utilize (Bb). These perceptions (Cc) will influence the person's or family's ability to draw upon those resources and the degree to which the person or family sees the crisis or pile-up as being manageable or overwhelming. The interaction of these factors will determine the individual's or family's adaptation to the situation. If the person or family can adjust the perceptions, draw upon existing new resources, and minimize the stressor effect of the pile-up, the outcome can be *bonadaptation* (adapting in a way that produces a good outcome for the individual, the family, or both) (McCubbin & Patterson, 1982). In the example described above, the person with the crying baby might "count to ten" or use a relaxation technique learned in a yoga class. These would be examples of resources (Bb). The person might also be able to perceptually sort out and separate the stressors so that they feel less connected, thereby easing the stress (Cc). The person may also be able to see the world through the other person's eyes, to see that the parking lot accident was, in fact, an accident and had no malicious intent. Instead of blowing up at the person, the two people exchange the names of their insurance companies in a less volatile atmosphere of human interaction. All of these would be examples of good coping strategies utilizing either one's resources (Bb) or perceptual skills (Cc), or both to achieve a positive outcome (bonadaptation).

However, another outcome is possible. If the person cannot separate the latest crisis event of the parking lot accident (X) from the other crises (the crying baby and the clumsy checker), the resulting pile-up (Aa) will be overwhelming. If the resources (Bb), such as having the flu or more generally having a low self-esteem, are depleted, there will be few aids from which to draw in coping with the pile-up. If the perceptions (Cc) include an element of helplessness and a touch of paranoia ("They're out to get me!"), the lack of good coping strategies and skills could lead to an undesirable outcome (Xx). This would result in *maladaptation*. In our example, a maladaptive response might be hitting the driver of the other car. Such a maladaptive response would only lead to a further crisis and add even more fuel to the pile-up.

As the individual or family experiences more bonadaption, there will be rewards for coping well. There will be a greater feeling of control over life, even in times of stress, crisis, and pile-up. Such individuals will increase their confidence in coping with life (Deci & Ryan, 2000). "That which does not kill me makes me stronger" becomes their motto. They will be better able to put the stressors of life into perspective. They will develop mechanisms for drawing upon their existing resources and be able to seek out or create new resources for their adaptation repertoire. The next time they are forced with a crisis or even a pile-up of crises, their bonadaptative skills will decelerate the momentum of the crisis and allow them to better process alternative methods of coping in a bonadaptive manner.

If individuals and families experience more maladaptation, the push toward further crises and pile-up will accelerate. They will feel less and less control over their lives and the world around them. This may develop into an "external locus of control" (Jurich & Polson, 1984). Under those circumstances people or families feel as if they have little or no control over their lives and the things happening in their lives. The "slings and arrows of outrageous fortune" accost them, and they believe they can do nothing to prevent it from happening. With this mindset, these individuals and families will fail to see many of their own resources and will take no initiative to develop new resources. Because they feel so little control over life, they will turn to their "tried and true" ways of doing things, even if those methods have not worked very well in the past. They become trapped in what strategic therapists refer to as a *maladaptive recursive cycle* (Wetzlawick, Beavin, & Jackson, 1967). It is a cycle because the stressor triggers a response from them that, in turn, creates more stress, which triggers the same response. It is maladaptive because it doesn't work to the person's or family's benefit. It is recursive because it happens over and over again. Being stuck in this cycle is liable to create a very defeatist attitude in the individuals and families involved. All of these pressures will accelerate any stressor into a pile-up and any pile-up into a lifestyle of maladaptation. This acceleration will exacerbate any negative situation into a crisis. The end result is an individual or a family who is multiproblem and feels like there is no way out.

THE TEETER-TOTTER MODEL

Further developments on the Double ABC → X Model (Burr, Klein, Burr, Doxey, Harker, Holman, Martin, McClure, Parrish, Stuart, Taylor, and White, 1994) have introduced multiple levels of abstraction of individual and family stress and difficult ways of coping with that stress. Drawing upon an ecological view of human experience (Bronfenbrenner, 1980), the phenomenon of suicide can be seen through multiple levels of abstraction as we proceed from the biological elements of the individual to the more macroscopic levels of the society. It is only at these multiple levels of influence that one can fully appreciate the complex nature of suicide. The ecological approach attempts to draw from a number of disciplines and types of theories to create a comprehensive approach to suicide, especially adolescent suicide (Hendin et al., 2005; Henry et al., 1993).

Jurich and Collins (1996) proposed a "teeter-totter" model of adolescent suicide to attempt a more ecological view of teenage self-destruction. Any conversation with an adolescent about how they cope in their world will immediately focus upon the adolescent's ability to balance the different aspects of their lives. A male teenager will complain of having to juggle his schoolwork, football practice, family demands, and the needs of his girlfriend. A female adolescent will speak of how exhausting the competing demands of school, home, friends, and her boyfriend leave her torn in different directions and exhausted. Most adolescents will describe their lives as an attempt to balance the demands of living with the resources upon which he or she can draw.

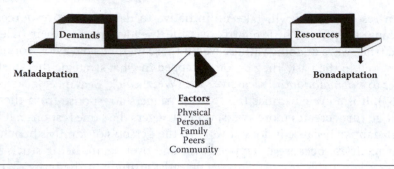

Figure 2.1 Balancing resources and demands.

Figure 2.1 demonstrates how this balancing act can be visualized as a "teeter-totter."

Although a truly ecological model would focus on all levels of an ecological system, including the macrosystemic and exosystemic levels of the adolescent's life space, the research literature has determined that, in the adolescent's effective environment, there are five factors that play the most influential roles in an adolescent's suicide. They are: (a) physical, (b) personal, (c) family, (d) peer, and (e) community levels of his lifespace. Each of these factors may put demands upon the adolescent but each may also serve as a resource for the teenager. An adolescent's youth may give him or her the energy to meet demands on many fronts. However, illness or the uncertainty of puberty may be significant stressors that demand attention. A good self-concept will act as an anchor against a tide of stressors. However, an external locus of control may leave the adolescent feeling helpless to change coping strategies. The family may support the adolescent on the road to development, but it may cramp the adolescent's style when it comes to leisure activities that compete with peers. Peers may support an adolescent's growing sense of independence from the family but demand conformity to the peer group's definition of what is "cool." The community may support a shopping mall with stores for adolescents to spend money but they may institute rules prohibiting groups of adolescents from gathering in that same mall to socialize. If these five factors place more demands upon the teenager than they provide resources with which to cope, the demand side of the teeter-totter goes down and the adolescent experiences maladaptation. The kinds of maladaptation that are the focus of this book include suicidal ideation, suicide attempts, and completed suicides. However, if the five factors provide the adolescent with an abundance of resources and only a minimum of demands,

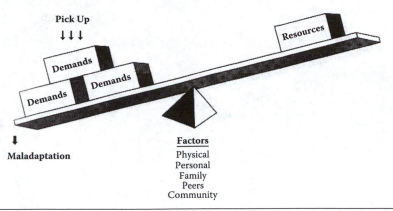

Figure 2.2 Tipping the balance toward maladaptation.

the teeter-totter will swing and lower the resource side of the model. The adolescent will then experience bonadaptation and will become satisfied with his or herself and with life.

Anybody who has ever played upon a teeter-totter knows that the person at the bottom of the teeter-totter, the one whose feet touch the ground, controls the mechanism of the apparatus. That person can push up with his or her feet to rise into the air while the other person descends to the lower position. He or she also can stay seated on the ground while the person in the "up" end of the teeter-totter sits helpless and powerless with feet dangling in midair. In our model, it is the forces in the "down" position that control life. If there are too many demands in proportion to the number and power of the resources, the individual will sink into maladaptation and will feel helpless to increase resources to rebalance the teeter-totter. Likewise, if there are more stressors, the person will tip the balance toward maladaptation (See Figure 2.2).

Those stressors may be normative or non-normative (McKenry & Price, 1994).

Normative stressors would include such universally occurring things as puberty, entering senior high school, or going on a first date. Non-normative stressors are idiosyncratic to the individual, such as family violence, poverty, or gang membership. In either case, a pile-up of stressors will push an individual adolescent toward maladaptation and accelerating crises, perhaps culminating in suicide. Likewise, Figure 2.3 demonstrates that adding to the resource side of the teeter-totter, especially by increasing coping skills, will tilt the device towards bonadaption.

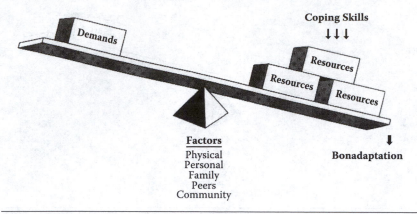

Figure 2.3 Tipping the balance toward bonadaptation.

In this situation, the adolescent will increase resilience and resist the temptations of suicide.

This integrative model lays out a framework to study the etiology of suicide and a blueprint for intervention into the suicidal process. The five factors form an outline to study the causes of suicide ideation among adolescents and the path to self-destruction. The notion of the teeter-totter, combined with elements of the Double ABC → X Model, lay out the points of intervention into the suicidal process. This model will serve as a theoretical framework for the rest of the book.

Three

ADOLESCENT SUICIDE
Why Is Adolescence Such a Fertile Breeding Ground?

HOW SERIOUS IS THE PROBLEM?
Adolescents Who Complete Suicide

As prevalent as suicide is for the general United States population, it occurs more frequently in the adolescent and young adult population than it does in the general population. As mentioned in Chapter 2, suicide is the eleventh leading cause of death in the general population, but it is the third leading cause of death among young people (Centers for Disease Control and Prevention, 2002). In 1999, more young people died from suicide than died from cancer, heart disease, AIDS, birth defects, stroke, and chronic lung disease combined. Almost 5,000 adolescents commit suicide each year in the United States (Henry et al., 1993). From 1952 to 1995, the suicide rate among adolescents and young adults nearly tripled. These numbers would indicate a crisis of monumental proportion.

Although suicides may occur over a wide range of ages and other demographic characteristics (Crosby, Cheltenham, & Sacks, 1999), there are some important demographics that are important to consider when discussing adolescent suicide rates. The suicide rate increases as the adolescent moves from early adolescence to middle adolescence (Pfeffer, 1986), and it rises again when the middle adolescent moves into the late adolescent years (Berman & Jobes, 1991). As the adolescent gets older he or she becomes more independent and autonomous. Although almost every adolescent strives for this more adult status, he or she also feels the weight of responsibility press heavier on their shoulders. The older teenagers can no longer blame their parents or their family for the mess they created. Such stressors exacerbate the negative feelings that most teens have during their adolescent years. However, in more recent years, 1980–1997, there has been a frightening increase among younger teenagers. Whereas the rate of suicide of those adolescents aged 15–19 increased 11 percent, the suicide rate for young adolescents aged 10–14 increased 109 percent (Centers for Disease Control and Prevention, 2002). As we as a culture speed up the developmental process and shave years off our children's childhoods, we create a multitude of problems, not the least of which is an increased likelihood of suicide at an earlier age.

Race is another demographic that is important to consider. Caucasian adolescents are more likely to commit suicide than are African-American adolescents (Berman & Jobes, 1991) or Hispanic teenagers (Kochanek & Hudson, 1994). As one African-American adolescent reported in an interview with me:

> You white people kill yourselves. We blacks kill each other. Either way, we wind up dead; so I guess it really doesn't make a difference. It's just a matter of who pulls the trigger.

However, as in the case of age, recent statistics appear to reflect a change in some of these demographic characteristics. From 1980 to 1996, suicide for young African-American males increased more rapidly than any other ethnic group, rising 105 percent (Centers for Disease Control and Prevention, 2002). Consistently, the Native American population has had the highest rates of suicide among any ethnic groups, ranging one and a half times the rates for the general population (Centers for Disease Control, 1996). It should be remembered that, as in the case with any ethnic group, different subgroups will differ greatly, depending on the nation, tribe, or band of Native Americans. These range from a low percentage for members of the Navajo Nation to rates over three and a half times higher for some Apache tribes (Berlin, 1987). Each Native American group has a unique culture with its own set of beliefs. Therefore, any attempt to understand or work with a tribal family must start with some quest for knowledge about those idiosyncratic tribal customs endemic to that tribal culture. This caveat should also apply to other groups designated by racial and ethnic characteristics (Andriolo, 1998).

Gender plays a significant role, also. The risk of suicide is highest among males (Centers for Disease Control and Prevention, 2002).

There are more than three completed suicides among males for every female who successfully commits suicide (Kochanek & Hudson, 1994). There are many speculations as to why more males commit suicide than females (Canetto & Sakinofsky, 1998). However, the research suggests that there are two key factors (Kirk, 1993). Many adolescent males report feeling a greater fear of failure than their female counterpart. As one young man (age seventeen) told me:

> Girls are different. Sure, a lot of them go to work or have careers, but they can always be a stay-at-home mom. If they screw up in their career, they can fall back on being a mom. Guys don't have a choice. You have to be the breadwinner. Everybody expects you to succeed. If you don't, you're screwed! There ain't no second chance.

Although this young man may not be entirely correct about gender roles in today's world, he does express a valid fear for many adolescent males. This fear may push more young males to consider suicide as an option (Kidd, 2004). The other key factor is the fact that males, as opposed to females, are more likely to use a more lethal means of suicide (Fisher, Comstock, Monk, & Sencer, 1993). This is particularly true for the use of firearms in a suicide attempt (Lester, 1996). With the increasing proliferation of guns in our culture, more suicidal adolescents have relatively easy access to firearms. Among young people, ages fifteen to nineteen, gun-related suicides accounted for more than sixty percent of the increase in the overall suicide rate from 1980–1997 (Centers for Disease Control and Prevention, 2002).

Adolescents Who Attempt Suicide

"Although the exponential increase in suicide completions for adolescents causes alarm, the increase in suicide attempts is mind-boggling" (Kirk, 1993, p. 9). During 1990, the Centers for Disease Control (1991) estimated that over 3.6 million young people ages ten to twenty-five seriously considered committing suicide. Although there is a wide range of estimates in the literature, studies typically have found that between six and thirteen percent of adolescents have reported at least one serious suicide attempt in their young lives (Garland & Zigler, 1993). Rubenstein, Heeren, Housman, Rubin, and Stechler (1989) reported that twenty percent of all of the adolescents in their study tried to "hurt themselves." In a Gallup Poll in 1991, fifteen percent of the adolescents randomly sampled reported that they personally knew someone who had committed suicide, but forty-five percent said that they personally knew someone who had attempted suicide and failed. In a sample of Midwestern high school students, almost sixty-three percent of the teenagers sampled admitted to having some type of suicidal ideation or behavior (Smith & Crawford, 1986). Some suicidal ideation is the norm, rather than the exception, for adolescents in our society.

In the previous section, it was pointed out that more male adolescents successfully completed suicide than females. This statistic reverses itself when we speak about attempted suicide. Adolescent women are three times more likely to attempt suicide than are adolescent men (Kochanek & Hudson, 1994). Part of this gender variance may be attributed to sampling technique. Most of the data on suicide attempts is gathered from patients at mental health or health care facilities (Berman & Jobes, 1991). As females are more likely to seek therapy and treatment for health problems from such agencies, the method of data collection may skew the data in favor of more suicide attempts among the female population. However, the main reason why women are less likely to complete a suicide is their use of less lethal means of suicide (Kirk, 1993). Men are more likely to use firearms or other more lethal means of killing themselves such as hanging. Women are more likely to try to overdose on some form of medication. Several things could intervene to make this type of suicide attempt less lethal than, for example, a gunshot wound. The medication may not be able to cause a fatality. I had a client who had planned to commit suicide by ingesting five hundred aspirin. Not only is it difficult to swallow five hundred pills of any kind, but it also would be doubtful whether the aspirin would be fatal. Secondly, the adolescent girl may have a potentially lethal drug but she may not have enough of it to be fatal. Lastly, even if dosage is lethal, few drugs can kill somebody quickly. Therefore, there may be time for emergency treatment. A bullet in a gun is not only lethal but, once fired, it takes away anyone's ability to intervene. The lethality of the firearm is higher.

On September 11th, 2001, our nation was shook to its foundations by a series of terrorist attacks at the World Trade Center and the Pentagon. It was a national tragedy that changed our lives forever. How many more adolescent lives are lost, not by the hand of terrorists but by their own hand in the form of suicide?

Why Are Adolescents So Vulnerable?

In the movie *The Virgin Suicides* (2001), a psychotherapist is interviewing a thirteen-year-old girl who has tried to commit suicide:

> He asks her: "What are you doing here, honey? You're not even old enough to know how bad life gets." She replies: "Obviously, Doctor, you've never been a 13-year-old girl." (Eugenides, 1993)

We, as a culture, forget how difficult adolescence is. Instead, we selectively remember only certain aspects of our teen years. For the most part, we recall only our triumphs. Sometimes, the occasional feelings of self-pity or self-righteousness may cause us to recall some terrible event or awful feelings we had. However, after those feelings have been sated, we return to the fictional past which we have created to sustain our ego. In some of my public presentations, I will ask my audience if any of them would like to return back to being a teenager once again. I seldom get any takers on my proposition. When I do, I typically get the following statement: "I would go back to being a teenager if I knew then what I know now!" My reply is that I did not offer that as an option. I reply that: "If you go back, you have to be just as stupid, awkward, and dumb as you were then." At that point I get no takers!

Adolescence isn't a time of change. It's a time of upheaval! Even a definition of what adolescence is supposed to be is problematic. When I teach my graduate level adolescence course, I begin the first class by asking my students to define "adolescence." Their answers can usually be placed into one of five categories: (a) age-span definitions, (b) biological definitions, (c) psychological definitions, (d) sociological definitions, or (e) social role definitions. I set each of these up as a "straw man" and proceed to knock them down by pointing out the inadequacies of each type of definition. What we are left with in the end is the populist definition that most of the culture uses to define adolescences: "Someone who is older than a child and younger than an adult." Although this is the most frequently given answer in our culture, and it is the answer on which most adolescents base their self-definition, it is obviously a very inadequate definition of who they are or are supposed to be. This is a "definition in absentia." It tells what people are by telling them what they are not. It's like defining an elephant by saying that it is shorter than a giraffe but larger than a mouse. Some information is conveyed but not much. Upon the shifting sands of this definition the rest of an adolescent's definition of self, and definition of the surrounding world, is built.

Stages of Adolescence

In order to understand the world of the adolescent, it is important to understand the way the teenager develops over the course of adolescence (Jurich, 1987). A thirteen-year-old and a nineteen-year-old are both labeled as "adolescents." However, they are very different and may be miles apart in their development. Each has a different set of needs and has different developmental tasks to perform. Each is at a different stage of development. Jurich (1979a) outlined four different stages of development over what is commonly labeled "adolescence." Although a description of each stage is given, specific ages for each stage are impossible, as each adolescent's journey is so idiosyncratic.

Preadolescence This is the stage of the "budding adolescent." Adolescents, while still considered to be "children" by most of the society, start to leave behind the trappings of childhood and begin to focus on their future roles as teenagers. Typically, this stage begins at approximately age ten and ends sometime around age thirteen. Less is known about this stage of adolescence than any other (Jurich, 1987). It is a "no-man's land" between childhood and the teenage years. For most preadolescents, this is a time of major physical changes (Reekers & Jurich, 1983). The child feels as if he or she has no control over these physical changes and their resultant psychological changes. Not only are those changes dramatic, but they also happen very quickly. Preadolescents change faster than their psychological ability to integrate those changes into their budding self-concept. This leads to a lower self-esteem and a heightened feeling of helplessness (Manor, Vincent, & Tyano, 2004). Self-consciousness and emotional outbursts accompany these rapid changes in body image, sexual functioning, and emerging secondary sex characteristics. They are thrust into a new sexual awareness that is overwhelming. Preadolescents have neither the intellectual sophistication nor the social skills to cope with their new, emerging sexuality. When they were children, if they were dissatisfied with their body size and type, they were given the hope that they would "outgrow it." However, in preadolescence, the young person is confronted with the biological truth of the type of body their genes have given him or her. As stated by one twelve-year-old girl, "This is the body I'm stuck with." Their feelings are mercurial, racing from elation to fear to despair, often in one evening. Preadolescents often see their family as a symbol of their childhood and feel that their family, especially their parents, are trying to prevent them from leaving their childhood roles. In an effort to begin establishing their own independent ego identities, which is their central task in adolescence, they begin to spend more and more time away from home. They begin to gravitate towards their peers, who are more likely to support them in their struggle to formulate a new identity which is independent from the childhood identity. This is perplexing to their family. Preadolescents put their parents in a terrible double bind. On one hand, they need the love, support, understanding, and stability of their family to help them through this difficult time. On the other hand, they may also push their family, especially their parents, away in order to form closer relationships with their peers. They may even rebel against family or community rules. They may view parents and community authority figures as "the enemy." This is a bitter pill to swallow for parents and community representatives (e.g., teachers). After giving them so much, parents often feel as if the preadolescent is being ungrateful. It is hard to readjust to your child who, since he or she has reached preadolescence, can no longer give you the unconditional love, respect, and obedience that once were freely given.

Early Adolescence   This is the stage of adolescence that covers the junior high school and early high school years. It is at this stage during which adolescents most typically become closely tied to the "teenage subculture." Early adolescents are finishing their physical growth and begin to solidify their body image. They also pass through their "intellectual growth spurt." For the first time they think in abstract concepts and hypothetical ideas. They leave the "world of what is" and enter into the "world of what if." They reach Piaget's stage of "formal concepts" (1954) and have the ability to formulate "postconventional moral reasoning" (Kohlberg, 1969). Teenagers reach a level of cognitive functioning at which they are no longer satisfied with accepting an "order" given by a parent. They feel that the justification, "because I said so," is totally inadequate. They want a logical reason for a parent's command or a community rule. They will argue against such commands or rules if they feel that the reason is inadequate or unjust. The peer group becomes increasingly important to the early adolescent. Peers support the adolescent in the quest for independence. Parents are the keepers of the flame of the past. Peers validate who the adolescent is right now and who the adolescent is becoming. They become what Gail Sheehy (1974) refers to as "testimonial people" to validate who the adolescent is becoming, and not the person who he or she has been in the past. Unfortunately, the peer group may also help foster resentment against any family restrictions or community rules. The early adolescent years may, in fact, explode into a high level of parent–adolescent hostility, in which parents and the peer group wage war over the adolescent's allegiance. Because early adolescents have the physical and intellectual tools to rebel successfully and also have the peer group's support to do so, this period of adolescence is often the low point in parent–adolescent relationships. However, an interesting paradox of adolescence is that the peer group, which encourages adolescents to rebel against parental and community rules in order to develop their individuality, also demands strict conformity to peer group rules. They pray to the great god "Normal" but "normal" is defined by what is important to the peer group. The latest in fashion, style, and music must be embraced or the adolescent risks expulsion from the group, which, for the adolescent, is a fate worse than death.

Middle Adolescence   This stage occurs in the late high school years, typically from ages fifteen to seventeen. During this stage, the adolescent starts to shake off the "cult of conformity" image imposed by the peer group. Instead, the adolescent begins to become his or her "own person." Middle adolescents begin to take more responsibility for their actions. They solidify their cognitive style and begin to view themselves as unique individuals who are less dependent on others, including parents and peers, for their ideas and values. They have become acclimated to their physical growth and changes, which are drawing to an end, and are formulating their own personality characteristics. The peer group is less influential because specific friends become more important. Instead of spending time with a group of peers, the middle adolescent prefers the company of a small group of really close friends. Dating becomes extremely important. Instead of "hanging out" in a group, the middle adolescent begins to pair off with a "romantic other." This obviously increases the likelihood that premarital sex will become an issue. This may precipitate conflicts between parents and adolescents over values and morals. Parents and adolescents can engage in bitter fights over "when" and "who" to date and the rules about dating. Although parent–adolescent conflicts may be fewer in number than in the early adolescent stage of development, their intensity may increase in the middle adolescent years. The intensity increases for the parents because the stakes are higher as their child grows older. Consequences of mistakes in preadolescence or early adolescence are painful but are less likely to cause as much permanent damage as those consequences of middle adolescence. In addition, most parents feel the pressure to "do something" as their time to intervene into their adolescent's life grows shorter with the passing of every day. The middle adolescents feel as they should have more autonomy than they did when they were younger. They feel as if they are entitled to make their own decisions as they are on adulthood's doorstep. Furthermore, middle adolescents have a wider range of resources from which to choose to replace their parent's support if it is withdrawn. If middle adolescents feel connected to their community, they will feel more drawn to community activities and more allegiance to the community's values. If middle adolescents feel alienated from the community, they are more likely to seek support from alternative communities, which may foster alternative values to society's values.

Late Adolescence This stage typically begins soon after the completion of high school and ends shortly after the assumption of adult responsibilities. This group would include college students, graduate trainees, and young workers in a variety of jobs. Late adolescents are attempting to put the finishing touches on their newly formed independent ego identity. During this stage, late adolescents shift their sights from the present to the future and begin to consider decisions about more permanent aspects of their lives. During this time, adolescents will make several crucial decisions in their life. They will begin to choose or actually choose a career. Because of their more mature and realistic view of the world, including their own abilities and needs, they are better equipped to make more informed decisions about what they want to do to make a living now and in the future. Likewise, these skills will be crucial in choosing a mate or a lifetime partner. In early adolescence, the teenager makes a choice of a dating or sexual partner based upon peer group values and will choose a partner who will garner him or her status in the peer group. Middle adolescents are more likely to consider their own values and needs. Late adolescents choose dating or sexual partners with an eye on longevity and permanence of the relationship. Late adolescents are more capable of understanding their parents' points of view and tend to be more tolerant of their wishes. Prior to this stage, many parents often feel they were poor parents because the adolescents frequently disagreed with them and their values. These parents often obsess about "What did we do wrong?" However, by the time the adolescent reaches late adolescence, parents often feel as if their adolescent has had some successes, even by their own standards. This feeling of accomplishment and success as a parent eases their fears. This, in turn, may make parents more tolerant of their late adolescents' differences. Thus, the tension between parents and their late adolescents eases and parent–adolescent relationships may become more pleasurable and rewarding. With their careers under way, late adolescents are more likely to have a more fully realized participation in affairs of the community. With the journey complete, the young adult can leave adolescence behind and more fully participate in life as an adult.

As we look at the factors that contribute to adolescent suicide, we must consider the stage in which the adolescent resides. Stressors may affect adolescent difficulty at different developmental stages. Jurich and Jones (1986) proposed that the stressors associated with divorce would have differential effect on adolescents at different stages of development. Likewise, the factors associated with suicide will affect different ages of adolescents differentially.

Four

FACTORS IN ADOLESCENT SUICIDE
The Seeds That Bear Bitter Fruit

Utilizing the model put forth in the previous chapter, any look into the causes of adolescent suicide must look at the dimensions of (a) stressors, (b) resources. (c) perceptions, (d) pile-ups, and (e) coping skills across the five factors that research has shown us are most important in the lives of adolescents: (a) physical, (b) personal, (c) family, (d) peers, and (e) community. It would be nice if we could place them into a five-by-five chart in such a way as to capture the etiology of adolescent suicide in one page. However, the complexity of the interchange of the above dimensions and factors makes such a table impractical and misleading. Part of the problem with suicide is that it is so idiosyncratic and complex. These characteristics contribute to the suicidal person's feeling both alone and overwhelmed. The remainder of this chapter will discuss the dimensions of suicidal adolescents within the domain of each factor in an attempt to give order to this often-chaotic journey to suicide.

PHYSICAL FACTORS

A number of researchers such as Mann, DeMeo, Keilp & McBride (1989), predominantly from the disciplines of medicine and psychiatry, have explored the biological and physical correlates of adolescent suicide. This type of research draws from a wide variety of research methodologies, including postmortem brain studies, cerebrospinal fluid studies, experimental drug studies on neuro-endocrine transmitters, and peripheral blood studies. Although much of the data are incomplete and even contradictory, there have been some physical factors associated with teen suicide (Arensman & Kerkhof, 1996).

A series of studies, such as those by Lester (1988), have attempted to identify biochemical factors in suicide. The majority of those studies have looked at variations in the chemistry of neurotransmitter chemicals such as serotonin. It has been suggested that alterations in neurotransmitter chemicals lead to an adolescent's greater vulnerability to psychiatric problems and, consequently, suicide (Shaughnessy & Nystul, 1985). These types of studies have been most successful when studying individuals with mood disorders (Beck, Steer & Braun, 1993; Flisher, 1999) or thought disorders (Reich, Yates & Nduagube, 1987). In addition to being subjected to a major series of stressors, adolescents who have psychiatric problems often lack the cognitive resources to call upon when facing these stressors and have little perspective to view their problems in any way other than being a chronic condition of stress. Other researchers have found correlations between low levels of growth hormones and suicidal behavior (Ryan, Puig-Antich, 1988). Low levels of growth hormones not only would affect the adolescent's emotionality but also the growth spurt that typically occurs in the early adolescent years, leaving the adolescent with significant stressors and a depleted battery of physical abilities to cope with those stressors. As a young man of age 15 related:

> It sucks to be the runt of the class. Everybody laughs at you and picks on you and you aren't big enough to fight back. When you play sports you're always picked last. What girl wants a boyfriend who has to stand on his tippy-toes to kiss her goodnight?

These types of studies has led researchers to consider the possibilities of a genetic predisposition to suicide that may be passed down through generations (Roy, 1986). This line of research merges into the recent trends of focusing the biochemical foundations of mental illness by the National Institution on Mental Health in the 1990s. The central theme of this body of research is that, as there seems to be a strong biochemical component to psychiatric illness, there would logically be a strong biochemical link to adolescent suicide, which may be the outcome of mental illness (Jurich & Collins, 1996). However, authors such as O'Connor and Sheehy (2001) have criticized this approach as being too simplistic, in that it minimizes the psychosocial factors.

A second set of studies has focused upon the reactions of adolescents to physical illness. Hawton (1986) found that suicide correlated significantly with medical illness in middle and late adolescents. The lack of significant correlations in early adolescents was attributed to the masking of any trends by psychosocial factors. However, when the illness is extreme, as in the case of epilepsy, the cataclysmic and long-term nature of the stressor was highly associated with both suicidal thoughts and behaviors in adolescents of all ages (Brent, Crumsime & Varma, Allman, 1987). The high levels of stress, together with the depletion of physical resources and a narrowing perspective, all combine to push the teenager towards suicide as an option. Similarly, adolescents with AIDS have been found to be at a very high risk for suicide (Marzuk, Tierney, & Mann, 1988). In addition to the suffering specifically associated with the disease, AIDS is a terminal illness with a great deal of fear and social stigma attached to it. This cuts off many adolescents from peer, family, and community resources. In addition, it also leaves adolescents feeling so out of control over the condition that the only thing that AIDS-infected adolescents do feel control over is the taking of their own lives. The third level of physical stress is the reaction that adolescents may have to their own physical development (Ladame, 1992). When an adolescent's physical development is out of phase with the peer group, either too early or too late, the adolescent no longer feels "normal." Their peers may ridicule them and the teenager feels out of place in his or her own life. In a similar fashion, for some adolescents, if their bodies don't measure up to their ideals and expectations, suicide may seem like the only way to change things. To an adult, this seems extreme. However, we must remember that, with adolescents having limited experience and no independent perspective on their own physical development, the finality of what they perceive as their limited physical maturation may be overwhelming enough to trigger suicidal ideations. If we add in the overwhelming feelings associated with the teens' inauguration into their sexuality, which is met with silence from the adults in his or her life, adolescents can easily feel betrayed by their own bodies. Suicide may be looked upon as an escape from this betrayal and as a method of punishing the betrayer, "my body."

Kurt Cobain, the lead singer and driving force of the grunge rock group Nirvana, died at the age of 27 from a self-inflicted gunshot wound (Strauss, 1994). He is a good example of how (Mundy, 1994). As a child, Kurt was diagnosed with bronchitis and had a mild case of scoliosis. He was given Ritalin to counteract hyperactivity. During his teenage years, he suffered from severe gastrointestinal pain (Handy, 1994). To counteract that pain, he self-medicated, turning to drugs and psychoactive substances. This led to a series of further physical problems attributed to the side effects of the drugs. This series of physical stressors piled up, sapped his resources, and blurred his perception to push him into maladaptation, culminating in his own suicide.

PERSONAL FACTORS

Among the personal factors that contribute to the etiology of suicide among the adolescent population, a large number of studies have looked at the incidence of psychiatric symptoms of young people who have either attempted or completed suicide (deWilde, Kienhorst, Dickstra, & Wolters, 1993). Some researchers have claimed that, in fact, there is only a small minority of suicidal adolescents who are free from any discernible psychiatric symptomatology (Shaffer, 1988). Although these researchers present reasonable data to support the claims that psychiatric symptoms are often present in suicidal adolescents, this does not necessarily mean that those adolescents who are or have been suicidal are actually diagnosed with a specific DSM-IV diagnosis. There is no specific DSM-IV diagnosis for suicide (American Psychiatric Association, 1994). Unlike the adults who attempted suicide, many of whom frequently were diagnosed with psychiatric disorders, the adolescent population was less likely to be diagnosed with such disorders (Jurich, 2002). Jurich found that an adult was more likely to be diagnosed with clinical depression (eighty percent) than the adolescent suicide attempter in the same study (twenty-nine percent). When adolescents were diagnosed, they were more likely to have received a diagnosis of some other kind (attention deficit hyperactivity disorder (ADHD), attention deficit disorder (ADD), bipolar disorder, or an affective disorder (forty percent of the time). In thirty-one percent of the cases, no formal diagnosis was made. No previous diagnosis was made in less than five percent of the adult cases (Jurich, 2002a). Adolescents who try to commit suicide, although less likely to be diagnosed than their adult counterparts, still are vulnerable to psychiatric illnesses and do exhibit psychiatric symptoms.

The psychiatric diagnosis most often linked to suicide, in general (Arensman & Kerkhof, 1996; Blenkiron, House, & Milnes, 2000) and among adolescents specifically, is major clinical depression (Hauton, Kingsbury, Steinhardt, James, & Fogg, 1999; Kidd, 2004; Ladame, 1992; Wodarski & Harris, 1987). In fact, some researchers have stated that they believe that depression is the single most powerful determinant of whether or not the adolescent completed suicide (Triolo, McKenry, Tishler, & Blyth, 1984). Estimates are that at least three out of every four adolescents are depressed at the time they committed suicide (Allberg & Chu, 1990). However, Ryland and Krues (1992) found that major clinical depression was officially diagnosed in only 17% of the cases in studies they reviewed. This is similar to the Jurich (2002a) findings cited above. It is interesting to speculate why it is that suicidal adolescents exhibit signs of depression but are not diagnosed as clinically depressed. Our society makes many assumptions about adolescents, and many of them are grounded in fact. Two such assumptions are that adolescents are very moody and that adolescents change their emotions rapidly and dramatically. Although these two assumptions have a strong foundation in the literature, the fact that we expect adolescents to act this way may, in fact, mask some underlying pathology that may be present. Their actions may be telling us that they are depressed but we treat it as "business as usual" because, after all, adolescents are moody. It is only after they attempt or complete suicide that we realize that they were manifesting some underlying psychopathology such as clinical depression. Twenty–twenty hindsight is almost perfect and, unfortunately, it is often useless to save the life of the teenager.

When an adolescent is depressed, what are the symptoms he or she manifests? Allberg and Chu (1990) listed a series of behaviors that are typical of depressed adolescents. These may be sleep and appetite disturbances, often resulting in either extreme (i.e., sleeping most of the time or sleeping little) or fluctuations between extremes (i.e., binge eating and nearly starving oneself). The adolescent is frequently inappropriate in his or her affect (i.e., crying or screaming binges). There is often social withdrawal. These adolescents feel angry with themselves, which makes them very vulnerable in the presence of others. The world becomes a much more dangerous place. Therefore, the safest course of action is to withdraw. There are often complaints of boredom and fatigue. Suicidal adolescents often exhibit pathological guilt. As one adolescent confessed to me:

> I have the King Midas touch in reverse. Instead of the "touch of gold," I have the "touch of shit." Everything I touch turns to shit!

Adolescents may demonstrate lasting changes in mood. The happy-go-lucky child of eleven turns into the morose, brooding adolescent of thirteen. Suicidal adolescents often lack a sense of spontaneity. They act as if they are unable to experience pleasure of any kind. It is almost as if they feel repulsed by the good things in life and eventually, by life itself (Cotton & Range, 1996; Orbach, Feshbach, Carlson, Ellensberg, 1984; Orbach, Feshback, Carlson, Gleubman & Gross, 1983). They simply see fewer reasons to stay alive (Ivanoff, Jang, Smyth, & Linehan, 1994). One of the problems with this "laundry list" of symptoms is that many people in our society will say "Gee, that sounds like a typical adolescent to me!" This is why so many adolescents go undiagnosed. It is difficult to separate out pathological behavior from typical needy adolescent behavior (Kaufman, Rohde, Seeley, Clarke, & Stice, 2005). This is why it is so important for those who know the adolescent best, parents and peers, to keep in close contact with the adolescent, both as a child, as a teenager, and as a young adult. When the adolescent is engaging in behavior that is not typical or is more extreme than usual, the warning lights need to go off. We need to be able to determine the difference between an adolescent's struggling and "business as usual." This is a major reason why I prefer to work with suicidal adolescents in the context of family therapy.

When an adolescent presents elements of a borderline personality with a major clinical depression, the young person's behavior can escalate even further (Berman, 1985; Kehrer & Linehan, 1996). Such adolescents are highly impulsive in their actions (Beautrais, Joyce, & Mulder, 1999). Most adults who are suicidal take some time to plan and think out their options. Many adolescents follow that same path. However, some adolescents may be very spontaneous about committing suicide, often with deadly consequences. A fifteen-year-old client of a colleague of mine was troubled but swore to his therapist that he had never given suicide a thought. The therapist believed him. There was no reason not to do so. One afternoon, the young client was walking with a friend down the highway; telling his friend about how rotten he felt. The cars were whizzing past and a truck was coming up behind them. The 15-year-old said, "Maybe I'll just kill myself." His friend responded in shock by saying, "You're crazy! You're not going to kill yourself!" The 15-year-old looked as his friend said, "Wanna bet?" Those were the last words of his life. He turned around and dove under the wheels of the truck without uttering another sound. It is frightening to think of adolescents as that impulsive, especially when the stakes, life or death, are so high. It is primarily adolescents who exhibit this type of spontaneous suicide.

Other actions that are typical of adolescents who have both borderline personality characteristics and major depression may also be alarming (Berman, 1985). Such adolescents may demonstrate inappropriate and uncontrolled anger and chronic feelings of emptiness (Kaufman et al., 2005). They will often overinterpret the words and behaviors of others as signs of rejection and unlovability (Kidd, 2004), thereby creating a maladaptative recursive cycle. If I am unworthy of love, I look for evidence that my feelings of being unlovable are, in fact, reality. When I overinterpret the remarks of others to prove I am correct, other people (e.g., peers and family) get frustrated with me and do not want to spend time with me. It becomes a self-fulfilling prophecy, as I sink deeper and deeper into self-recrimination. At this time, death may cease to become frightening but, instead, begin to look like an attractive alternative to a life of misery.

Some professionals do not consider the pain of the depression itself to be the salient precipitating factor in adolescent suicide. Instead, they posit that the feelings of helplessness and, therefore, hopelessness have a far greater impact on the adolescent's path to suicide (Beautrais et al., 1999; Beck, Brown, Steer, Dehlagaard, & Grisham, 1999; Beck, Steer & Brown, 1993; Beck, Brown, Berchick, Stewart, & Steer, 1990; Beck, Steer, Kovacs, & Garrison, 1985; Cotton & Range, 1996; Duberstein & Conwell, 1997; Hawton, 1986; Hawton et al., 1999; Kidd, 2004; O'Connor & Sheehy, 2001; Rubenstein et al., 1989; Rutter & Behrendt, 2004). In a unique sample of people, who were accidental survivors of a serious suicide attempt, Jurich (2002a) found that the key factor in their decision to commit suicide was not the pain of their depression but their feelings of helplessness and, therefore, the hopelessness they experienced. As one eighteen-year-old male recalled:

> You know, Doc, if you take two guys, one who's feeling lots of pain but feels like he's got a handle on life, and one who's feeling a lot less pain but feels out of control to do anything about it, the latter guy is a better candidate to commit suicide than the former.

These feelings were confirmed, to some extent, by the fact that the Hopelessness Scale by Beck, Wiessman, Lester, and Trexier (1974) is better at predicting suicide than the more popular Beck's Depression Inventory (Beck, Steer & Brown, 1996; Westefeld, Range, Rogers, Maples, Bromley, & Alcorn, 2000). So, for many adolescents, it is the hopelessness of the depression and the feelings of helplessness to change their lot in life that is the key factor in deciding that suicide may be an option to explore.

Feelings of helplessness and hopelessness are especially disturbing to an adolescent whose central developmental task is to establish his or her independent ego identity. At a time where adolescents are seeking autonomy, they feel as if they have no control over their lives (Beautrais et al., 1999). In a desperate effort to exert some control over their lives, adolescents may engage in some maladaptive behaviors. For example, a depressed female adolescent may turn to an eating disorder in order to exercise some control over her life (Allberg & Chu, 1990). She may feel totally helpless in all other aspects of living but she can control what she eats in order to obtain society's image of a perfect body (O'Connor & Sheehy, 2001). Therefore, anorexia becomes a pathway in which she at least has some control. An adolescent male may attempt to self-medicate himself though the use of illegal drugs or pharmaceuticals (Arensman & Kerkhof, 1995; Kidd, 2004). As a clinician, I believe that many adolescents who come to the attention of the mental health system because of drug use are really self-medicating their psychiatric illness. However, without medical supervision, the use of drugs to self-medicate may only exacerbate the problem. The use of a sedative or barbiturate may temporarily blot out the pain of the depression but, in the end, taking depressives without being monitored by a physician for depression only creates a downward spiral. Taking amphetamines may give the adolescent temporary relief from his depression but the psychological addiction to escape his depression is very high. As most psychoactive substances are illegal to minors, there is the risk of getting into legal trouble. The drugs also may provide the adolescent with an easy means of committing suicide. Lastly, the adolescent could accidentally commit suicide by a drug overdose. All of these outcomes make the original feelings of helplessness and hopelessness even worse. As an example, we have mentioned above that rock musician Kurt Cobain was notorious for using drugs as self-medication for his physical maladies and as a way of numbing himself from his psychosocial problems (Mundy, 1994). In this way he chose to take a maladaptive coping strategy. Many adolescents have used his inappropriate example as a model for their own maladaptive coping strategies and after him.

Researchers have also shown that depression may lead to other problematic behavior, such as panic disorders, aggression, and both personality and psychotic disorders (Kaufman et al., 2005; Ladame, 1992). Once an adolescent's depression grows, many of these behaviors will result from the maladaptive methods of coping with both the pain and the hopelessness and helplessness of the depression. It creates a downward maladaptive spiral. As would be expected of adolescents who are prone to clinical depression, many suicidal adolescents also are diagnosed with affective disorders (Berman, 1985; Chance, Kaslow, & Baldwin, 1994; Ryland & Krues, 1992). Other diagnoses cited by mental health professionals include substance abuse, conduct disorders, personality disorder, adjustment disorder, and schizophrenic disorder (Aresman & Kerkhof, 1996; Duberstein & Connell, 1997; Jacobs, Brewer, & Klein-Benham, 1999; Kullgren, Tengstroem, & Grann, 1998; Ryland & Krues; 1992). Such diagnoses not only add stress to the adolescent's life but they also isolate him or her from potential resources. They also make it difficult for the adolescent to get an accurate perspective on both the stressors and potential resources. When one is under the siege of mental illness, it is hard to look beyond the moment to plan a strategy for coping. Coping strategies are called upon to insure the individual's survival in the present moment, and little thought is given to the ultimate consequences of a survival strategy, which is desperately felt to be needed now. Hence, adolescents may make poor choices in their selection of survival strategies (Kehrer & Lineman, 1996). For example, drug use as self-medication may seem like an excellent strategy for the momentary relief of stress but the individual might not think about the consequence of addiction in the future. Likewise, an adolescent may feel that the threat of suicide can have short-term effects that are desirable, like the offer of resources from people who are startled into action by such a threat. For the moment, the adolescent feels as if the coping strategy of threatening suicide has had the desired effect. However, in the long run the effect may be far less desirable. After a number of threats, other people such as peers and family may no longer respond to what they would label "overdramatic responses" by the adolescent. This leaves the adolescent with fewer resources and those who supported them previously with a bitter taste in their mouths, feeling they were being manipulated by the adolescent. In order to recreate the shock value of the suicide threat, the adolescent may resort to more dramatic and lethal means of getting attention. This escalation in the lethality of the threat could lead to more dangerous behavior in which the adolescent could be maimed or even killed by accident. Either way, that strategy ends up in tragedy (Berman, 1985; Garland & Zimgler, 1993; Shafii, Carrigan, Whittinghill, & Derrick, 1985).

Some personal factors may not be a dramatic or serious diagnosable mental illness. An adolescent's primary developmental task during adolescence is to develop an independent ego identity (Jurich, 1987). To adolescents, a key element of that is to achieve autonomy and differentiate themselves from parents whose images of them are still as preadolescent children. If the adolescent is unable to achieve a differentiated sense of self, he or she may remain in an "identity diffused" state (Sands & Dixon, 1986). In this state, adolescents are still actively searching for an identity to which they can commit. Whereas this diffused state is typical of an adolescent in the preadolescent or early adolescent stages, if it still persists into the middle and late adolescent developmental stages, the adolescent will feel incomplete and out of step with peers. This can lead to an inhibited personality (Shafii, 1985) as well as higher trait and state anxiety (deWilde et al., 1993). In any case, the adolescent will have lower self-esteem because of his or her inability to achieve the principal developmental task of adolescence—achieving that independent ego identity. Consequently, low self-esteem has been shown to be associated with greater suicidal risk in adolescence, especially in the middle and late adolescent years (Beautrais et al., 1999; Collins, 1990; deWilde et al., 1993; Neuringer, 1974; Rutter & Behrendt, 2004; Wilburn & Smith, 2005).

Another danger of this undifferentiated self for the middle or late adolescents is that they may feel so much pressure to develop an independent ego identity that they "foreclose" into an identity prematurely (Marcia, 1980). The adolescent chooses an identity to reduce the anxiety experienced by not having developed an ego identity as expected and as demonstrated by his or her peers. Often there is little thought given to this choice. It is often chosen somewhat impulsively, based upon meeting the adolescent's immediate needs. Therefore, there is no true commitment to this foreclosed identity. It is a convenient port in a storm. An adolescent may foreclose into a negative identity as a gang member or a "loser" (Kidd, 2004). However, even if he or she forecloses into a positive identity, there may still be problems. An adolescent may choose a foreclosed identity by acquiescing to a career of the parents' dreams, like a doctor, but may feel empty because there is no true commitment to that identity. The teenager may choose an identity by foreclosing into a relationship with a boyfriend or girlfriend whom the parents or peers push but with whom there is nothing in common. Billy Joel describes such a relationship with the story of Brenda and Eddy in "Scenes from an Italian Restaurant" on the *Stranger* album:

> Billy Joel describes them as "the popular steadies" and mentions that they were the "King and Queen of the Prom". They were their peers' most popular couple and the envy of all their friends.

The song goes on to describe how the relationship that appeared to be so perfect to their peers falls apart into divorce. It is a foreclosed relationship with little commitment; so when the going gets tough, the relationship dissolves. As bad as a diffused identity may feel to a teenager, if that same teen forecloses into an identity that disintegrates in late adolescence or young adulthood, the strain of feeling out of place with one's peers will be even more stressful (Neuringer, 1974).

Using Freud's work as a foundation for ego development, some psychologists have emphasized the role of *shame* in identity development (Kalafat & Lester, 2000; Shreve & Kunkel, 1991). They describe shame as a sense of personal inadequacy stemming from a failure to reach one's own internalized ideals. It is not bad feelings about what one has done. That is *guilt*. It is feeling bad about who one is—an inadequate self. In adolescence, this sense of shame can result in a lack of cohesiveness in the newly formed self. The adolescent develops a good set of ideals as to who he or she wants to be but feels such shame about failing to reach those goals that a sense of self-loathing begins to emerge. To an adolescent in this circumstance, suicide may seem like a good coping strategy. It simultaneously ends the pain while, at the same time, punishes oneself for being shamefully inadequate. This is an example of taking a maladaptive coping strategy to its tragic and final extreme. Because of the pain involved, together with feelings of helplessness and hopelessness, an adolescent's judgment is skewed so that a maladaptive coping strategy is employed, often with tragic consequences.

An adolescent's cognitive development may also help create a situation in which an adolescent may be more vulnerable to suicide. Adolescents are fully capable intellectually of understanding the universality and finality of death. They have the cognitive development to understand those concepts. However, adolescents are also very egocentric and believe that their newly found identities are indestructible (Jurich, 1985). Therefore, paradoxically, adolescents may fail to grasp that, if they take their own lives, they really will die and not return to life (Hawton, 1986; Manor et al., 2004). Consequently, it is questionable as to whether adolescents who use suicide as a coping technique really know that they are going to die, in the full sense of what death is (Jurich & Collins, 1996). They may be egocentrically deluded into thinking that, if they commit suicide, they really won't die and everyone will feel sorry for them. This brings to question whether adolescents who commit suicide really have full emotional knowledge of their actions.

The personal factors may also contribute to the adolescents' resources. Just as a physically healthy teenager contributes to the potential resources that can be called upon in times of stress, a healthy self-concept contributes greatly to the adolescent's resource tool box (Crockett, Randall, Shen, Russell & Driscoll, 2005; Jurich, 1987). Flexibility and the ability to adapt to change are important personal traits which may be of use in times of stress and crisis.

A sense of humor may give the adolescent a sense of perspective during a crisis. Humor creates distance. Sometimes, an adolescent who can distance himself or herself from a crisis with humor can get a better perspective about the stress and muster the resources to cope with it. An internal locus of control, in which the individual feels as if he or she controls most of what happens in life, has also been shown to be an excellent resource in coping with stress (Jurich & Polson, 1984). Using personal resources to supplement one's coping strategies is very beneficial to the individual under stress, crisis, and pile-up. Two broad coping strategies used by individuals are *imperviousness* and *resilience*. Each has its place in coping with life's stressors. Imperviousness is the ability of the individual to withstand small stressors. A person who is good at being impervious "lets things roll off like water off a duck's back." Resilience is the ability to bounce back after being knocked down by some more major stressors. An adolescent needs to have both of these coping strategies at his or her disposal in order to best cope with the adversity of stress. If an adolescent is good at being impervious but not at being resilient, he or she will be able to handle the common stressors of life but will have problems with major pile-up. If a person is resilient but not impervious, he or she will handle life's pile-ups will but will be tortured by small stressors in life. The adolescent is optimally situated when he or she can draw upon both impervious and resilient coping strategies when necessary. Thus, the personal factors of individuals are key components in deciding whether they will cope with stressors, crises, and pile-ups in a bonadaptive or maladaptive manner (O'Connor & Sheehy, 2001).

FAMILY FACTORS

A number of researchers have stated that the family may be the single most important factor in an adolescent's entertaining suicidal thoughts or actions (Triolo et al., 1987). This may be especially true for preadolescents and early adolescents who have fewer resources outside the family than do middle and late adolescents. Theoretical models that focus on normal family interaction patterns attempt to elaborate about the normal family processes. Once those are established, these models examine the pathological processes of families in order to link those patterns with the etiology of suicide in adolescents (Orbach, 1988). For example, utilizing the Circumplex model of family interaction, research has shown that moderate degrees of cohesion (family connectedness) were present in healthy families (Olsen, Sprenkle, & Russell, 1979). Extremes in cohesion have been found to be associated with a multitude of problems. Families who were disengaged and distant from one another produced adolescents who felt disconnected and isolated. Those who came from enmeshed families often produced adolescents who felt smothered and felt like they were a prisoner to their own family.

A number of studies found suicidal adolescents came from families who were either enmeshed or disengaged (Collins, 1990; Corder, Page, & Corder, 1974) or found that their families vacillated back and forth between both extremes in cohesion (Pfeffer, 1986). Families who have had a suicidal adolescent and have been described as disengaged were characterized by a lack of warmth (Corder et al., 1974), a lack of empathy (Miller, King, Shain, & Naylor, 1992; Wodarski & Harris, 1987), and a lack of supportive adults in the home (Morano, Cisler, &

Lemerond, 1993). The adolescents described these families as "a house but not a home." Conversely, families who were engaged with their adolescents and were aware of their daily activities produced adolescents who were better adjusted (Waizenhofer, Buchanan & Jackson, Newman, 2004). Families with suicidal adolescents who were described as being enmeshed with their families were characterized as being overcontrolling (Corder et al., 1974) and as stunting the adolescent's quest for differentiation and individuation from the family (Pfeffer, 1986; Wenz, 1979). These adolescents felt that their parents tightly controlled them in an effort to keep them from growing up so that they would still be dependent on their parents. In this way a family trait such as cohesion, which in normal families is moderate, can be correlated to suicidal adolescents if the cohesion is too extreme in either direction, too enmeshed, or too disengaged.

In similar fashion, the other main dimension of the Circumplex model, adaptability, functions in a similar manner (Olson et al., 1979). Moderate levels of adaptability have been associated with normal functioning families. Extremes in adaptability have been associated with more pathological families who have produced a suicidal adolescent (Collins, 1990). Chaotic families who have a suicidal adolescent tend to be disintegrating, multiproblem families, with few functioned coping skills (Miller et al., 1992). Rigid families who have suicidal adolescents are so frozen in ritual and roles that are "tried and true" methods of coping that they do not have the ability to adjust to changes within the family, especially those changes brought about by a maturing adolescent (Pfeffer, 1986). In either case, the developmental needs of all family members, especially the adolescent, go unrecognized or unmet by the parents or by the entire family. This results in the adolescents' developing poor interpersonal and social skills and impaired problem-solving skills, which are often linked to suicidal behavior (O'Connor & Sheehy, 2001).

If we combine extremities on these dimensions together, we can see where such pathological extremes of family characteristics can lead an adolescent to commit suicide. In a family which is rigidly disengaged, the adolescent experiences the pain of being isolated from one's own family along with an inflexible family system, which limits both the possibility of change and the probability that change will be employed to lessen that pain (Miller et al., 1992). To the adolescent in this situation, suicide may seem like the only way out.

When rigidity is combined with enmeshment in the adolescent's family, the adolescent feels as if all of the decision-making power resides in the hands of the parents, with little or no input or involvement by the adolescent (Corder et al., 1974). In this situation, the adolescent feels little or no power over his or her involvement with the family and, therefore, feels trapped in a child-like developmental stage. Because any sign of autonomy or individuation will be seen by the parents as disloyalty and, therefore, betrayal of the family, the adolescent feels powerless to change the family environment that has stunted his or her growth (Pfeffer, 1986). Suicide becomes the adolescent's desperate effort to restore some sense of personal power in an attempt to meet his or her own developmental needs.

When families are chaotically disengaged, the family is so scattered in its interpersonal focus that the adolescent feels lost in the shuffle. There is no sense of order in the family and chaos reigns. Because the family is disengaged, nobody seems to care what the other family members are doing or feeling. As one adolescent described it, "I don't have a home; I have a boarding house to flop in." Because adolescents are trying to establish their own sense of independence, such a description of "home" has, on one hand, a lot of appeal to them. There seem to be few rules or no rules and nobody seems to "get in your business." For many adolescents from more typical families, this might seem like a dream. Adolescents in such chaotic disengaged families might even brag about the autonomy they have. However, the adolescent soon comes to realize that the reason why they have so much autonomy is that the rest of the family doesn't really care about them. They are chaotically bouncing through life by themselves, with little thought about the other family members. When adolescents finally realize that this is the case, they feel unloved and abandoned. Their peers might give them support but that support ebbs and flows with the whims of the peer group. This is especially true of preadolescents and early adolescents who are more in need of parental support and less likely to have formed close friendships at that age. Many adolescents described themselves as being "abandoned" or "orphaned" by their families. If an adolescent takes this abandonment by the family as a sign that he is "not worth caring about," he or she may seek suicide as a way of not burdening the family with his or her needs (Kidd, 2004).

When families are chaotically enmeshed, adolescents receive a very confusing double message. They are told that they must be loyal to the family at all costs, but the family is so chaotic that there seem to be no rules on how to make that happen. Family loyalty is paramount, but the chaos of the family is so overwhelming that no pattern or predictability is apparent in the family's interactions. Loyalty issues seem to pop up out of nowhere and fade in importance without any sense of resolution. This type of family interaction is "crazy making" (Watzlawick et al., 1967). To the adolescent, it is impossible to create an independent ego identity because to be independent is to be disloyal. However, the circumstances in which loyalty questions arise are confusing at best. The adolescent has no anchor point because of the family chaos. There is also no modeling of negotiations or conflict resolution for the adolescent to follow. As one adolescent explained:

Everything would be quiet. I would be doing my own thing and then, *wham*! Either Mom or Dad would get on my case about how our family was first, and I was betraying the family by wanting to go out for the track team. They would yell and nag and then, *poof*! Everything would be dropped. Nothing I could say or do would change anything. I was helpless to do anything! Then it would start again. One time, when mom was ragging on me, I picked up the gun and threatened to shoot myself just to shut her up

Suicide can be a way of ending the chaos and ceasing the feeling of disloyalty. "If I don't know what else to do, killing myself at least takes me out of the equation."

Extremes in such basic family dimensions as cohesion adaptability make it dangerous to speak openly and honestly within the family system (Olson et al., 1979). In families with suicidal adolescents there is often a scarcity of communication among family members (Cordor et al., 1974; Wodarski & Harris, 1987). When the rules are unclear or are very rigid, any communication among family members may break a rigid rule or may violate a principle of which the adolescent was unaware. Many family members simply find it easier not to communicate at all, except for light chitchat of no consequence. When confronted with the prospect of walking through a minefield, the best path to take may be no path at all. Some families with suicidal adolescents communicate but do so very poorly (Asarnow, 1992; Pfeffer, 1986). If the family with extremes in cohesion and adaptability make it dangerous to communicate, a family member must develop "survival techniques" in order to be safe in the family. Family members may use secrecy in order to withhold information from other family members who might react badly to such information. Incongruent and disqualifying messages let a family member make statements but also allow him or her to escape the consequences of those statements by reducing the clarity of what was said. This obfuscation of meaning, to quote a fifteen-year-old male client, "turns up the fog index and lets me escape into that fog if I have to." Non-supportive messages protect the person sending them by attacking the listener ("the best defense is a good offense"). Double-binding communications take away the power of the listener by backing him or her into a corner with both choices benefiting the speaker, and neither necessarily benefiting the listener. When such patterns of communication are present in the family or the family doesn't communicate at all, stress is elevated in the family, and the family members lose each other as resources. This also restricts family members from sharing their perceptions about family matters and gaining new insights into family dynamics and themselves. Such a shut down of viable communication among family members works to the detriment of all three dimensions of Hill's ABC → X model (Hill, 1949).

Such flawed communication patterns also increase the level of hostility within the family (Pfefer, 1986; Rubenstein et al., 1989; Wodarski & Harris, 1987). Because everyone in the family is "walking on eggshells," everyone feels tension in the family on a continuous basis. Nerves are frayed, and everyone is irritable. Many family members begin to blame each other for these negative feelings, and the hostility within the family rises. Because adolescents are seeking their own autonomy, they are often at odds with the parental rules of the family (Jurich, 1979). This makes them the perfect scapegoats for the hostility. If something goes wrong, blame it on the adolescent (Buehler & Gerard, 2002). At a time when adolescents are trying to formulate their own independent ego identities, they are branded with an identity by their own family as "troublemaker." Adolescents can respond to this in one of two ways. They might fight back and attack those family members who are being hostile to them. If they take this course of action, they are validating to their families that they are, in fact, troublemakers. A second course of action is that they will believe that they are, in fact, a troublemaker, and they will accept the label. In either case, adolescents can easily begin that cycle of depression in which they loathe themselves and seek to punish themselves. As explained above, such anger turned inward will often begin the process that culminates in suicide.

Suicidal adolescents have often been subjected to emotional, physical, and sexual abuse (Allberg & Chu, 1990; Hamton, 1986; Shafii et al., 1985; Slaby & McGuire, 1989). Sexual abuse may be especially disturbing and damaging to the preadolescent population who have suicidal ideation (Jurich & Wearing, 2004; McHolm, MacMillan & Jamieson, 2003). A disturbing finding in the literature was that, regardless of whether the family hostility was directed towards the adolescent or not, forty-three percent of all adolescent suicide attempts were preceded by a family fight (Litt, Cuskey, & Rudd, 1983).

Because of this degree of hostility and the types of dysfunctional interaction patterns within the family, many families try to close off their boundaries in an effort to shield the family from the critical gaze of outsiders (Leigh, 1986). Making the family's boundaries somewhat impermeable does eliminate at least some of the outside criticism. However, unless the family can totally shut off any contact with the outside world, including all forms of mass media, some information from the outside world will creep into the conscience of the adolescent to tell him or her that something in this family is very wrong. It only exacerbates the adolescent's perception of the extremity of the family's dysfunctions. In addition, closing off the family's boundaries may cut the family off from any external resources (Sands & Dixon, 1986). As a result, suicidal adolescents see their families as being totally alone and isolated, with no hope of changing their present interaction patterns. The adolescent sees his or her family as being stuck in a world of pain with no way out (Asarnow, 1992). In these circumstances the adolescent may view suicide as the only option available to force the family to open up its boundaries.

The origin of much of the hostility and closing of the family's boundaries seems to stem from the inability of the parents to accept and perform parental roles (Pfeffer, 1986). Parents of suicidal adolescents often demonstrate a marked inability to deal with their own childhood trauma (Sands & Dixon, 1986). Some of these parents were abused when they were children. Many suffered through some highly stressful times, such as poverty, crime, loss of a job, divorce, or premature deaths in their own family of origin. This can often lead to the parents' being depressed (Forehand, Jones, Brody & Armistead, 2002; Hammen, Shih, & Brennan, 2004). It is very typical that the adolescent may model this depressive behavior, thus transmitting the depression from one generation to the next. Now that they have established their own family (family of procreation), they are so egocentric in trying to meet their own unmet needs that they have a difficult time comprehending the normative parenting expectations placed on them by society (Wenz, 1979). Therefore, they struggle to accomplish the duties of parenthood and are inadequate in offering much guidance about values or coping skills to the adolescent (Asarnow, 1992; Peck, 1982). With no role model to follow, adolescents may have little to guide them in establishing resources or developing coping skills. Consequently, the adolescent attempts to create coping techniques through trial-and-error (Wenz, 1979). Although some of these resources and coping skills may be functional, a number of them will be maladaptive. Suicide may become one of these maladaptive techniques of coping that an adolescent may explore when he or she is trying to make sense of an extremely confusing world.

Many parents have trouble, not only with their parental roles but with their spousal roles as well (Buehler & Gerard, 2002; Pfeffer, 1986).

Families with suicidal adolescents often have severe marital discord (Berman, 1985; Sands & Dixon, 1986). A home with marital fights (either physical or verbal) produces high levels of stress for the adolescent. What adolescent wants to experience two of the most important people in his or her life hitting each other or calling names? It is very easy for the adolescent to become triangulated into the spousal relationship under these circumstances. If this does occur, it is also very easy for the adolescent to feel some sense of responsibility for the marital problems and perhaps even blame himself or herself for the parents' spousal problems.

Even if the adolescent is not triangulated into this spousal relationship, the adolescent may still be affected by marital discord. Adolescents are at a time of life where they are exploring the vast possibilities of coupling relationships, be they heterosexual or homosexual. They are learning what it is like to fall in love. Once they have established a solid ego identity, the next developmental task for them is establishing intimacy (Erikson, 1968). An adolescent who is working on his or her own feelings of intimacy has to live in the same house as parents who are modeling intimate spousal relationships by fighting all of the time (Jurich & Jones, 1986). This is not the model that young people want to have of an intimate relationship. Sadly, I have had a number of students and clients who tell me that they never want to get married because they saw the way their parents turned out. This is a difficult decision to hold, considering the peer pressure and pressure from the media to be romantic, sexual, and intimate. The adolescent may feel caught in a vise in which suicide looks like a solution to the problems.

In many cases marital discord can lead to marital separation or divorce (Allberg & Chu, 1990). We have previously discussed how cataclysmic a stress or divorce can be to the whole family. As one adolescent girl, age 13, told me:

> Divorce is a bummer. Your stress is doubled and your friends are halved. Your future drops to zero.

The stressors surrounding divorce are great (Videon, 2002). The animosity and uncertainty of parental divorce keep the adolescent's life in a constant state of upheaval. Because of divorce, many adolescents may spend part of their life in a single-parent family (Garland & Zigler, 1993). Not only is one resource, the noncustodial parent, taken away but, because of the burden of having to perform the duties of two parents, the custodial parent is also lost to the adolescent as a resource (Jurich & Jones, 1986). For the adolescent, especially the preadolescent and early adolescent, the lack of a stable home environment leaves them with a profound sense of loss.

It is this sense of loss that characterizes many suicidal adolescents when they speak about their families (Arensman & Kerkhof, 1996; Henry et al., 1993; Morano et al., 1993). This loss may be due to a parent's death (Allberg & Chu, 1990), parental absence because of work (Shafii et al., 1985), or drug or alcohol use (Henry et al., 1993). The loss may be particularly disturbing if a parent committed suicide (Arensman & Kerkhof, 1996; Rubenstein et al., 1989). Not only does the adolescent experience the loss of a parent but he or she watches, up close and personal, how to commit suicide. That is a very powerful maladaptive model to expose to an impressionable young person. If a parent commits suicide, there is a five times greater chance of his or her child committing suicide. That type of modeling is overwhelming to many adolescents. A parent may fall victim to chronic illness (Hawton, 1986) or may be trying to cope with his or her own emotional problems (Berman, 1985). In these situations, the parent may feel unable to meet the emotional or interpersonal needs of the adolescent. Once again, the adolescent is left with sharing his or her parent's stress while they lose that parent as a resource (Forehand et al., 2002).

Even if both parents are present in the family and seem to be unburdened by these stressors, they may be psychologically absent and unavailable to the suicidal adolescent (Hawton, 1986). It is hard for the adolescent not to feel ignored (Henry et al., 1993). Their troubles and tribulations do not even make it onto the parent's radar screen. Many adolescents feel unwanted and unloved by their families (Triolo et al., 1984). Even worse, they may feel unlovable (Kidd, 2004). In such families, suicides or suicide attempts may be more about being a symptom for the family's dysfunction rather than the adolescent's own pathology. An adolescent's suicide attempt diverts attention away from the family's problems (Henry et al., 1993) and may push the family further toward maladaptation.

PEER FACTORS

Peers are important relationships for all of us. However, they hold a place of central importance for the adolescent because the peers provide a counterpoint to the influence of the family in the adolescent's establishment of his or her own ego identity (Jurich, 1987). Therefore, peers are inordinately important to adolescents. If the adolescent is accepted or even well liked by his or her peers, all is right with the world and the adolescent has a very strong set of resources to help cope with stress. However, a lack of peer acceptance may be devastating, both causing stress and eliminating resources. What makes this situation worse is the fact that adolescents can often be hypersensitive to any messages about nonacceptance from friends, acquaintances, or the peer group as a whole (Kirk, 1993). Early adolescents are especially vulnerable to this dynamic (Jurich, 1987). They seemed to be trapped by their own inability to internalize peer acceptance to validate themselves. Because of this developmental lack of skill in internalizing, they need the constant validation of the peer group. This makes them very vulnerable to the whims of the group and takes away the adolescents' control over their own ego development. As the adolescent matures through middle adolescence and late adolescence, skills in internalizing validation and self-validation grow and help the adolescent be less vulnerable to the caprice of the peer group. However, even in the latter stages of adolescence, adolescents who find themselves without peer acceptance, belonging, and affirmation, may find their own self-esteem diminishing and their minds turning to thoughts of suicide (Kidd, 2004; Sands & Dixon, 1986).

When adolescents differentiate from their parents, they approach peer relationships and friendships on their own terms (Jurich, 1987). They diminish their allegiance to the peer group and begin to choose friends for their mutually beneficial relationships with them. There is an identification with these friends and a natural support develops. However, when adolescents fail to differentiate from their parents, they are likely to feel either enmeshed or cut off from their families (Bowen, 1976). If they are still enmeshed with their parents, adolescents will feel disloyal to identify with their peers. If they are cut off from their families, adolescents will often feel that they are inadequate in relationships. "After all, even my family turned away from me." In either case, when adolescents fail to differentiate from their parents, they also fail to differentiate from their peers (Sands & Dixon, 1986; Wodarski & Harris, 1987). Adolescents who feel inadequate in social situations but feel that they are surrounded by socially competent peers will, most likely, decrease their self-esteem (Holinger & Offer, 1981; Sands & Dixon, 1985). Suicidal adolescents often expressed less satisfaction with their peer relationships and friendships (Forrest, 1998). However, they also expressed a need to have a social group of peers in order to enhance their self-esteem (Rubenstein et al., 1989). This poses a serious problem for suicidal adolescents. They almost desperately want what they are poorly suited to pursue (Neuringer, 1974). Another problem exacerbating this situation for the early adolescents is that they also want their parents to approve of their peer group (Triolo et al., 1984). Especially if the adolescent is feeling either cut-off from or enmeshed with his or her family, the parents will not likely give up their power in the parent–adolescent relationship by validating the peer group, which is their potential rival for the control of the adolescent. The suicidal adolescent may feel "painted into a corner" as far as peer relationships.

When these adolescents do come into social contact with their peers, they lack the necessary social communication skills to be very successful at establishing mutually beneficial peer relationships (Allberg & Chu, 1990). Contacts with peers are often awkward and may be even humiliating (Blumenthal, 1990). Because of these experiences, an adolescent may isolate himself or herself (Allberg & Chu, 1990; Rutter & Behrendt, 2004) and become a "loner" (Wodarski & Harris, 1987). Not only is this painful but it leaves the adolescent with fewer interpersonal resources and poor social supports (Blumenthal, 1990; Slaby & McGuire, 1989). This gives adolescents a feeling of emptiness in their lives (Hawton, 1986). This can lead to loneliness, depression, and further withdrawal from contact with their peers (Allberg & Chu,, 1990; Forrest, 1988). A suicide attempt may be the adolescent's only way of dramatically attempting to communicate his or her pain to peers and family (Allberg & Chu, 1990). Therefore, the suicidal adolescent may become the victim of his or her own conflicting social pressures, resulting in alienation and marginalization (Sands & Dixon; Young, 1985).

There are a number of situations that exacerbate the adolescent's vulnerability to peer stress. Romantic relationships can be a great source of support and validation to an adolescent who has trouble relating to peers (Jurich, 1987). What better validation is there than to have a person tell you, "I love you and I want to spend the rest of my life with you"? Unfortunately, the entire adolescent population has read too many fairy tales and, unfortunately, believes in many of the modern myths of romantic relationships. For instance, adolescents believe that the hard part about relationships is "finding the right person." Once you've found the "right person," "relationships are easy and everything just falls into place." Nothing could be further from the truth. Once you've found the "right person," then the hard work starts. People have to work at making a romantic relationship successful. It just doesn't "just happen." Many adolescents expect their relationships to be problem-free. That is just not a realistic picture of intimate relationships. Therefore, they are surprised, shocked, and disappointed when they have to negotiate with an intimate partner and cope with differences of opinion. For adolescents who have inadequate social skills in their peer relationships, believing in this myth can have terrible consequences. The intimate relationship means more to those adolescents because it makes up for and substitutes for the relationships with peers that did not work. If the adolescents come to view their intimate romantic relationship as being unstable and problematic, even if their expectations of that view are fueled by unrealistic mythical assumptions of an overly romantic society, they will assume that, once more, they have failed at peer relationships (Berman, 1985; Henry et al., 1993).

There is another societal myth which comes into play at this point. Overly romanticized society tells us that there is only one true, perfect person for you—one soul mate. For those who believe in this myth, if they meet this "soul mate" and the relationship fails, they have blown their one chance at true happiness. For a thirty-year-old, a divorce can be a terrible, painful experience. However, in many ways it is easier than the break-up of a first intimate romantic relationship at age sixteen. Even though the divorce at age thirty will be much more complicated and signifies the termination of a relationship that was pledged to last a lifetime, in many respects, it is still easier than the sixteen-year-old's break-up of a three-month relationship. The thirty-year-old knows he or she will survive and that there is probably someone out there with whom he or she can create another, more functional relationship. The sixteen-year-old doesn't know that. Because of the lack of dating and intimate experiences prior to this relationship, the sixteen-year-old relies on the societal myth that says that there is one perfect soul mate. If the adolescent has blown that one chance, what is his or her future? Should he enter into a monastery or she into a convent to make wine or translate manuscripts for the rest of his or her life? They imagine they can't get into another intimate romantic relationship. Society has told them that they blew their one chance! Is it any wonder that adolescents whose romantic relationships have broken up are even more susceptible to the kind of peer stress that may result in suicide (Arensman & Kerkhof, 1996; Blumenthal, 1990; Canetto & Lester, 1999; Hawton, 1986; Sands & Dixon)? If these adolescents do not break up their romantic relationships and decide that they need each other so much that they will get married and try to raise a family in their teen years, their life will still not be "perfect" along the lines dictated by the societal myths. Trying to be a teenage spouse or, even more, a teenage spouse and a parent creates a life which is so filled with stress that it, too, is more likely to make them a candidate for suicide (Henry et al., 1993).

Sexual identity differences have been linked to a higher risk of suicide (Ryland & Kruesi, 1992). There does not seem to be anything inherent in the specific nature of homosexuality or bisexuality that seems to be causally linked to the etiology of suicide. However, because of our society's negative attitudes toward homosexuality, there is often a great deal of peer censure and even ridicule. This seems to be linked to the elevated rates of suicide among homosexual, lesbian, and bisexual adolescents. As one fifteen-year-old homosexual male related:

> Once you come out of the closet, you're a target. People stop talking when you approach a group. As you leave, someone softly mumbles the word "queer" behind your back. I've still got friends—good ones. But there are people I don't want to be around in an isolated situation. Look what they did to Matthew Shepard.

Such pressure cannot help but make peer pressure build and, with it, peer stressors. In addition, many peers are too scared of peer censure to support a gay friend. This takes away a lot of resources from the homosexual or bisexual adolescent. If these stressors are frequent and resources are weakened, suicide may seem like a viable alternative.

Many adolescents, who feel as if they don't fit in with the mainstream peer group, may attempt to cope in maladaptive ways. They may decide that using or abusing drugs is a way to cope. Such behavior may also give them a sense of acceptance with a specific subgroup of the population—the drug users. Although this may have some short-term benefits for the adolescent, there are also some long-term consequences. Aside from addiction and legal trouble, drug abusers feel inadequate because they are not able to cope with life without the psychological crutch of drugs (Jurich, Polson, Jurich, & Bates, 1985). This diminishes an adolescent's self-esteem. Drug use also teaches an adolescent to seek immediate relief from anything unpleasant by using drugs. Therefore, it teaches the adolescent to be highly impulsive. This combination of low self-esteem and high impulsivity makes the adolescent very vulnerable to seeking an immediate, impulsive release from pain by committing suicide (Arensman & Kerkhof, 1996; Beck & Steer, 1989; Garland & Zigler, 1993). Adolescents who feel inadequate to fit into the mainstream peer group, may turn to delinquent behavior and seek acceptance from "the hoods" or a juvenile delinquent gang. Despite all of the apparent bravado and independence from society, many delinquent adolescents often feel trapped by society's rules on one hand and the gang's rules on the other hand. Suicide may be looked upon to provide an avenue of escape (Kidd, 2004; Sands & Dixon, 1986).

When there is a difference between an adolescent's intellectual development and his or her social development, problems can arise (Delise, 1986). Although adults may treat these adolescents according to their intellectual age by giving them advanced academic standing or skipping a grade or two, these adolescents are very well aware that they are inferior to their peers when it comes to social skills. Despite adult kudos on their academic performance, they feel immature in their social skills and do not identify with their peers' needs and values. In fact, when one considers the fact that many peers may feel intellectually inferior to those adolescents, these peers may look upon the social arena as a way to "get back" at them or "bring them down to size." This creates tremendous stress and cuts off adolescent peer resources. It is for these reasons that gifted adolescents, especially females, have been found at a higher risk for suicide attempts (Delise, 1986; Shaushnessy & Nystul, 1985). For students who are having trouble in school, declining grades and failing in school can also be a source of personal and peer embarrassments, often leading to a suicide attempt (Henry et al., 1993; Rubenstein, 1989; Wodarski & Harris, 1987).

Even the simple act of residential mobility may pose severe problems for adolescents. Residential moves will disrupt relationships with peers, forcing the adolescent to be the "new kid on the block." The adolescent's ignorance of the new peer group rules and previous social relationships puts him or her at a tremendous disadvantage in making new friends. This induces new peer stress without the assistance of familiar resources to help the individual cope (Henry et al., 1993). This will increase the vulnerability of the adolescent to turn to suicide to cope with the pain (Arensman & Kerkhof, 1996).

The most dramatic example of the influence of adolescent peers on each other is the phenomenon of "cluster suicides" (Davidson, 1989; Gould, Petric, Kleinman, & Wallenstein, 1994). Cluster suicides occur when one adolescent commits suicide and the peer group is greatly disturbed by the event. As stated previously, since our culture has simply decided not to think about death, it always seems to catch us by surprise. Two other factors make this event even more problematic:

1. The death of an adolescent is an "out of time" death. Adolescents are not supposed to die at that age. They are supposed to grow old and eventually die during their geriatric years. This enhances the stressor event.
2. A suicide is a purposeful choice to embrace death. As this is so contrary to our normal fear of death and our treating death as an enemy, it is more shocking and more stressful. Guilt and blame may be present because the peer group will try to place the blame of the adolescent's suicide on someone in order to understand it better.

If the adolescent who committed suicide was well liked and thought of as highly competent, a peer might think, "God, if he committed suicide and he had his shit together and everyone liked him, how can I not commit suicide, too?" If the adolescent who committed suicide had problems, a peer might reason: "She was just like me. Maybe suicide is an alternative for me, too. Everybody says 'She's in a better place now.' Maybe that's where I should be, too."

If the suicidal adolescent was a "loner" and relatively unknown, how the peers and school handles the suicide might have a major impact on the possibility of future suicides. A school needs to have empathy for the victim, but it needs to label his choice as a foolish one and speak about the cost of such an absolute choice. If the school lionizes the suicide victim, puts his picture on the front page of the paper, and is effusive in praising him, a peer might think, "He was a nobody! Yet, look at all the attention he got from his suicide. He ate lunch by himself four out of five days a week but everyone is saying that he was their best friend. Look at the attention he's getting. I bet they would do the same for me if I committed suicide."

These are not the kinds of internal dialogues we want our adolescents to be having. The results can be deadly. For example, on February 19, 1983, a seventeen-year-old male was killed in what was reported to be a drag racing incident in Plano, a suburb of Dallas, Texas. Within the next eight weeks, three other Plano teenagers, including the seventeen-year-old's best friend, took their own lives (Gelman & Gangelhoff, 1983).

Studies have shown that just knowing somebody who has committed suicide (Blumenthal, 1990) or somebody who was murdered (Berlin, 1987), especially a peer, is enough to increase the risk of suicide. However, in cluster suicides the initial adolescent who commits suicide seems to breed a contagion among other adolescent peers in a manner that mirrors the spread of an infectious disease (Gould, 1990). The identification with the adolescent who has just committed suicide is very powerful for the adolescent who is formulating his or her own identity. Adolescents are very vulnerable to the influence of peer modeling (Davidson, 1989). This major peer influence can tip the teeter-totter towards maladaptation for not only one suicidal young person but for many others as well (Jurich & Collins, 1996).

COMMUNITY FACTORS

At the broadest level, the term *community* refers to the culture in which an adolescent lives. Many scientists have wondered if adolescent suicide is a uniquely American phenomenon. We in the United States are not alone about our concern for adolescent suicides. In the *International Handbook of Adolescence* (Hurrelmann, 1994), excluding the United

States, one half of the 30 countries about which a chapter was written felt the need to have a section on adolescent suicide (Jurich & Collins, 1996). Each country responds very differently to the phenomenon of adolescent suicide (Hawton, 1986). Some cultures, especially those of an agrarian nature, seem to change at a slower pace. Others, especially highly industrialized countries, change rapidly. It is these rapidly changing cultures which create more turmoil for their adolescents, increasing the number and magnitude of stressors (Ryland & Kruesi, 1992).

Within the greater culture, there are a number of subcultures that view death, dying, and suicide in different ways (Irish, Lundquist, & Nelsen, 1993). Within a pluralistic culture such as the United States, this is certainly true. Certain tribes within the Native American population have the highest suicide rates in the United States (Berlin, 1987; Centers for Disease Control and Prevention, 2002). This population has a number of factors that contribute to the stress of Native American adolescents (Henry, et al., 1993). Poverty and economic hardship poses a major problem. Not only does it create stressors in the life of the adolescent but it also limits the adolescent's access to resources. For many Native American adolescents, their life on the reservation is compared to the life in the culture at large, as depicted for them on television. This may breed dissatisfaction among the adolescents who believe the unrealistic image of how people in the culture at large live. The Native American population is still feeling the effects of the forced displacement of children and adolescents to boarding schools, engineered by the federal government. There are also conflicting and sometimes even paradoxical messages given to the Native American youth by the culture of his or her tribal heritage and the culture at large. In addition to these factors is the prejudice and discrimination suffered at the hands of the majority culture. These all serve to add stressors to the Native American adolescent's life. In addition, poor coping techniques, in the form of alcoholism and drug abuse are sometimes modeled for the adolescents by tribal adults (Henry et al., 1993). Finally, many Native American tribal cultures do not have the same negative view of death and suicide that is generally found in the larger society. The removal of the larger culture's negative attitudes about death and suicide lowers a barrier against using suicide as an active coping technique (Jurich & Collins, 1996). Considering these factors, it is little wonder that, for some Native American adolescents, the suicide rate is so high.

Even for those ethnic minority groups where the suicide rate has been historically low, such as the African-American population, there are problematic conditions that have recently caused the suicide rate of young African-American adolescents to rise (Centers for Disease

Control and Prevention, 2002; Murry & Bell-Scott, 1994). With the history of slavery and oppression in the background of many African-American families, it is no surprise that many in the African-American community have felt a strong sense of alienation from the majority culture. Many have sought to distance themselves from the culture at large because of this sense of alienation. Although this attitude may serve to lessen stress by isolating the African-American adolescent from societal discrimination, it also has the unintended consequence of cutting off many African-American adolescents from needed resources. This situation is worst in the urban ghetto. In the inner city or "the 'hood," poverty, overcrowding, crime, violence, and social isolation from mainstream society can create feelings of powerlessness, depression, and despair among young people. Adding to these problems is the psychological distress caused by both real and perceived discrimination because of their race (Cassidy et al., 2004). Facing these stressors with few resources is difficult and, increasingly, adolescents are turning to suicide as a possible way out. Thus, for the subcultures at either end of the continuum of suicide rates, there are still pressures that can lead to a variety of forms of maladaptation, including suicide.

Within the larger society, communities vary significantly in the degree to which they value their young people and support them through this very difficult period of life, their adolescence. If a community is quick to punish or arrest an adolescent, it will not be looked upon by its adolescents as being "user friendly" (Kirk, 1993). Instead, it will be viewed as yet another sign that theirs is a hostile environment in which to live. If the community is a highly transient one, where many families move in and move out, adolescents will be under stress and feel no allegiance to such a community and its rules. If there are no social supports to help the teenager cope with these stressors, the adolescent will be more likely to become maladaptive (Hawton, 1986). If the community's adolescent population is large, it may stretch the community's resources to assist them (Holinger & Offer, 1981; Ryland & Kruesi, 1992). Competition for prized commodities, such as jobs, good grades, and status positions, may become fierce and adolescents may resort to maladaptive coping techniques such as violence. On a trip to the mall, adolescents may find themselves being courted by merchants to spend their money in their stores, yet the same adolescents may be chased out of the mall by the same merchants for "loitering too long" if they don't buy anything. The adolescents receive a paradoxical mixed message as to their worth to their community.

Many of a community's values are taken from those of the greater society. The greater society condones taking medications to cope with illness, either physical or psychological. This attitude is mirrored in individual communities. Adolescents see this portrayed on television and modeled by their parents, so many adolescents self-medicate by taking psychoactive substances, either legal or illegal (Beck & Steer, 1989; Geller & Luby, 1997). Therefore, the risk of a suicide by drug overdose is increased (Hawton, 1986), especially if a mental illness is involved (National Institute of Mental Health, 2001). The societal acceptance of violence creates a community atmosphere where violence is promoted as a problem-solving technique for young people (Berlin, 1987; Kreitman & Casey, 1988). That violence may be directed towards others or it may be directed towards oneself. In a society that allows for the widespread availability of firearms (Boyd & Moscick, 1986), researchers have found a positive correlation between the accessibility and use of firearms and suicide rates (Garland & Zigler, 1993; Lester, 1988). Since 1950, the number of firearms per person in the United States has dramatically risen, and the number of suicides by firearms has increased three times faster than all other methods of suicide (Boyd & Moscick, 1986). For adolescents who commit suicide, there is a greater availability of firearms in their homes than in the homes of their peers (Brent, Perper, Moritz, Baugher, & Allman, 1993). Thus, the effect of the society filters down from many levels to affect the individual suicidal adolescent (Bronfenbrebber, 1970; 1986).

How a community newspaper, television, or radio station reports an adolescent's suicide will have a great effect on any subsequent suicide attempts by the adolescent's peers (Henry et al., 1993). Suicides among adolescents seem to rise sharply if there is more media coverage of the event (Blumenthal, 1990; Garland & Zigler, 1993). The suicide rate in the broadcast region covered by the television or circulation region covered by the newspaper tends to increase for one to two months after a suicide has been covered by the media (Phillips, Carstensen, & Paight, 1989). This is particularly true for adolescents who see themselves as similar to the suicidal victim. How an individual community will respond to these societal values and how that community values its adolescents will have a major role in determining the community's adolescent suicide rate. If the adolescents in a community feel that they are cared for and cherished by the community, they will utilize their community resources to find other bonadaptive ways to cope with the stress of adolescence. However, if the adolescents feel alienated by their community, they will demonstrate no loyalty to their community and will exhibit a wide range of maladaptive coping strategies, including suicide.

These previous chapters have served to give the reader the background that I feel to be necessary to understand the very complex nature of suicide as it applies to adolescents. Applying even one therapeutic technique to all of the possible permutations of adolescents and problems, including the five factors outlined above, would be an impossible task. The remainder of the book will focus on therapeutic strategies and techniques. It is my hope that these strategies and techniques, when cross-referenced with the above information on suicide, adolescent development, and salient factors in the adolescents' lives, will help guide the reader in conducting therapy with suicidal adolescents.

Five

THE THERAPEUTIC FRAMEWORK
FOR INTERVENTION
A Strategy for Family Therapy

FOUNDATIONS

The theories of the etiology of adolescent suicide give the therapist some direction in doing therapy with this population. The "Teeter-Totter Model" presented by Jurich and Collins (1996) suggested that the bonadaptation could be nourished if stressors could be eliminated or their impact be lessened or if additional resources could be utilized. For example coping skills could be taught. In addition, borrowing from Hill's original ABC $\rightarrow$ X Model (1949), a therapist could change the client's cognitions about the client's stressors or resources. This would suggest that cognitive therapy or cognitive behavioral techniques would be useful. Perhaps this is why these two approaches are so popular in treating suicide (Berman & Jobes, 1991; Hendin et al., 2005; Sueidman, 1998; Westefield et al., 2000). All of these types of intervention will be explored later in subsequent chapters.

In my own style of therapy, working with suicidal adolescents and their families, I have blended these approaches with my basic strategic approach to therapy. Although similar to the strategic therapy espoused by the Mental Research Institute (MRI) Group (Watzlawick et al., 1967), Jay Haley (1976) and Chloe Madaness (1981), and the Milan Group (Selvini, 1988), I came to my formulations about strategic therapy along a different path.

As a graduate student at Pennsylvania State University in the late 1960s and early 1970s, I read what I could about family therapy to augment my background in individual therapy. However, many of the seminal works had not yet been written (e.g., Jay Haley's *Problem Solving Therapy* (1976), Salvidor Minuchin's *Families and Family Therapy*, 1974; and Murray Bowen's chapter in *The American Handbook of Psychiatry*, 1975). I was well trained by two of my mentors, Bernard Guerney, Jr., and Louise Guerney, in what has come to be known as Relationship Enhancement Therapy (Guerney, 1969, 1977). Therefore, I knew client-centered interventions (Rogers, 1951) well, especially as they were applied to work with family systems. I was also trained in the behavioral work of Gerald Patterson (1971). Lastly, my other mentor, Carlfred Broderick (Broderick, 1993; Broderick & Schrader, 1991), taught me his techniques of insight-oriented intervention with families to show them the dynamics of the family system in order to change their perceptions about their family problems.

As useful as these techniques were in my work, they all had liabilities. My attention-deficit hyperactivity disorder (ADHD) personality makes me impatient to work exclusively within a client-centered approach. Furthermore, although I do believe that Roger's principles of *warmth, empathy,* and *genuineness* (Rogers, 1957) are necessary conditions for change in therapy, I do disagree that they are always sufficient to bring about change. Carl Whitaker has remarked that optimal therapy occurs when the therapist is interested and fully engaged in the therapeutic work (Whitaker & Bumbercy, 1988). I've always done effective behavioral work, but I find strictly behavioral work with clients to be relatively boring. I once had a client family where, over the course of therapy, we had created a loose-leaf binder with 46 specific behavioral contracts to guide the family's interactions. The therapy helped the family a lot but they seemed unable to generalize from one contract to a different situation. Good therapy but not very stimulating for the therapist. Insight therapy worked well except in cases where the client was incapable of using the insight or refused to use the insight. In those cases, I found myself wanting to break through to the client to bring about change.

In the third year of graduate school training, I attended a workshop with Albert Ellis on Rational-Emotive Therapy (Ellis, 1962). His postulation is that individuals have the ability to determine, in large part, their own behavior and emotional experience. He expressed this in his A-B-C theory of behavior and personality disturbance. "A" is the activating event or experience. It is objectively what happens. "B" is the Belief System of the person. "C" is the consequence of the interaction of the activating event (A) with the person's belief system (B). For Ellis, it is important to understand that "A" does not cause "C." In fact, Ellis would argue that, in situations which are pathological, "B" is likely to have as much or more causative power to produce a "C" that is inappropriate or irrational than does "A." To add my own interpretation to this formulation, I redefined the three elements to reflect the individual's types of thoughts during each situation. "A" is the individual's perception of the activating event or experience. "B" is the individual's interpretation of "A," based upon his or her belief system, and "C" is the individual's strategy for action, based upon the occurrence of "A" and the interpretation of "B." As in Ellis' formulation, the key to therapy is the "B" term.

For example, suppose I bring one of my cats into a room. A simple perception is "Tony brought a house cat into the room." This is a fairly simple "A" statement of the perception of the event. There may be times where a person's perception is faulty, such as an individual's forgetting to put on his or her glasses, but, for the most part, there will not be much variation or "error" in the "A" factor. However, the "B" factor, the interpretation of the "A," is based upon the individual's own idiosyncratic belief system and is, therefore, highly subjective and may be situation specific. Suppose the individual in the room into which I bring my cat is a "cat lover"? This person will experience my cat as a special event to make an animal connection with another cat. His or her "C" will be to pet my cat and maybe even ask to hold it. The "C" logically flows out of the "A" and "B." What if that person is a dog lover whose belief is that "dogs are great but cats are just okay."? This person's "C" will be to tolerate the cat and maybe even give it a pat or two. Once again, the "C" is determined by the same "A" but a different "B." What if the person is allergic to cats? The "A" is the same but the belief will interpret a "B" that my bringing a cat into the room is problematic. Who wants to be forced into a sneezing fit? This person's "C" will be avoidance, perhaps with an explanation to me about his or her allergies. Finally, suppose that the person in the room is phobic about cats (has ailurophobia)? The same activity event (A), my bringing my cat into the room, will trigger fear and panic responses as a "C" reaction. The same activating event (A) will trigger four distinct consequent strategies for reaction, based upon the individual's interpretation of "A." Each "C" is quite logical or rational, given the individual's "B." The irrationality lies in the variations possible in the potential interpretations (B). This formulation gave me a mechanism for understanding the process of the systems theory concept of "multifinality."

Ellis' strategy in therapy is to challenge the rationality of the client's interpretations (B) of activating events (A), in order to produce action strategies (C) that will be bonadaptive. His method for accomplishing this is to label client's "B" statement as being irrational, and encourage the client to replace these irrational statements with "B" statements that are more rational. Ellis has postulated eleven ideas or values universally inculcated by Western culture that are "irrational," "senseless," or "superstitious" (Ellis, 1962). If the client is rational and cooperative, Ellis' therapy closely mirrors that of Broderick. It gives insight to the client and asks the client to reformulate his or her interpretations. There may be some emotions involved and even encouraged but the process is primarily cognitive in nature. However, if the client is reluctant to change irrational ideas and beliefs, Ellis "attacks the irrational beliefs" and encourages the client to become very emotional about those interpretations. In his therapy, Ellis can be very confrontational and use the client's emotions to analyze and change those beliefs. Thus, Ellis' therapy is both "rational" and "emotive," hence its name.

What I experienced Albert Ellis doing in the workshop was creating "cognitive dissonance" in the client concerning his or her belief in general and in the interpretations spawned from those beliefs. Any two cognitive elements (bits of knowledge or beliefs) may be consonant, dissonant, or irrelevant with respect to each other (Festinger, 1957). If two cognitive elements are irrelevant to each other, they are unrelated. If they are consonant, the person holding those thoughts or beliefs feels congruent and, therefore, feels a general sense of well being. However, if the two cognitive elements are dissonant, the individual feels anxiety and imbalance. Dissonance occurs when one cognitive element follows psychologically from the contrary of the other. The person has difficulty in holding these two mutually incompatible beliefs at the same time. Therefore, cognitive dissonance creates an internal motivation for the person to change his or her beliefs so as to create a more consonant situation. Therefore, "states of dissonance have motivational properties" (Smith, 1969, p. 91). I believe that Albert Ellis creates cognitive dissonance in his clients to internally motivate them to change their beliefs. By labeling a belief or interpretation as "irrational," Ellis was saying to the client, "Surely a rational human being like yourself can see the folly of holding such an irrational belief?" The double bind is set. If the client is rational, he or she must change the belief. If the client is reluctant to change the belief, Ellis will label him or her as being irrational, a label few of us are willing to apply to ourselves.

Why is it so important to provide this "internal motivation" for the client? Any therapist has had the nightmare of a client who refuses to change. Therapy is a very difficult endeavor when the therapist works harder than the client. Some would say it is impossible. Adolescents are notorious for creating therapeutic situations in which they appear to be comfortable with the state of inertia, while the therapist or parents try endlessly to get him or her to change. Unless the therapist can change this dynamic, therapy is bound to fail. In the case of a suicidal adolescent, this means he or she will die.

Why do clients do this to the therapist who is trying to help them? Early in my career, when I was a volunteer drug counselor, a sixteen-year-old male client said that he dreaded seeing me twice a week. I asked him, "Why?" He replied:

> Nobody in this world spooks me like you do! First you try to get me to look at myself and then you push me to change. I know who I am! I may not like it but I know what I'm about. Pushing me to change scares the shit out of me! I wouldn't know what to do or who I am? That's some heavy shit to lay on me. Man, you're dangerous!

I had to think about that quite a while. I don't see myself as dangerous or scary. I see myself as helpful and as a nice guy. This brought home the point that "change is scary." Therefore, if my job as a therapist is to push for change, that makes me a dangerous person, indeed.

Freud (1955) postulated that resistance was the client's attempt to derail the therapeutic process, and it needed to be conquered. I came to the opinion that resistance is a normal response of a client or a client's family to the fear of change. One of the things that drew me to strategic therapy was the writings of Don Jackson and John Weakland (1971) in which they described the resistance, demonstrated by the families of schizophrenic clients, as being normal and understandable, given the stress under which they lived. Asking them to step into the unknown and change is a frightening request. I generalized their observations to all clients, although resistance would obviously be less severe in families which were less stressed. My formulation was:

$$Change = Pain/Comfort$$

As the client's pain increased, he or she would be more likely to embrace change and overcome resistance. If the client were too comfortable, the client would embrace inertia and use resistance to thwart change from occurring. When resistance is low, direct interventions, such as Rogerian Theory (Rogers, 1951), Behavioral Contracts (Patterson, 1971), and Insight-Oriented Interventions (Broderick, 1993) worked very well for me. However, if resistance was high, the techniques I borrowed from Ellis' Rational-Emotive Therapy worked well. Thus, these are the foundations for my therapeutic approach to adolescents and their families.

FORMULATION

At this point, I would like to provide a brief overview of my formulation of the therapeutic process as I would typically utilize it with a family in therapy. This process will be revisited in the following chapters specifically dealing with families in which an adolescent member is having suicidal ideation.

JOINING

The initial step in the therapeutic process is joining (Jurich, 1990). Many therapists and researchers consider the initiation and nurturance of the therapist's relationship with the clients to be the single most important factor in determining whether the client will be successful in therapy (Duncan, Hubble, & Miller, 1997). When doing family therapy with adolescents and their families, I dress down to the teenager's level. My grey hair, my clinical marriage and family therapy license, my Ph.D., and the fact that I am a university professor all give me credence with the parents in the family. It is the adolescent whom I must win over. For an initial meeting, I never wear a jacket and tie. If I'm in the mood to dress up, I'll put on Dockers and a golf shirt. If not, jeans and a t-shirt or comfortable shirt is typical. I also wear a lot of black, with which teens feel comfortable. I shake everybody's hand and make sure I understand each name. If the parents call the adolescent by one name and he or she uses another name, I will specifically ask the teenager which is preferred. If a pejorative name is used for the teen (e.g., Jimmy or Billy), even if everyone is using it, I will ask the adolescent if that is the name he or she prefers. If I am going to ask this adolescent to participate in therapy as an adult, I do not want a pejorative name getting in the way. My purpose is to break down barriers and to invite the family into a therapeutic situation that will shake up any preconceived notions they may have had of therapy.

At this point I ask the family what brings them to therapy. In most cases the parents will begin. Before the first session is over, I need to hear each family member's thoughts and, if possible, feelings about "the presenting problem." This means that I many have to encourage some people to speak and may have to ask some people to let others speak. Regardless of how the family has defined their rules in the past, I need to win the "battle for structure" (Minuchin, 1974) and redefine the rules and structure of the therapy session as being more equalitarian than they may be at home. During this process I try to employ the essence of Client Centered Therapy (Rogers, 1957). I try to be engaging and will give each family member unconditional positive regard, no matter how much animosity they exhibit among themselves. I try to demonstrate empathy with each family member so that each can feel heard and sense that I am trying to make both an intellectual and affective connection with him or her. Lastly, I try to be genuine. I try to be myself, with all the psychosocial bumps and bruises included. A number of years ago, a student watched me do therapy for the first time. After the session was over she came over to me and said:

> You fraud! You're no different in therapy than you are in class or in the hallways. I expected to hear some words of wisdom. Instead, I got just regular old you!

I smiled and asked her who she thought I was going to be? She smiled and said, "Maybe I can do this after all." Part of being genuine is being you. If you're putting on an act, the adolescent will smell it out immediately. The other part of being genuine is keeping the family, both the parents and adolescents, in reality. The fifteen-year-old adolescent who wants a three a.m. curfew on a school night needs to know that, in our culture, that is an unrealistic expectation. Parents who complain that their seventeen-year-old daughter is seldom home on the weekends need to be reminded that the adolescent's primary task is to establish her own independent ego identity. These anchors to reality are important.

I need to leave enough time at the end of the session to complete paperwork and schedule the next session. However, I also have to negotiate who will attend the therapy sessions. Most families have the expectation that you will do something to "fix their kid." As a family therapist, I often have to "sell" the family on everyone's participation. The family and the therapist have to redefine who the family is in therapy (Jurich and Johnson, 1999). I try to tell them how important it is to have everyone's input in the therapeutic process. I also tell them that I'm a better therapist with all family members in the room. I've often found that fathers are most reluctant to participate. Many men feel that it is their wife's job to deal with the psychosocial aspects of the family. Some men feel that their own role as "protector of the family's boundaries" has already been violated by coming to therapy. At that point I need to tell the family how important it is for everyone to participate in therapy. In the case of reluctant fathers, I often tell them that "It's hard to turn a double-play in baseball if the second baseman won't cover second base. We're here as a team, working together on this problem." In a world where the medical model insists on identifying an individual patient to be cured, it is hard for the family to abandon that model and focus on family dynamics. Hard though it might be, it is necessary.

Even in the first session, I want the clients to be thinking about their goals for the therapeutic process. Most often they will simply say that they want the presenting problem to "go away." At that point I will ask them, "What would you like to see in that problem's place if we eliminate it?" For me, getting rid of a problem is not enough. I want the family to articulate what will fill the vacuum that the absence of that problem will create. This accomplishes two things. First, it helps me analyze the function of the system within the family. How does this problem help the family in such a way that they hold onto the problem? This will help in my subsequent analysis of the family dynamics and give me clues to what may trigger the family's resistance to changing when I switch to strategic therapy. Secondly, if I can understand what the family wants the "problem-free future" to look like, I can better understand what direction they wish to pursue. As the solution-focused therapists argue, setting goals will give the clients and the therapist a sense of direction to guide the process of therapy (deShazer, 1985; Selekman, 2002, 2005). It is easier for both clients and therapists to decide what to do in therapy when they both know where they want to go.

Finally, I believe that it is my therapeutic duty to give the family a gift in each session. In the first session, I believe that I need to give them "hope." It is the hope that things can change and that there is a future without the debilitating problems that brought them into therapy. I don't want to sound like a Pollyanna or that change will occur with no work and no pain. That would not be genuine. Most families come to therapy believing that their problems are overwhelming and that they are the only family ever to face such obstacles. Although not wanting to rob the family of its uniqueness or denigrate their pain, I want to reassure them that there are things they haven't tried that have a good possibility of working. "You will work and sometimes work hard, but it is doable." If they feel that their situation is hopeless and you do nothing to dissuade that idea, why should they come back? Giving them a sense of hope makes it more likely that they will return for a second session.

ANALYZING FAMILY DYNAMICS

Drawing from my background in family systems and utilizing concepts from strategic therapy, I begin to analyze the family dynamics and individual behavioral patterns from the moment the family enters the therapy room. Who sits with whom lets me know where there are coalitions and potentially cut-offs. Who speaks first, who speaks most, and who gets the last word all give me indications of power hierarchy. I've always found Minuchin's work on structural therapy (1971) to be a good starting place. I especially want to watch how they respond to me and my cotherapist (if I have one). Am I looked upon as an ally or as an invader into the family system? Are they buzzing with chaos or do they rigidly try to fit me into their mold of whom they think I should be? Do they take responsibility for their behavior or do they blame someone else? Very often families will point fingers at each other and say, "Fix him, her, or them, because it's their fault, not mine." All of these impressions give me the "flavor" or "style" of family interactions.

The content of the discussion will be the presenting problem. I never specifically ask for the "identified patient." The family's discussion will make it obvious whom each family member will nominate to fill that role. I avoid labeling a specific family member as the identified patient because pathologizing one family member does not fit with my family therapy paradigm in which pathology either springs from faulty family interaction patterns or has its origins within the individual but is exacerbated by the family's interaction patterns. If it is necessary to label one family member as the identified patient, as in the case of filing an insurance claim, I prefer to use the label "symptom bearer" to describe the person in the eye of the storm. Although still conveying that person's centrality to the problem, it lets the family know that the presenting problem does not belong to that person alone but is shared by everyone in the family.

Following the strategy put forth by strategic therapy (Watzlawick, et al., 1967), my main focus is to look for *maladaptive recursive cycles* within the family's interaction patterns. These patterns are cycles in that they are interactions between and among family members, which exhibit "circular causality." There may be a starting place in the interaction but who started it is not a relevant aspect of the pattern. Most of the time, in a cycle between two family members, each person will declare that the other person started it and will be able to give evidence to prove the point. Getting to the "root cause of the problem" is, therefore, minimally useful. The more important fact is that the cycle keeps going, with each family member triggering a response from his or her partner until the cycle escalates and often becomes unstoppable. The important question isn't who started it but how to stop it. The cycle is maladaptive because it doesn't work. It causes additional pain and doesn't promote bonadaptation. Lastly, the maladaptive cycle is recursive because it happens over and over again. Therefore, we have a maladaptive recursive cycle.

A legitimate question to ask would be, "If it doesn't work, why keep doing it?" There are a lot of potential answers to that question. From Transgenerational Theory we know that many interaction patterns are learned in the family of origin (Bowen, 1976). Ivan Boszornenyi-Nagy coined the phrase "invisible loyalties" to describe the phenomenon in which family members cling to certain interaction patterns in an attempt to demonstrate loyalty to their family, despite the obvious problematic consequences of trying to cope in that way (Boszornenyi-Nagy & Spark, 1973). Many times these invisible loyalties are engaged without the individual's ever being conscious of doing so. Sometimes family members keep maladaptive recursive cycles going because they are engaging in a power struggle. Sometimes people cling to an interpersonal pattern because, without it, they may feel that they will lose their "sense of self." For them, the continuance of this pattern forms the basis of an existential crisis. Sometimes family members simply don't know what else to do. In any of these situations, it is important for me, as the therapist, to recognize them and strategize about ways to interrupt these maladaptive recursive cycles in order to bring about therapeutic change.

I also look for "leverage points" in the family system (Jurich, 1990). A leverage point is place in the family where I can apply pressure or change the flow of energy to help the family bring about change. Many of these leverage points come from an understanding about family systems, adolescents, and (in the case of this book) about adolescent suicide. This is the reason for the previous four chapters in this book. They will help the reader identify the leverage points within the family system. However, not all leverage points spring from the well of typical family systems and adolescent behavior. Many leverage points are idiosyncratic to the individual and the individual's family. These must be learned from the clients. They may make no sense in any context other than this client family at this point in time. They are so tied to the individual client family that the only way to fully appreciate them is though a case study. My best example for the reader to explore is a chapter which I wrote for David Baptiste's *Clinical Epiphanies in Marital and Family Therapy* (Jurich, 2002b).

As the primary tools in my therapeutic arsenal are insight, behavioral contracts, cognitive dissonance, my relationship with the clients, and me as the therapist, my search for leverage points is geared with these five tools in mind.

- How might I teach them a new coping skill or strategy?
- At what point in the family system is it most likely to be most effective?
- What kind of behavioral contract will work with which family members in which situations?

- Who might be most vulnerable to change by increasing cognitive dissonance?
- With whom is it most important for me to form a close therapeutic relationship so that the family won't bolt from therapy?
- Upon what part of my being, both as a person and as a therapist, can I call to change what part of the family to help promote therapeutic change?

These are some of the key questions to ask when analyzing the family dynamics.

TEACHING INSIGHT

Because of my professional training, reading, attending workshops, and professional experience, I, as a therapist simply have a lot more knowledge about adolescents, family interactions, and individual motivation than my clients. These are my areas of expertise and study. This is not true for most of my clients who have gathered their information base from their families, friends, and the popular media. Therefore, I can frequently assist the family to bring about change by teaching them some of my broader knowledge base. I become an informational resource for them.

Some insight that I import to my clients comes from the fact that, although I have become part of the therapy by being their therapist, I am not *in* their family. Therefore, I can be more objective about their family interactions. Notice that I did not say that I could be totally objective. No therapist can be completely objective (Anderson & Goolishian, 1988). By doing therapy with the family, the therapist becomes part of that family. Therefore, the therapist can't be completely objective. However, because the therapist is new to this family system, has a background in family dynamics and human development, and only spends an hour or two with the family per week, the therapist is much more likely to be more objective about the family's dynamics than the family members. This more objective sounding board for the family allows the family members to gain perspective about their family's interactions.

Many family dynamics hold great power over family members, as long as they are kept hidden and covert. However, if they are identified and overtly discussed, they often lose their power. For example, strategies of "guilting" or "pouting" work best if they are covert or subtle in their use. People being "guilted" or "pouted at" feel as if they are in a double bind. The "guilter" or "pouter" has overtly told them to have a good time without him or her. However, the way that that overt message was delivered (the tone of voice, facial expression, and body posture) gave a contradicting but more covert message of, "but I really don't want you to go without me, regardless of what I just said." This puts the guilted party or "poutee" in a classic double bind. He or she does not know which message to believe, the overt message of "go without me" or the covert message of "take me with you"? A therapist can drastically effect the power of such messages by making both messages overt and giving both family members insight as to their interactional pattern. In essence, this is actually quite a strategic intervention. The guilting or pouting creates a maladaptive recursive cycle. Making the covert overt disrupts this cycle and takes away much of the power. The perception of the guilter or pouter is changed from a "generous and long-suffering victim with no power" to "a very powerful and calculating manipulator." Once this image is unveiled for both parties, the strategy loses power and can more easily be discarded. Therefore, insight about family dynamics and development can serve as a strategic intervention also.

Lastly, the therapist can often give insight to a family by giving a voice to all of the members of the family. For instance, parents often assume that they are in agreement with parenting jobs, such as discipline. However, the reality is that one parent is comfortable with physical discipline but the other parent is not. If the parent who favors physical discipline is more vocal and more powerful in the family system, the other parent may feel disenfranchised from his or her own point of view. The therapist can give insight to the family by asking the disenfranchised parent if he or she really feels the same as the other parent. If the disenfranchised parent is allowed to voice his or her opinion, the underlying tension can rise to the surface and can be explored and negotiated objectively. Many of my clients have told me that the most important aspect of their therapy was that they felt safe to express how they really felt about family members and family dynamics. These new insights for the family don't come from research or theory but instead blossom from the family members themselves. Therapy simply provides them a "safe haven" where they can be discussed openly.

BEHAVIORAL INTERVENTIONS

There are some families who do not benefit from insight. They are often concrete thinkers who see the world as a series of discrete events. Therefore, insight is less useful to them. They also may be families who have staked out such oppositional adversarial positions that any insight would be used as a weapon, rather than as a resource. In the 1989 movie *War of the Roses*, the husband and wife are so adversarial that they see themselves as combatants. Any insights into the other person's feelings or thoughts are simply looked upon as another weapon in the battle. Some families are so overwhelmed by their problems that insight is not useful to them. For these families, I turn to behavioral interventions and, especially with adolescents in the family, behavioral contracting.

Some problems lend themselves better to behavioral interventions. Bed-wetting responds well to behavioral strategies and the purchase of a device placed under the sheet that wakes the child up if he or she wets the bed. This behaviorally teaches the child to be more conscious of the physical sensations that surround bed-wetting and, hopefully, to eventually be able to feel those sensations before wetting the bed. Similarly, phobias respond well to behavioral techniques such as "reciprocal inhibition" and "systematic desensitization" (Wolpe, 1973). In these techniques, clients are taught relaxation techniques to relax their muscles when they begin to feel anxious. Once the techniques are learned, the therapist and client make a list of events that would trigger the client's phobia. These events are placed in order, ranging from those events that would trigger a mild phobic response to those which would trigger major anxiety. The therapist, over time, asks the client to imagine each event, starting with the least anxiety-provoking and progressing to more anxiety-provoking events. While imagining each event, the client is asked to employ the relaxation techniques he or she was taught to lessen the anxiety. When the client reports having no anxiety with an event, the client and therapist move to the next most anxiety-provoking event. This process is repeated until the client feels little or no anxiety. These types of problems lend themselves well to behavioral interventions.

Many presenting problems in families with adolescents stem from areas of rules and discipline. Either the rules are nonexistent or parents are arbitrary and inconsistent in how they apply the rules, or parents have not formed an executive system to make and enforce the rules (Minuchin, 1974). In any of these situations, the rules need to be formulated, consistently applied, and effective consequences must be designed. Many families are incapable of or unwilling to do these tasks. In this situation, I turn to creating behavioral contracts with the family members. The way I do this is to tell the parents and adolescent that we will enter into a contract to formulate rules and how they will be reinforced. When we are done, I will have the clinic secretary type up the contract and have everybody sign it. It's amazing how an adolescent's arguments end when confronted with a contract with his or her signature on it. Everybody gets a copy of the contract and one is kept in their case file. In this way, no document can be lost or altered.

Let me provide an example. A seventeen-year-old boy is constantly violating his weekend curfew. The adolescent, his parents, and I sit down together to create a behavioral contract. As the negotiator, I start the process. I turn to the parents first and ask them to come up with a time for the curfew. They respond by saying nine p.m. The adolescent responds by exploding, "Nine p.m.! What do you think I am? Twelve years old?" Ignoring the emotion of his outburst, I respond to him by asking him to give his parents a counteroffer. He chooses two a.m. The parents begin to mumble about the adolescent's irresponsibility. Ignoring their response, I ask the adolescent if he would compromise and reduce his two a.m. curfew to midnight. Sarcastically, he responds that "they won't buy that!" I take a one-down position and suggest, "I don't know? Let's see!" He agrees to a midnight curfew. Now his parents are upset, and they protest that "he must be made to comply to a nine p.m. curfew!" I ask them if they would consider a ten p.m. curfew? At first, they are reluctant but, when I ask them if they want a nine p.m. curfew about which they perpetually fight or a ten p.m. curfew he follows, they acquiesce. I turn to the adolescent and ask him to lower his curfew request to ten p.m. It doesn't take a mathematical genius to figure out that he gave up four hours but his parents only gave up one. The adolescent complains, "It's not fair!" My response is "Life isn't fair. Furthermore, they pay the bills and are the adults. However, look what you got—an extra hour. If you follow that curfew and don't screw up, we might be able to raise it later."

We move on to negotiate the consequences. I tell them that I want three consequences: one for up to fifteen minutes late, one for sixteen to sixty minutes late, and one for over an hour late. Dad responds by saying, "Why? Late is late." I respond by telling him:

> No it isn't. At your work you can come in fifteen minutes late and still be okay. Your boss won't be happy but it's a lot better to be fifteen minutes late than three hours late. Furthermore, remember back to when you were your son's age. If the consequence for being twelve minutes late is the same as the consequence for staying out all night, what's your son's incentive for walking in the door? I would be willing to bet that he would turn around and spend the entire night out. His motto would be "Let's eat, drink, and be merry for tomorrow we're grounded."

This typically stops any further objections, and we negotiate consequences.

This process has several advantages. The rules are clear and unequivocal. Mom and dad have the power to make exceptions but, unless an exemption is specifically granted, the rule stands. If the contract isn't working, any party has the right to bring it up in therapy and ask to renegotiate the contract. Both the parents and the adolescent negotiated together, somewhat as coequals. This engenders respect for the adolescent in the parents and teaches the adolescent how to negotiate and form contracts, a basic skill he will need as an adult. Because I constantly explain the process, together with their individual thoughts and feelings, my use of behavioral contracting takes on the form of cognitive behavioral contracting. I not only work to change and shape the family's behavior but also their thoughts and attitudes about those changes. In this way I try to create a situation where both cognitions and behaviors change and mutually reinforce respective changes. Most families will accomplish only two or three contracts before they generalize these negotiating skills to the rest of their inter-actions. In this way, a short duration of therapy can have far-reaching therapeutic effects.

STRATEGIC THERAPY

At the first sign of any resistance on the part of any client family member, I switch to strategic therapy. Remember that, as a strategic therapist, I expect that most clients will have some resistance to change. Therefore, I am not alarmed by the client's resistance nor do I feel threatened by it. In fact, I believe that, if the client demonstrates some resistance, it probably means that I am on the right track. If a client is asked to change something that is of only minor importance, anxiety will be low and there will be little resistance. If, however, clients are asked to change something of central importance to their lives, the stakes are much higher, which leads to more anxiety and, consequently, more resistance to the danger of change. Therefore, resistance by the client is a "normal" response.

If the client begins to demonstrate resistance, it means one of two things:

1. The client wants to change but the course of therapy has gone "off target."
2. The client has been frightened by therapy in some way that his or her security is threatened. Therefore, the need for security begins to outweigh the pain of the presenting problem.

The therapist must be aware of both of these possibilities. If the therapist is aware of (1) and not (2), every time the therapy starts to explore a core area of the problem, the resistant client will find a way to manipulate the therapist from pursuing it further and therapy will be sabotaged. If the therapist is aware of (2) but not (1), he or she will egocentrically assume therapy is always "on track" and may pursue several "dead ends," much to the frustration of the client family.

As a therapist, I go back to the client family goals for therapy. I will ask the family to revisit their goals, both individually and as a family. I will then check with them if the course of therapy is moving them along to their goals for life. I invite them to tell me if they think that the course of therapy is "off track." I need to be open-minded and to realize that, in fact, I may have "lost the way" and therapy may be "sidetracked." If the family can convince me that we need to change direction, we change direction. If we all agree that we are "on course," we will discuss why things are "slowing down." If they think we are "off track" and I don't, we will try to proceed according to their wishes but I will reserve my opinion until I see how therapy proceeds. I have to be open to the fact that I may be wrong and therapy may have "wandered." Even with my expertise, the client family members have lived in their family longer than I have and therefore may know their family system better than I do. Furthermore, as the therapist, I am "a guest in their house" and should respect their rules.

However, if I feel that the family is, indeed, resistant and I have checked out that our present course of therapy is congruent with their goals, I will validate that therapy is hard work and is often a painful process. I will often suggest that we do some "experiments" to see if we are, in fact, "on track" with their goals. In this case, I will recap what we have accomplished, summarize the family members' feelings, and validate that they all, each in his or her own way, have worked hard. The stage is set for utilizing Strategic Therapy (Jurich, 1990).

The Hook

When clients begin to feel resistance they tend to pull away from therapy and the embodiment of therapy, the therapist. If a person begins to feel a lack of security, one way he or she can cope with it is by distancing himself or herself from the object or situation that is causing that insecurity, in this case—therapy. The attempt to distance is an attempt to make therapy less important and, therefore, have less investment in the change that therapy is demanding. If the therapist lets this happen, he or she may soon be dismissed as impotent and find himself or herself with greatly diminished effectiveness as a change agent.

When the therapist first joins with the family, part of that joining process is to "hook" the family into therapy. At a later time of resistance the therapist needs to hook the family once more so that therapy can continue. However, there is a second purpose for hooking the family at this time. Hooking the clients makes them feel at ease with the therapy process and will disarm them, giving them a sense of security. This hook is accomplished by encouraging existing patterns of interaction. Most typically, I accomplish this by summarizing what I have understood to be each family member's point of view and feelings. I then go on to specifically validate those thoughts and feelings by stating that I understand those thoughts and feelings, and that they are reasonable under present circumstances in which the family finds itself. Even if the feelings and thoughts of different family members contradict each other, the systemic therapist can still validate each person's point of view and, with all sincerity, recognize each family member's perceptions as being part of the entire family picture (Jurich, 1990).

The therapist's ability to hold multiple viewpoints as being valid is the key to the therapist's genuinely believing even contradictory views and feelings as being able to coexist at the same time. If the family can also accept multiple realities as existing within the family, resistance will lessen. If they are incapable of accepting multiple realities, each family member will at least hear the therapist's validation of his or her own reality, even if it means ignoring the rather obvious fact that the therapist has also validated other family members' realities as well. This feeling of acceptance affirms each family member's worldview of the family and sets the family up for the next step in strategic therapy.

The Slam

The "slam" is a sudden and dramatic change in the interaction between the therapist and the family (Jurich, 1990). This shift in interaction is specifically geared to disrupt the family's maladaptive recursive cycle of interaction. Because family members have been lulled into security and complacency by the hook, the slam catches them off guard and is more likely to disrupt previous rigid interaction patterns. Once this is done, old coping devices lose their power and underlying beliefs and feelings are allowed to emerge. The therapist creates a cognitive dissonance between old, rigidly held beliefs and feelings and a new reality which has emerged from the therapeutic process. I could catalog an entire chapter of slams that could be used by therapists. A slam need not smack of confrontation. Some can, in fact, be quite gentile and relatively unobtrusive. Others can be flamboyant and outrageous. The only requirement for a slam is that it be different from "business as normal" and create cognitive dissonance within each family member.

Some examples might help enlighten this process. As most families coming into therapy assume that, in therapy, the therapist will "lead them out of their problems," a therapist may slam the family by taking a "one-down" or "not knowing" position. Once that is done, the family can no longer be passive and wait for the therapist to "bail them out." The family will have to assume responsibility for their actions and have to express their rationale for how their interactions are logical and rational in order to accomplish the family's goals. Because the slam has projected them into a state of cognitive dissonance, the motivation for change has been shifted from "the therapist is trying to get me to change" to "I need to change to remove these yucky feelings of cognitive dissonance." The locus of control to change has been given back to the family, where it belongs, and the family's motivation to change has been enhanced by their added desire to reduce their cognitive dissonance.

Another therapist may produce a slam by reframing a family member's behavior in a way that is different than the family's existing hypothesis of the behavior. On one hand the therapist appears to align himself or herself with the family's status quo. However, the reframe also suggests that there might be some flaw in the family's logic upon which that status quo is based. For example, an adolescent boy who destroys physical property in his family's house can be labeled as being out of control and a delinquent by the entire family, including himself. However, if the therapist has discovered that the only time the young man does these destructive things is when his mother and father argue, the therapist might suggest a different motivation for this behavior. Instead of a delinquent, the therapist might label the adolescent as a "white knight" who is attempting to save his parents' marriage by trying to distract them from their argument and forcing them together to act as an executive parental system in order to deal with his behavior. This twist of the family's logic serves to disrupt their previously held maladaptive recursive cycle. "He's putting his fist through the wall in order to help us?" As crazy as that logic may seem, it is consistent with the facts of what takes place when parents argue. Furthermore, labeling the adolescent as a "white knight" gives him a positive social role that is steeped in everyone's childhood fairy tales. It dramatically relabels the adolescent's identity in a positive fashion, much to the surprise of the entire family, including the adolescent. It also gives the family a "shorthand" by which they can refer to this type of behavior for the adolescent at a future time. When the adolescent does something similar at school, the therapist can say, "Here he goes trying to be the white knight again," and everyone, including the adolescent, will know exactly what that means without having to explain the whole process again. Once this pattern is labeled, the therapist and parent can explain to the adolescent how his logic is flawed and that his mother and father have the strength to handle their own problems without his help. In essence, they can fire him as their white knight and allow him to return to being a teenager again.

A therapist can use a metaphor as a slam. The metaphor may increase the family's understanding of the maladaptive recursive cycle and even give added insight to the person in the center of the storm. For example, we may have a seventeen-year-old girl who is fighting an alcohol addiction. She's not sure why she drinks and her parents are at a loss as to why their daughter just can't say "no." Suppose the therapist describes this alcohol addiction, using the metaphor of a jealous lover?

> You know, when you describe how you like to drink, it sounds like you are describing a relationship with this really hot guy. He makes you feel good about yourself and tells you you're beautiful. All your friends think that it's so cool that you're going out with him. It makes you feel like a real adult. Your parents can't tell you not to go out with him because your dating life is your choice. He's a great boyfriend. Let's just call him Jack Daniels. The only problem with going out with old Jack is that he's the jealous type. He wants you to himself—completely. He wants to fix it where he monopolizes all of your time. No time or energy for other guys. No time for your family and goodness knows no time for school-work. You see, if he isolates you from everyone else, you're all his. You won't be your own person. You'll be a reflection of him.

This is an involved metaphor but look what it accomplishes. It validates the good feelings drinking alcohol does for her and explains those motivations in a way which is more accessible to her parents. However, it also elaborates on the paradoxical nature of alcoholism, that it eventually takes you over and you lose yourself. For an adolescent who is trying to formulate an independent ego identity, this is a very powerful metaphor.

A therapist can use rituals as a slam. In the above example, the therapist could use a funeral ritual to help the adolescent conquer her addiction. Eulogies could be read about the death of her boyfriend Jack Daniels. Each family member could eulogize Jack and talk about the good things he had done for the adolescent. Prayers for those loved ones he left behind can be said. A graveside service could be held at which a bottle of liquor could be buried as proxy for burying Jack. Because of the family's familiarity with our cultural rituals of death and burial, this ritual may make it easier for the family to share their adolescent's pain of separation from, and grieving for, her habit of addiction. The adolescent can hear her family speak about the good and bad aspects of her drinking. Even the most hardcore alcoholic will be intrigued with the possibility of describing her drinking as her lover. The very outlandishness of this ritual will give it power to disrupt the maladaptive recursive cycle which the family had previously described as normal.

The therapist may use a paradoxical directive as a slam. A young man who is twenty-two and still lives with his parents is having a hard time finding a job. His parents describe him as lazy because he rarely tries to find work. When he does get a job, he manages to get fired within two or three days for "screwing something up." They think that he would be happy just sponging off them for the rest of his life. In therapy, their expressions of dismay are met with his telling them, "Get off my back! You're always telling me what to do." The therapist could ask the young man what his parents think of him. His answer is, "They think I'm a royal screw-up!" The therapist would ask, "Do you like that?" His response is, "No! Would you?" At that point in time the therapist could say the following:

> I'm puzzled. If you don't like your parents to call you a screw-up, why are you trying so hard to prove them right? You seem angry with your parents but you seem to do everything in your power to show them that they have the right idea about you. You're making it easy on them. They can complain to their friends about you and call you lazy when you come to therapy. You must be very loyal to them to put up with such grief just to show them that they are right. If you were really angry with them you would get a job just to prove them wrong. Then they would have nothing to complain about, and they would have to go through the very hard work of rethinking their ideas about you. Boy, you are a very loyal son. Since loyalty is such a wonderful trait to have, I think you should practice being loyal by screwing up even more.

Such a paradoxical directive will force all of the family members to reevaluate their contributions to their family interaction patterns.

The Juice

If families are still exhibiting a lot of resistance, even after the therapist administers a slam, it is time to "juice" the system further. In order for a slam to have the intended effect of disrupting the maladaptive recursive cycle, it must cause enough cognitive dissonance to motivate the family members to overcome their fear of change. If the cognitive dissonance does not reach a critical threshold, the family members' need for security and comfort will not overcome the pain of the maladaptive recursive cycle. No change will occur. What the therapist needs to do is make the clients feel less comfortable by "turning up the heat." Add more electrical juice to the family system to shock the family members into changing. In the previous example, if the young man was not moved to find a job by the slam, I would juice the system by suggesting that letting a twenty-two-year-old man stay at home was causing everyone problems because most twenty-two-year-olds work. The image of a twenty-two-year-old nonworker in the home is just too incongruent and is causing everybody pain. Therefore, I would suggest that the young man stop acting like a twenty-two-year-old and, instead, act like a ten-year-old. Nobody expects ten-year-olds to work. However, if I ask him to act like he's ten, I should (to keep things congruent) ask the parents to treat him like he was ten, with ten-year-old responsibilities and restrictions. My hypothesis is that, if I make the slam extreme enough, I will create so much cognitive dissonance in everyone that they will embrace change instead of escalating levels of anxiety due to increasing cognitive dissonance.

When this cycle of hook, slam, and juice is completed, I rejoin with the family and start the process all over again to address the next maladaptive recursive cycle. I am always overt about what I am doing and will never try to "trick" a client by withholding information about my therapeutic process. I sincerely believe that disrupting the maladaptive recursive cycles is the key to effective therapy. Whether I accomplish this through my therapeutic relationship with the client, teaching insight, creating behavioral contracts, or conducting strategic therapy, my goal is always the same: disrupt the maladaptive recursive cycles so that the clients will embrace change so that they can accomplish their goals.

Six

CRISIS INTERVENTION
Balancing on the Edge of the Cliff

RATIONALE

It may seem odd to begin a discussion of therapy with the topic of suicide crisis intervention. There are two reasons for starting out with crisis intervention. First, if a therapist is going to do therapy with suicidal adolescents, he or she must be aware that, at any point in the therapeutic process, the adolescent may become actively suicidal, thereby drawing the therapist into a crisis intervention situation (Callahan, 1998). Therefore, before therapy even starts, the therapist must be planful about how he or she would proceed with crisis intervention, if that situation should arise. With a crisis intervention strategy in place, the therapist can make a rational decision as to when to shift into "intervention modality" as the situation dictates, and when to shift back to "therapeutic modality." If there is no crisis intervention plan of action, therapists are often thrown off balance when the young person mentions suicide as an option, often overreacting to the adolescent's suicidal ideation as an imminent suicidal event. Not only does this derail the therapeutic process but it also reinforces for the adolescent the fact that they have a very powerful manipulative tool to use any time therapy gets "too hard" for him or her. Planning out a course of action for suicidal crisis intervention ahead of time will allow the therapist to remain more rational and less emotional in determining the seriousness of the suicidal threat.

Secondly, if a therapist is clear about how to handle an explicit suicidal crisis, the course of how to proceed in therapy will become more focused in the therapist's mind. Identifying the "worst case scenario" helps the therapist to ask the therapeutic question, "Does this intervention take me closer to or away from the suicidal crisis point?" If it takes the therapy further away from the point of suicidal crisis, then the therapist's crisis intervention plan will be a more remote contingency. If an intervention brings the therapy closer to the suicidal crisis point, the therapist has three further questions to ask:

1. Will this intervention eventually move the client away from the suicidal crisis point?
2. What is the risk involved if I pursue this intervention?
3. Will my suicide crisis intervention lower that risk to an acceptable level if it must be employed?

In a way, all of therapy with suicidal adolescents is conducted with the "worst case scenario" in mind. If this is done explicitly, the therapist can be more rational in planning out a course of therapy.

OCCURRENCE

Suicidal crises may occur in a number of ways. A particularly difficult therapy session may sow the seeds of suicide, which may explode in a suicide attempt that night or over the next weekend. Although it is rare with adults, adolescents may become actively suicidal within the therapy session. Perhaps because of your reputation of working well with adolescents, you get an emergency phone call in the middle of the night from a police officer, a social service professional, a frightened parent, or a suicidal adolescent, asking you to become immediately involved in a suicidal crisis. Sometimes the situation may be hypothetical. For example, an adolescent female client asks you how you would respond to a young girl who tried to take an overdose of pills. Your answer may have a major impact on whether your client decides to become that hypothetical person. A teenage male client may tell you that he has a buddy who has talked about shooting himself. He asks you what you think he should do to help his buddy. This may be a veiled hypothetical about himself or he may truly want your advice to help a friend. In either case, how you respond to his request will have a major impact on some young person's life. You could get a two a.m. phone call from the police to talk your teenage client off of a bridge or a window ledge. In this case, every word you say can mean the difference of life or death. Therefore, before we cover the course of therapy, I feel the need to address the issue of suicide crisis intervention.

Opening

My metaphor for a young person who is to the point of taking action to commit suicide is that of a man standing on the edge of a cliff. His toes are dangling over the lip of the precipice. There is a 200-foot straight drop onto jagged rocks. If he falls, he's dead! He is staring off into space, suspended between the inertia to remain on the cliff and stay alive and his desire to step out into the unknown and embrace death. Even if he decides not to commit suicide, he has put himself in a precarious position. He could lose his balance and fall. Some of the rocks under his feet could give way. A strong gust of wind could blow him over the edge. In any of those cases, he will die, not because he wants to do so, but because he placed himself in harm's way. If I am called to help this person, my first priority is to back him off the cliff.

We have all seen enough action movies to know that Clint Eastwood in *Dirty Harry* or Mel Gibson in *Lethal Weapon* will do something dramatic or even outrageous to save the life of the person who is standing on the ledge of the building, threatening to jump. I'm not suggesting that we punch the suicidal person in the face or handcuff our wrist to his. That is Hollywood and there is a modicum of fantasy at work. However, if we analyze their "interventions," utilizing strategic therapy, they most certainly did interrupt the maladaptive recursive cycle. The suicidal person in both cases expected the police officer to talk to him and argue with him why he should not commit suicide. Both police officers subverted that expectation by telling the suicidal people that they're not going to do that. As therapists, we can do something similar without all of the macho histrionics.

When a person confides to a friend or group of friends that he or she is suicidal, what is the typical reaction of the people who just received that news? Some will end the conversation as quickly as they can and leave. They do not want the responsibility of their friend's death on their hands, and they are afraid that they might, in fact, say the wrong thing and push their friend "over the edge." Some friends will respond, "You're kidding!" and not take their friend's talk of suicide seriously. Some friends will launch into the numerous reasons why their friend should want to stay alive and commence a litany of positives about being alive. It is almost as if they were afraid of letting their friend say anything more about suicide. Seldom will a suicidal person be allowed to express his or her own pain and suffering. Even if the person's friends would sit and listen, he or she is often so embarrassed by suggesting something like suicide, which is so culturally taboo, that he or she will be afraid to bring the matter up. In any case, a therapist who invites the client to "tell his or her story, his or her own way" is breaking the maladaptive recursive cycle. The therapist's invitation to let the client talk in whatever way the client sees fit to do is different from what the client had expected the therapist to do. It derails the maladaptive recursive cycle and opens up at least one more possibility for action other than "life as it was" or "death."

In addition, listening to the client tell his or her story, his or her own way, takes time. To return to my metaphor, the man on the cliff feels that time is very short and is rapidly running out. Letting him talk in his own way about what brought him to the edge of the cliff takes time. Strategically, it works counter to his expectation that "time is short." This opens up a new possibility: "Nothing needs to be hurried or rushed." Towards this end, the therapist needs to keep a calm presence with the client. This will bring down the tension in the situation and will model a calmer affect for the client. Metaphorically, for every minute the client keeps talking, he backs up a foot from the edge of the cliff. Twenty minutes backs him off twenty feet. He is still in danger. He can take off, sprint for the cliff, and still dive over the edge. However, he is a lot safer twenty feet from the precipice than he was when his toes were dangling over the edge.

Letting the client tell his or her story his or her own way also takes energy. In my framework of strategic therapy, I believe that it takes energy to act. This is the reason why there are cases of severely depressed people who describe themselves as so depressed that they do not have enough energy to go through with their suicide. Tragically, there are cases of depressed clients, who are immobilized by their depression, who attend therapy, relieve some of their depression, and subsequently commit suicide "on the rebound." The therapy helped relieve enough of their depression to free up enough energy to commit suicide but not enough for them to choose life as an alternative. It takes a certain amount of energy to commit suicide. By encouraging the client to talk, the therapist is asking the client to expend energy. This lessens the possibility of committing suicide at that time and further disrupts the maladaptive recursive cycle.

Let me illustrate this principle by way of an example. A young man, age 20, who was stationed at a nearby military establishment, had decided to commit suicide. He had discovered that he did not like military service but was still obligated to the Army for another two years. His wife missed her family and left him to go "home." Living at her parents' home, she started an affair with an old boyfriend and had asked the client for a divorce. In addition, his dog was hit by a car and died. Therefore, the client had rigged a noose in his garage and put a chair under it. His plan was to stand on the chair, put the noose around his neck and jump off the chair to hang himself. However, being a religious man, he had doubts if he would go to heaven if he did commit suicide. Therefore, he called the local phone crisis line. The crisis volunteer on the line had been trained to let him tell his story his way and respond empathically to his expression of thoughts and feelings. Carl Rogers' principles of warmth, empathy, and genuineness were employed well by the volunteer. As this was going on, I was contacted as the "supervisor on-call." The volunteer asked the client if he would consent to my coming out to his house to speak with him in person. He agreed and I drove out with a second volunteer to his house, while the first volunteer continued to speak to him on the phone.

Once we arrived, we released the first volunteer from continuing the call and told the client that the phone volunteer had "passed the baton to us." We remained calm and asked him to tell his story his way. He spoke of his pain and suffering, and his frustration that he did not seem to be able to do anything about it. His initial descriptions of his feelings were that he was angry: angry at his wife, angry at the Army, angry at God, and angry at himself. This was to be expected from a young man in our society, especially one whose career was in the military. Working from a client-centered approach (Rogers, 1951), we helped him see that there were other feelings underlying his anger: feelings of hurt, helplessness, and despair. He commented that he found strength in the Bible and wanted to read some of his favorite passages to us. He proceeded to tell us why a given passage was important to him. He told us about his situation, his life, and why he was presently to the point of committing suicide. However, he did it by reading and subsequently discussing passages from the Bible. This was his way of telling his story. This did not take place within the confines of a 50-minute therapy session. It took almost four hours. However, using my "man on the cliff" metaphor, at the end of four hours, he had backed 240 feet from the edge of the cliff. He was safer, didn't feel the urgency to choose life or death immediately, and was exhausted, too exhausted to go through with his plan of suicide that night. I will refer back to this case as we move through this chapter.

WHO'S IN CHARGE?

I have a philosophical belief that is informed by research and theory but is still a belief at its core. I believe that suicidal people, especially suicidal adolescents, are in such pain and feel so hopeless that they are incapable of making any major decision with the requisite degree of rational thought. This is especially true for a decision so all-encompassing and final as choosing life over death. Such an existential decision cannot be made by a person who is so intellectually and emotionally debilitated by their suffering and feelings of helplessness.

As a therapist, I consider empowering my clients to be a major goal of therapy. However, empowering a debilitated teenager when he or she is in an actively suicidal crisis can lead to tragic results. Therefore, in contrast to therapy, crisis intervention with suicidal adolescents requires me to take much more responsibility for the client. I will try to work together with the client as a team, just as I would in therapy. However, in therapy, the ultimate force for change must come from the clients. In suicide crisis intervention, I will shoulder the responsibility for keeping the client alive long enough for the client to enter into therapy. Then, we can focus on empowerment. If necessary, I will tell the client, "I will not let you die today." Clients will often retort, "Don't I have a right to kill myself if I want to do so?" My response is:

> Yes, you do, but not when you call me in for help. You asked for help. That means that you have at least a "moment of doubt" as to whether you really want to die. If you are going to choose something as permanent as death, don't you want to be entirely certain about it?

To a degree this is a paradoxical intervention in that, in Western society, seldom is anyone "entirely certain" about an act that is labeled as taboo as suicide. Calling me has identified for me that the client has at least a "moment of doubt." As a good strategic therapist, my task is to amplify that "moment of doubt" to disrupt the maladaptive recursive cycle.

If I believe that the client does not have the capacity of choosing death over life in the middle of a suicidal crisis, I also must believe that he or she also does not have the ability to choose life over death, either. For many suicidal clients, choosing life over death "forever" is just as overwhelming as choosing death over life. It is still an existential decision. Instead, I ask them to choose life over death for a limited period of time upon which we can agree. I will ask the client to choose life over death for "a month," or "a week," or "forty-eight hours," or "twenty-four hours." We will discuss what time frame is appropriate for that specific client with his or her own specific problems and circumstances. Sometimes, all I have to do is get them through the night. Often something that seems so sinister in the dead of night seems much less draconian in the light of day. As a therapist, I have to be reasonable and grounded to push for a timeline during which there can be some change accomplished. A "forever decision" is too overwhelming. A decision that has time limits is much more "handle-able" for a client. I tell them:

> If you choose death over life, it's the last choice you will ever make. If you choose life over death for a specified period of time, you open up more choices for yourself. If you still want to choose death after our agreed time limitation is over, you can then choose death over life at some later time.

As I've spoken to professionals and parents, that last sentence startles them. They often respond by saying, "You mean that you actually tell them that they can commit suicide later?" Do they think that I'm putting a new idea into the client's head? The client already knows that he or she can commit suicide whenever they want to do so. All that I am trying to do is create a "safe zone" of time in which suicide is not an option for them. Most clients appreciate my honesty and feel empowered by the fact that, if they choose life over death, at least on a temporary basis, it opens up other choice points for them to make decisions. However, since they have called me at the time of this crisis, I will do everything in my power to keep them alive.

The term "everything in my power" means not only what I personally can do but it also means that I will call upon whatever resources I can muster to keep the client alive. It may mean calling in the police to file a report or assist with physical restraint, if necessary. I may ask for the police to put the client into protective custody or transport the client to the hospital. I may seek hospitalization for the client. In fact, once a client mentions suicide, I tell them that the natural course of events will lead me to seek hospitalization for them, unless they can prove to me that they have the ability to stay alive until our next appointment. I then take a very cautious and skeptical stance to judge their safety. It is always fascinating to me to watch an adolescent client, who fifteen minutes ago threatened suicide, struggle to convince me, the skeptical therapist, that they no longer feel suicidal in order to stop me from hospitalizing them over the weekend. I tell them that I have the final word on hospitalization, not them.

If I do call in other professionals, either from law enforcement, mental health, or social services, I feel that I must work with both the professionals and the rules which they must follow. Conflict among professionals does not help a suicidal adolescent. Mutual respect among the professionals involved is necessary. Because of my work in this field, many of the professionals in my community and surrounding communities will defer to my expertise and let me take an ascendant role in the crisis intervention. In fact, the law enforcement community has called me in on several cases to assist them in suicide crisis intervention. However, I need to defer to proper police procedures while doing so. If I hospitalize a client, I must follow the hospital's rules on treatment regimen and staff assignment. There is no room for bruised egos when a young person's life is at stake.

Determining Lethality

As the client begins to tell the therapist his or her story in his or her own way, the therapist must begin to assess the suicide threat for lethality (Jurich, 2001). Because the therapist does not have the benefit of time as he or she would have in therapy, the therapist does not have the ability to utilize assessment instruments that, in therapy, would help to determine the seriousness of this threat. Therefore, the therapist must utilize his or her interview skills to form an impression as to how potentially lethal this suicidal episode is. Following the nonverbal behavior of the client is crucial. How agitated is the client? Does the client engage or avoid eye contact? Does the client exhibit facial expressions which indicate anxiety about talking to the therapist or does he or she appear calm and determined? Likewise, the therapist should study the client's non-lexical verbal expressions. These are the verbal qualities that surround the text of the client's speech, such as tone and pitch of the client's voice (Jurich & Jurich, 1974, 1978). All of these nonlexical or nonverbal cues help the therapist to place the lexical messages of the client into a context. They are the meta-messages that help us understand the client's messages (Watzlawick et al., 1967).

As therapists, because most of our work exists in the world of words, our focus is typically on the lexical content of the client's communication. Many clients, in the process of telling their story their way, will talk openly about the method they have chosen to end their lives. Some will only hint at how they plan to kill themselves. Still others will be silent about how they plan to commit suicide. It is the task of the therapist to open up the discussion about the method of suicide the client has chosen. Many people speak of death in euphemisms. Phrases like "passed away" or "no longer with us" refer to death as if it really isn't there. I have always felt that therapists needed to address death and suicide directly and with no sugar coating. I will ask a client, "How do you intend to kill yourself?" If that sounds harsh, that is good. I want to jolt the client, especially an over-romantic adolescent, into the reality that they will be dead, not "passed away" but dead. Using words like "suicide" and "killing yourself" is designed to slap the adolescent suicidal client in the face with reality.

If the adolescent is reluctant to discuss how he or she intends to commit suicide, I will ask them "Why, what have you got to lose?" If the adolescent answers that he or she doesn't want to tell me the method of suicide because I will try to stop him or her, I admit that that is exactly what I would do with that information. There's no sense in lying. If the therapist did lie, the suicidal client wouldn't believe him or her, anyway. However, I then add that this situation puts the suicidal client into one hell of a bind. If he or she tells me the method of suicide, I may have more power to stop the suicide. However, if clients don't convince me that they are serious about the method of suicide, how will they get anyone to believe that this is truly a suicidal crisis? This is a paradoxical maneuver from strategic therapy. There seems, to the objective observer, to be a flaw in logic. If the suicidal client is serious about committing suicide, wouldn't the best course of action be to say nothing, commit suicide, and have his or her actions confirm that he or she was serious about ending his or her life? Fortunately, most suicidal clients, especially adolescents, are not that logical. When confronted with the emotional double-bind, "show me you are serious about committing suicide by telling me how you are intending to do it" most suicidal clients, especially adolescents, tell the therapist how they intend to kill themselves. Their need for validation that they are in pain, and it appears "hopeless," is so strong that they will share their method of suicide just to prove to the therapist that they are serious about killing themselves. Any other reasons for not telling the therapist their method of suicide can be countered with a similar double-bind. In a life-or-death situation like suicide, by using this type of double-bind—even if it doesn't work—the therapist has not lost anything. However, it has been my professional experience that this strategic technique, especially with adolescents, works most of the time.

Once the client gives the therapist his or her method of suicide, the therapist must judge lethality based upon several factors:

1. Is the method lethal?
2. Is the plan of suicide well thought-out?
3. Does the client know the details?
4. Is the client hesitant?
5. How helpless does the client feel?
6. How hopeless does the client feel?
7. How realistic is the client, in the therapist's judgment?

Taken together, these seven questions need to be answered by the therapist to judge the lethality of the threat.

Let me juxtapose two examples. I had a young fourteen-year-old female describe her method of suicide as follows:

> I don't know. I figured that I'd poison myself. My mom has a bottle of 500 aspirins. I figured that I'd chug the bottle and just die.

I also have had a seventeen-year-old male who told me how he would kill himself:

> I will shoot myself in the mouth with my father's .38-caliber nickel-plated pistol. He keeps it in the top left drawer in his bureau under three rolled-up pairs of socks. One's black, one's blue, and one's brown.

The young woman in the first example has a far less lethal plan of suicide than does the young man in the second example. Her plan is not well thought-out and shows hesitation. She knows few details. Her method of suicide, "chugging 500 aspirin" is impractical. Swallowing 500 aspirins is a laborious and time-consuming task. Her method is not lethal. Taking several hundred aspirin will make you sick, and your liver will not like you very much afterwards, but it probably will not kill you. Compare this method with the young man's plan in the second example. He is direct and certain in his description. There is no hesitation. He has a very lethal means of killing himself—a gun. His plan is well thought-out in that he has selected to shoot himself in the mouth, which, using a .38-caliber pistol would almost certainly be fatal. In addition, he knows the details right down to the color of the socks!

Judging the client's levels of helplessness and hopelessness will give the therapist an indication of the desperation the client feels to put the plan into motion. Even a less lethal plan of suicide, in the hands of a client who feels very helpless and hopeless, may prove to be very lethal. A client, who has a more lethal plan, but feels more in control of life and more hopeful, has other options from which to choose instead of the lethal plan for suicide. Under those circumstances, the latter client may actually have a less lethal situation than the former client.

Lastly, when judging lethality, especially with adolescent clients, the therapist must remember how naïve and unrealistic many adolescents are about life. I had a seventeen-year-old as a client who announced that she was suicidal because she was to have her "glamour shot" photo taken for the yearbook and she had a blemish on her nose. Any adult would be flabbergasted at such a declaration, myself included! However, I had to remember that I was dealing with an adolescent whose experience with real problems of the world was limited. In her life, this was a very big deal. The therapist has to remember what it was like for him or her at that age. It is a lot easier for the adult therapist to try to remember what life was like at age seventeen, than it is for a teenage client to try to project what it will be like as an adult. I dealt with this suicidal threat by asking the client what photographer was doing the photo shoot. She told me the name of the photographer, I called him up, and he explained, first to me and then to her, that he could easily airbrush out any blemishes. My client smiled, and there was never any other suicidal threat again. This is one of my most extreme examples of a threat of "suicide over nothing." However, it was not a "nothing" to my client. Had I not taken her threat seriously or, even worse, laughed at her dilemma, what might she have done? Maybe she might have done nothing. However, she also might have worked herself up into an emotional frenzy in which she might have lost all perspective and done some serious harm to herself or even killed herself. We need to remember how impulsive adolescents are. That, together with their lack of perspective, can be a deadly, lethal combination.

Once the therapist has determined the lethality of the suicidal crisis, he or she can gauge the urgency with which this crisis must be handled. A suicidal crisis of less lethality means that the therapist has the time and space to intervene by means of a method that is closer to therapy, rather than crisis intervention. The higher the lethality of the suicidal crisis, the greater the sense of urgency for the therapist to disrupt the maladaptive recursive cycle that has brought the client to the brink of suicide. Because, in a high lethality suicidal crisis, the time for intervention is so short, many therapeutic techniques that require a longer duration of time cannot be employed. It is not that they are not effective, they simply take too much time to implement in this urgent situation. For example, although the client's extended family may be the root of the suicidal episode, traditional Bowen Family Therapy (Bowen, 1975) is not feasible in this urgent crisis. Once the crisis is resolved, a course of therapy following Bowen's Theory may be very helpful. However, the urgency of a high lethality suicidal crisis limits the options available to the therapist. At this time I rely upon the Hook and Slam I put forth in the previous chapter. However, because of the urgency of the suicidal crisis, I have to be very careful about how I employ each.

THE HOOK—USING THE CLIENT'S PERSPECTIVE

When a therapist is conducting therapy, the client will provide much information on what the therapist might use to hook the client. The therapist must choose which information to use in disarming the client's defenses in order to set up a disruption of the client's maladaptive recursive cycle. In family therapy, the family members will also give the therapist information to establish a good therapeutic hook. Even if no other information is provided, when working with adolescents, the nature of adolescent life will provide the therapist with several openings to try to hook the client into lowering defenses. However, in a suicidal crisis, many of these sources of information may be lacking. If the therapist has never previously seen the suicidal teenager who is in crisis, the therapist may have little or no background upon which to create an effective hook. Even if the suicidal adolescent is or was a client of the therapist, many of the aspects of the young person's life, which were important in therapy, may recede into the background at the apex of the suicidal crisis. In this crisis, the "here and now" is most important. In most suicidal crises for adolescents, the family is not present to contribute information. Even if family members are present, they are often so frightened and stressed that they cannot provide much in formation upon which the therapist can formulate an effective hook. Lastly, the circumstances which brought the adolescent to the brink of suicide may be so unique that much of the information on typical adolescent development may simply not fit the present situation. Therefore, many of the ways that a therapist gains information to formulate a good hook may not be available in a suicidal crisis.

To hook the adolescent client, who is experiencing a suicidal crisis, I borrow a technique from neurolinguisitic programming (Bandler & Grinder, 1975). Bandler and Grinder proposed that each person has a preference for one of the three primary senses: visual, auditory, or kinesthetic. They felt that a person was most at ease in their preferred primary representational system (PRS). Therefore, they suggested that therapists should adjust therapy to communicate within the client's PRS to ensure the greatest ease for the client and the maximum communication between the client and the therapist. Although this theory has achieved a strong following among some therapists, many of principles surrounding PRS have not been supported by research (Darn, 1983; Graunke & Roberts, 1985). However, the principle of putting the client at ease and connecting with him or her by speaking his or her "language" can be borrowed by the therapist to form a quick bond with the suicidal adolescent and may hook that adolescent into letting his or her guard down. By their language, I am *not* referring to clients' vocabulary or speech patterns. The therapist's trying to mimic the argot of the adolescent's words and slang would sound phony and, if anything, push the adolescent away. However, using the client's metaphors and life experiences *can* accomplish the neurolinguisitic programming goals of putting the client at ease and enhancing client–therapist communication.

I had a case of a young suicidal teenage male who made money after school and on weekends as an auto mechanic. He was proud of those skills and of the responsibility he demonstrated by having that job. I asked him what he did when a customer said they had a problem but couldn't describe it well enough for the client to know what was wrong. The client said that he asked the customer to take him for a drive so he could see what was wrong. I replied:

> Ok, that sounds like a good idea. Something is wrong with your life and I don't have a handle on what it is. Can you take me for a drive in your life so that I can see if you need a new carburetor or a fuel pump?

For the first time in our interaction, the young man smiled at me and said "Buckle up!" The metaphor of troubleshooting an automobile and doing therapy made sense to him and put him at ease because we were "in his ballpark," speaking his language. This metaphor ultimately led me to a wonderful slam that disrupted his maladaptive recursive cycle. I asked him:

> When you have a car with a faulty carburetor, what do you do with it? Do you fix the carburetor, or replace it, or do you just junk the whole car?

> He replied: "I fix it. It would be crazy to junk the whole car because one part was bad."

> I answered: "Then why are you ready to junk your whole life when only one part is broken?"

> He smiled.

We did therapy subsequently, and he always referred to therapy as "jacking him up to see his underbody."

Previously, I had elaborated the case where the young man was suicidal and had constructed a noose in his garage to hang himself. He wanted to read his favorite Bible passages to me and the crisis center volunteer who accompanied me on the emergency call. Because I was in my client-centered modality of therapy, letting him tell his story his way encouraged him to do the bulk of the talking. At one point he sat frustrated and challenged me:

> You're the damned counselor! Don't you have any advice to give me that will make all of my problems go away? Why are you so damn quiet?

I responded quietly:

> Well, the way I figure it, God gave us two ears and one mouth. Maybe, in times like this, He wants me to listen twice as much as I talk.

He immediately got quiet and became contemplative. He said, "You know, I never thought of it that way." My client's religious conviction led me to a series of mini-slams when he asked me to read several of my favorite Bible passages. I chose verses which emphasized hope and forgiveness. After the Sermon on the Mount, when the Pharisees asked Jesus to name the greatest of the commandments, he replied that there were really only two commandments and the second one was to "Love thy neighbor as thyself." I pointed out to him:

> It doesn't say "Love thy neighbor *better* than yourself." It says "Love they neighbor *as* thyself." If you can't love yourself, how can you love your neighbor? What kind of love can you show your family or your wife if you are ready to kill yourself?

My series of mini slams gave way to a major slam. He responded, "So, I guess I can't kill myself and be very Christian."

In both of these examples I was able to use something the client had given to me at the time of his crisis. I used the auto mechanic metaphor and the Bible to speak the client's language. We stepped into their respective areas of expertise. Once the client felt at ease and felt that I was deferring to their worldview, I created cognitive dissonance within their worlds to suggest that their own occupation, in one instance, and religion, in the other, would come to the conclusion that suicide is not a logical alternative for a good mechanic or a good Christian. This cognitive dissonance broke the maladaptive recursive cycle which had led them to the point of suicide.

THE SLAM—DISRUPTING CYCLES

In a suicidal crisis that is highly lethal, the therapist's main objective is to disrupt the maladaptive recursive cycle that has led the client to the brink of suicide. There are a number of ways to accomplish this. However, all of them are predicated upon a solid therapist–client relationship. Unlike therapy, where the luxury of time allows the relationship to grow and season over time, the suicidal crisis demands a quick joining process and hooking of the client, and an equally expeditious intervention to try to change the client's stated course of action.

Utilizing the Teeter-Totter Model discussed in chapter two, the therapist has two broad strategies: (1) reducing stress or (2) adding resources (Jurich & Collins, 1996). Hill (1949) gives the therapist a third strategy, that of changing the client's perception of the event, in this case suicide.

Reducing stress is an excellent way to disrupt the client's maladaptive recursive cycle. However, in most cases there is little that a therapist can do to reduce stress at the time of the suicidal crisis. Despite this reality, the therapist should still consider methods of reducing stress as an option. For example, I was called to one of the university dormitories for a suicidal crisis involving a young woman who was threatening to stab herself with her boyfriend's hunting knife. Although she had a number of problems, the event which had triggered the suicidal crisis was that this was the Friday evening of the last day to drop classes without a withdrawal–failure (WF) being recorded on the student's transcript. She confessed that, due to her depression over her "on again–off again" relationship with her boyfriend, she couldn't study and was, therefore, flunking all of her classes. Therefore, she said that she would be kicked out of school and have a permanent blot on her academic record which, before this semester, had been a B+ average in two years of college. After joining with her and listening to her tell her story her own way, I asked the following question: "Would you still be suicidal if I was able to get you released from all of your courses without a failing grade?" I told her that she might have to take some courses over and that money laid out for this semester was gone but she would have no Fs or WFs on her transcript. This stopped her maladaptive recursive cycle. She replied, "Probably not." I asked her to give me until Monday evening at 5 p.m. to see what I could do to make things better. I asked her for her permission to speak with her professors and instructors. I also asked her to allow me to check her into the student health center for medication and observation for her own safety until that time. Eventually, after some discussion, she said "yes" to all three requests. I started calling up her instructors on Saturday morning and, by 4 p.m. on Saturday afternoon, I had some form of accommodation from each professor that would allow her to either drop the class, subsequently do the work for the class, or retake the class with no permanent consequences to her academic record. I told her this on Saturday evening, and we started therapy on Tuesday morning. Utilizing the Teeter-Totter Model, I actually did two things:

1. I reduced the primary stress which precipitated the suicide crisis.
2. I gave her a resource she had not previously had—me.

Although situations in which the therapist can lessen the client's stress are rare, they shouldn't be overlooked because they can have significant impact on the suicide crisis.

Adding resources is more typically the strategy for disrupting the maladaptive recursive cycle in a suicide crisis. The very act of the therapist's talking with the client gives the client a resource he or she has not had before. The therapist's knowledge, experience, training, and resource network is now accessible to the client. That is quite an increase in resources. I often tell a client that "the entire mental health community of professionals is here in this room with me, ready to give you a hand." This dramatizes the increase of resources to the client. I will also speak with the client about specific resources about which the client may be unaware. I had a suicidal young man, age fourteen, who had multiple problems, one of which was school. He told me that he just couldn't see the blackboard but that his family couldn't afford to buy him glasses. I informed him that the Optimists Club would provide him with a pair of glasses free of charge. I gave him another resource.

Many resources arise from the client's own network of interpersonal relationships. I will often suggest the adolescent's mother or father as a resource. Many adolescents do not consider going to their parent because they feel as if such a request would force them back into the child role again and that would make them feel like a failure as an adolescent. I try to tell adolescents that, no matter what their age, they will still be the offspring of parents. I try to give them an example of how I, at the ancient age of fifty-eight, still ask my mom for advice. I also add that it makes parents feel wanted if they can help. I have had suicidal adolescents refuse to seek their parent's help to meet their own needs, but will ask for parental assistance because it will make their parents feel good. Their rationale is important. The fact that I've reminded them of a new resource is important. Sometimes parents *are* the problem for the adolescent. This is an ideal time for the therapist to ask the client how they would feel if the therapist did family therapy with the adolescents and their parents to see if "we can turn them from a liability to an asset." Many suicidal adolescents, especially early adolescents, are intrigued by that idea. Some adolescents totally reject the idea of their parents as an asset. A suicidal crisis is not the time to argue that point. Drop it and move on. Ask about siblings or extended family members. I had a client who, in telling his story his way, said, "My whole family's screwed up. I have no use for any of them."

I asked, "Isn't there anyone in your family that makes you feel warm inside or makes you laugh?" He responded, "No! Well, Aunt Mary from Salina used to make me laugh. She had that twinkle in her eye." I asked,

"When was the last time you spoke to Aunt Mary from Salina?" He proceeded to tell me that it had been almost two years. I asked him to speculate how she might respond if he called her up or even visited her. He thought that she would like that and he launched into a ten-minute monologue of nostalgia that brought a smile to his face for the first time. I had given him another family resource with whom he had lost touch. Sometimes resources can be a member of the client's circle of friends, or a roommate, or a member of the basketball team. Don't overlook coaches, teachers, or ministers as potential resources. The more encompassing the network of resources, the less isolated the adolescent will feel and the more options the client will be able to exercise.

Changing the client's perception of the suicide will often be the most dramatic way to disrupt the maladaptive recursive cycle. Working with the client's metaphors, as was demonstrated in the two examples cited above, can give the therapist the opportunity to create a cognitive shift in his or her thinking if cognitive dissonance is created. A therapist can reframe the suicidal crisis as a "cry for help" for the adolescent. If the client rejects that notion, ask him or her if the suicidal crisis is a cry for help for the family and he or she is acting as the "standard bearer" for the family. Many adolescents will reject the notion that the "cry for help" is for them but will embrace the idea that they are, almost heroically, threatening suicide to help his or her family. At that point the therapist can tell the client that his or her mission is accomplished and that the need to threaten suicide is no longer necessary. Many adolescents will in fact, be relieved to relinquish their role as standard bearer and be willing to turn over the responsibility to the therapist, especially if family therapy is suggested as an alternative.

Many adolescents come to the brink of suicide expecting it to be painless and easy. They have been seduced by the countless hours of watching antiseptic deaths on television and the movies. In those deaths, the "good guys" die either quickly or peacefully for a noble cause. In the James Bond movie *Thunderball*, James is dancing with a female enemy agent whose henchmen are trying to shoot him with a pistol with a silencer attached. He sees the pistol. At the last moment, he wheels his dance partner around so that she is shot in the back by her own henchmen. The audience sees a small red dot appear on the back of her dress and, with a slight sigh, she seems to faint and fall limp in Mr. Bond's arms. She shuts her eyes as if she were asleep. Never skipping a beat, James waltzes her over to a table at which is seated a young couple. He sets her down on the seat and tells the couple, "Would you be so kind as to watch over my girlfriend. She's dead on her feet." He briskly walks away. This is a quintessential "antiseptic death." No pain, no agony, and no suffering is seen. The dead woman is cavalierly abandoned with a bad pun. As teens have an unrealistic expectation of not only death but also what the process of dying is like, they do not understand what the reality of death truly is. On some level the adolescent believes that he or she will die an easy and peaceful death and somehow will be able to come back and see their own funeral like Tom and Huck in *Tom Sawyer* (Twain, 1876).

In cases like this, a good slam would be for the therapist to describe the adolescent's potential death in a more realistic manner. Such a description will often be enough to disrupt the maladaptive recursive cycle leading to suicide. When Clint Eastwood in *Dirty Harry* describes for the man who is on the ledge of the building threatening to jump the bloody mess he will make on the pavement, the man gets nauseous and instinctively backs off the ledge. At that moment, Harry grabs him. When the man struggles, Harry punches him in the mouth, knocks him unconscious, and takes him off the ledge. Not exactly therapeutic in nature, but it does illustrate the effect of making death and dying more real to the client.

I had a case where a seventeen-year-old young Kansas woman called me in my office at about 4 p.m. She explained that she had heard me talk on a radio interview about suicide and wanted to tell me that she was going to kill herself before her parents came home at 5 p.m. I listened to her tell her story her way and ruled out that it was a prank call. I asked her how she was planning to kill herself. She responded that she was going to drive her car off a cliff. My first thought was that there are no cliffs in Kansas. However, she described that she lived in the Flint Hills and knew of a road that had a curve around the side of a hill that had a 45-degree drop off for 100 feet. She would drive her dad's Chevy Impala through the guardrail and "just die." I asked her how she thought she would die. She replied, "I'll just die. That's it." I proceeded to describe how she would die. I described the most bloody and awful scenario of her death that I could conjure up. I told her that her face would crash into the windshield and be embedded with glass, the steering wheel would cut her in half, and she would have the pleasure of watching the bottom half of her body detached and burning to death. Is that really what would have occurred? I don't know. I told the bloodiest story I could to shock her into the fact that she would not "just die." She said, "Yuck! I don't want to do that!" I replied, "Good! Let's talk." I kept her on the phone until her dad came home. We set up a vigil by Mom and Dad to watch over her. We made an appointment to come into therapy for the next day. As I was on the phone and did not even know where she was, I felt the necessity to strongly disrupt her suicidal maladaptive cycle. I did so dramatically because I felt I needed the impact to derail her path to suicide.

Many adolescents will not forgo their attempt at suicide for their own sake but will do so for others. For example, I have asked a young man, "If you commit suicide, how will your little brother make sense of it?" This adolescent, who had been talking to me with a loaded .45-caliber pistol in his mouth, took the gun out of his mouth when I asked that question. A young woman of seventeen, who had an infant daughter, had determined that her daughter would be better off living with her parents. She decided to kill herself. Nothing I could say seemed to dissuade her from suicide. I asked her the following:

> Would you take a revolver with three bullets in the six chambers, spin the chamber, point it at your baby daughter, and pull the trigger?
>
> I had asked her if she would play Russian roulette with her daughter. She replied, "Of course not! That's sick!"

I responded by saying:

> Well if you commit suicide, that is exactly what you would be doing to your young daughter. Statistics show that when a parent commits suicide, their children have a five hundred percent greater chance of committing suicide themselves!

She sat in stunned silence. I had derailed her maladaptive cycle of suicide. She was willing to put her own life on the line, but like the good mother that she was, not her baby's life. The statistic is a true representation of the research. Families in which a parent has committed suicide run a five times greater risk of having one of the children commit suicide (Jacobs et al., 1999). Why did I say "five hundred percent"? I did so because "five times" and "five hundred percent" is the same number but "five hundred percent" sounds bigger. One of the advantages to being at the same university for thirty-three years is that you sometimes have the ability to follow up on cases. Fifteen years after I had first seen this client in a suicidal emergency situation, I was supervising behind the two-way mirror in a clinic. A woman, who looked to be in her early thirties had come in for an initial therapy session. She was married with three children and was having marital problems. A standard question on the clinic's intake forms asked about suicidal ideation. Her reply was as follows:

> Suicide. Yeah, I felt suicidal once but I can't commit suicide because it would hurt my babies. Do you know a son-of-a-bitch named Tony Jurich? He told me that, if I killed myself, my kids would

have a five hundred percent better chance of killing themselves, too. That son-of-a-bitch took away my right to commit suicide.

From behind the mirror I thought to myself, "Yes!" after fifteen years, my strategic slam still had the power to disrupt her suicidal maladaptive recursive cycle.

If nothing else works, I use my research (Jurich, 2002a). I tell the client that I have collected data from 128 subjects who genuinely tried to commit suicide. I go on to say:

These were not "suicidal gestures" but lethal means of killing themselves: The man who shot himself in the temple of his head, the woman who jumped off a five-story ledge, the woman who took thirty-five sleeping pills. Each of these people in my study said that they genuinely chose to die. They are only alive by a quirk of fate or by God's will. However, each person in my study told me that there was a moment, usually after the point of no return, that they had doubts as to whether they really wanted to die. The woman who took the sleeping pills said that she didn't know if she was certain of her choice of death. She tried to crawl across the bed to the phone to call for help but the pills had taken effect and she couldn't move. The only reason she is alive today is that her roommate came back home from her date because she forgot something and found her lying there. The woman on the ledge said that she wanted to die until she felt her rear foot leave the ledge. She said she thought, "Oh, God, don't let me die!" She even tried to reach back for the ledge with her hand. That gesture probably saved her life because it kept her body from rotating on the way down. She broke both her legs and fractured her hip but she survived. The man who shot himself said he wanted to die until he felt the hammer go down on the pistol. He said that it seemed like an eternity in slow motion. He tried to pull the gun away form his head, but he wasn't quick enough. Maybe he changed the direction of the barrel of the gun, just enough to shoot through his temple rather than completely through his brain. Someone immediately called 911, and they saved his life. He has a plate in his head, but he's still alive! I could tell you another 25 stories like these. Do *you* want to try to commit suicide, reach the point of no return, have doubts about really wanting to die, and not be as lucky as the people in my study?

I have never had a person answer "yes" to that question. This rather long intervention has the power to disrupt the client's maladaptive recursive cycle of suicide by using the power of research to validate an extreme probability that they will have cognitive dissonance after the decision to kill themselves, and it will be too late to stop it. This creates cognitive dissonance in the "here and now" because the client still has the power whether to proceed any further to the edge of the cliff or not to do so. As the same study (Jurich, 2002a) demonstrated that feeling powerless, hopeless, and helpless are such a strong factor in pushing a person to commit suicide, this use of the stories of my subjects basically throws down the challenge to the client to "act now because later you may be even more powerless to act!" It heightens the client's cognitive dissonance by focusing on the variable of control over one's life, a variable that the research has shown to be extremely powerful at the moment of final decision to commit suicide or not. This is a powerful mechanism to disrupt the client's suicidal maladaptive recursive cycle.

POST-INTERVENTION SAFETY

After the maladaptive recursive cycle has been disrupted, the therapist must ensure the safety of the client. Most often hospitalization is warranted. The therapist must arrange for the transportation to ensure that the client will get there. If an ambulance or the police transport the client to the hospital, the client is guaranteed to arrive. They also will if the therapist transports them. I believe that it is a bad idea for the client to transport himself or herself or have a family member or a friend transport him or her to the hospital. A manipulative client can talk a friend or family member from delivering him or her to the emergency room.

The therapist may feel that the suicidal crisis episode is over and that the client need not be hospitalized. I still think that it is a bad idea to leave the client alone for the night. I believe that the therapist should make arrangements with a friend or a family member to spend the night with him or her. I also believe that the therapist should speak with that caretaker about what to expect, how to act responsibly, and how to handle an emergency if the client should regress back to suicidal behavior.

Lastly, the therapist needs to take care of himself or herself. The therapist will probably be exhausted after the crisis. The therapist needs to rest. Cancel appointments if necessary. I believe that the therapist has to decompress. Part of that process is to talk over the crisis and how he or she handled it. Talking it over with a colleague or supervisor would be ideal, preferably within 24 hours of the crisis. As Billy Joel sings in a song called "James": Do what's good for you or you're not good for anybody.

Seven

JOINING

Convincing the Adolescent That This Does Not Have to Be a Solitary Battle

WHY FAMILY THERAPY?

A legitimate question for the reader to ask at this point in the book is, "Why family therapy?" Much of what I have written can be used in therapy with both families and individuals as clients. The previous chapter was specifically written to be used primarily with individual adolescents, as families are seldom present at the time of the suicidal crisis. I have tried to appeal to both individual and family therapists in addressing suicidal adolescents. However, when it comes to therapy, I believe that a family therapy approach will produce the best results when working with suicidal adolescents.

In the past, the preferred mode of therapy with suicidal adolescents has been individual therapy. The prevailing opinion seemed to be that because suicidal ideations were indicative of internal turmoil, the individual should be the only client who enters into therapy. In addition, this point of view fits nicely with the medical model of therapy in which an "identified patient" (IP) should be treated for an individual problem. Therefore, the prevailing opinion has been that therapy should be conducted with suicidal adolescents, prevention should be stressed with groups of adolescents in settings such as schools, and emergency services should be instituted and be made available to suicidal adolescents (Hendin et al., 2005; Sneidman, 1998, 1999; Wekstein, 1979).

The families of adolescents are much more likely to be involved in therapy when discussing grief reactions to death or suicide (Lattanzi-Licht, 1996). Contrary to the implications of these writings, families are involved with a suicidal family member both before and after a suicide. The reader might be directed to a book called *Small Mercies* by Barbara McCauley (1998) for an excellent depiction of the intertwining of family relations within a family before and after the suicide of a family member.

The lack of inclusion of families in the therapeutic process is puzzling, however, when one considers the crucial role played by families in the etiology of suicide, especially suicides by adolescents (Henry et al., 1993; Jurich, 2002a; Jurich & Collins, 1996). If parents play such a crucial role in causing or contributing to adolescent suicide, I believe that mental health practitioners need to strongly consider family therapy with the suicidal adolescent and his or her family to be indicated by the research findings on the genesis of adolescent suicide. In a study of accidental survivors of suicide attempts, sixty-three percent of the adolescents listed "family" as the primary long-term cause of their suicide attempt (Jurich, 2002a). Trying to conduct therapy without major participation by the suicidal adolescent's family seems to be leaving out a crucial piece of the puzzle. Even if the adolescent is greatly helped by the individual therapy, he or she still must go back to his or her family to reintegrate into that family. I believe that reintegration is much better carried out if the family has accompanied their adolescent on the therapeutic journey. They can witness, first-hand, the type and magnitude of the stressors and pain that the adolescent is experiencing. Family therapy cannot only change the adolescent's ideas and behaviors but also can alter the attitudes and behaviors of the rest of the family members, especially the parents. In this way, the therapist can efficiently reduce the stressors in the adolescent's life. The therapist can also present to the suicidal adolescent a new resource—his or her parents. For some families, it may be a struggle to help the parents become resources but their very presence in the therapy room will go along way in convincing the suicidal adolescent that his or her parents are truly on his or her side and are not the enemy. To put it in the parlance of the street, by participating in family therapy, the parents are not only "talking the talk" but they are "walking the walk."

There has been a great emphasis recently on "evidence-based therapies." There are several studies that have demonstrated the effectiveness of family therapy in a multitude of adolescent problems, such as addiction (McGovern, Fox, Xie, & Drake, 2004), eating disorders (Powers & Santana, 2002), psychiatric disorders (Mattejat, 2005), delinquency (Breuk, Sexton, Van-Dam, Disse, Doreleijers, Slot, & Rowland, 2006), and general adolescent difficulties (Carr, 2000; Hogue, Dauber, Samuolis, & Liddle, 2006). However, there are few studies that specifically focus on the family therapy treatment of suicidal ideation. Therefore, I will try to point out when there is evidence-based therapy research available. However, this field has not been researched well up to this point in time.

From the standpoint of cognitive interventions, the very act of having the entire family expressing their thoughts and feelings openly in the same room is a powerful intervention. The family members may find that they agree with each other and are more similar than they thought they were. The parents may find that their suicidal adolescent sees the world quite differently than they ever thought possible. Many families discover that one parent (most typically, Mom) is very aware of the adolescent's thoughts and feelings and the other parent (often, Dad) is less in touch with his spouse and his teenager (Jurich, Bollman, & Schumm, 1984). In any of these cases, the discussion under the guidance of a family therapist will be crucial to the understanding of the suicidal adolescent's situation.

If the therapist is utilizing some form of behavioral intervention, having the rest of the family present in therapy has several advantages. The family hears the adolescent's behavioral contracts and can support the adolescent at home as he or she tries to "work his or her program." The mark of a good behavioral program is not the time the adolescent spends in therapy but the time the adolescent spends during the other 167 hours of the week when he or she is in "the real world." The therapists can't spend that time with the client. However, the adolescent client's family can spend time with their suicidal adolescent in "the real world" just living. In addition, within a family therapy context, the rest of the family becomes part of the behavioral contract and each member has his or her own roles to play. Therapy is no longer a solitary activity but a group process. The adolescent no longer feels as if he or she must make this therapeutic journey alone.

From a strategic point of view, family therapy is a much more powerful form of intervention than strategic therapy with an individual. Strategic takes a flow of energy, such as the inertia that holds a maladaptive recursive cycle in place and seeks to redirect the flow of energy in a more useful or positive (as defined by the client's goals) direction. In that way, it is truly an exercise in therapeutic jujitsu (Jurich, 1990). The question becomes, "What if you have a depressed, despondent, suicidal adolescent?" There appears to be very little energy flow with such a client. Strategic therapy can be done with this client. The therapist can use a very Freudian definition of depression as being "anger turned inward" (Freud, 1955). This bifurcates the adolescent into the anger perpetrator and the anger victim and allows for some dynamic tension to be explored between the client's two "warring personae."

However, if the therapist has the client in family therapy with his or her family, lots of energy flow can be observed and altered among the various family members. If a suicidal female adolescent client is silent about her motivations for suicide, it will be difficult to conduct individual therapy. However, if that same adolescent is in family therapy with her family, the therapist has other options. As the client is being silent, I can ask the other family members why they think the client is contemplating suicide. The therapist can justify this question by telling the family that they understand the client far better than the therapist does because they have known her longer and they live with her. When the client's kid sister, whom the client thinks is the "favorite child," responds to my question by saying, "She's just a big baby who's too chicken to live life!," this will trigger a much more vocal reaction from the client than anything the therapist could have said. Even if the client's sister's reaction is way off base, it is still valuable because it provoked a reaction from the client. If the client tries to dismiss the sister's analysis by saying, "That's ridiculous!," the therapist can reinvite the client to refute her sister's remarks by informing the therapist and her family as to what her true motivations are. Most adolescents will be only too happy to oblige in proving the sister wrong. If the client is still reluctant, the therapist can inform the client that, since there is no competing theory put forth by the client, the therapist has no choice but to accept the analysis of the sister as being valid. This process is a slam and a juice that will typically cause such a degree of cognitive dissonance in the client that even the most sphinx-like adolescent will volunteer information. None of that intervention could be accomplished without the family in the room.

In addition to this logic and rationale about the advantages of family therapy with suicidal adolescents, there is also some research which demonstrates some advantages to family therapy over individual therapy with suicidal individuals. Jurich (1983a) conducted a comparison study of sixteen suicidal clients who received family therapy and eighteen suicidal clients who received individual therapy. A Tennessee Self-Concept Scale (Fitts, 1965) was administered as a part of the initial assessment of the suicidal client and after the termination session, following a pretest–post-test design. All of the clients in both groups significantly increased their (1) total self-concept, (2) self-criticism, (3) identity, (4) self-satisfaction, (5) behavior, (6) physical self, (7) moral and ethical self, (8) personal self, (9) family self, and (10) social self.

The conclusion to be drawn from this data? Therapy, whether individual or family therapy, works well with suicidal people. However, when the scores were compared across therapeutic modalities, there were three significant differences. Suicidal clients who had family therapy, improved their family self, self-satisfaction, and total self-concept scores significantly better than did their counterparts who had participated in individual therapy. As the therapist was the same in all thirty-four cases, these results could reasonably be attributed to the mode of therapy with family therapy's being better in these crucial three areas. Obviously, both modalities of treatment, individual and family therapies, worked well with suicidal clients. However, family therapy had some significant advantages over individual therapy in several crucial areas that are extremely important to adolescents: total self-concept, family self, and self-satisfaction. Consequently, in my work with suicidal adolescents, family therapy is my treatment of choice.

JOINING WITH CLIENTS WHERE SUICIDE IS THE PRESENTING PROBLEM

When the presenting problem is the adolescent's suicidal ideations, the initial family therapy session will be dependent upon whether this is the first time the therapist has seen any member of the family or whether the therapist has seen the suicidal adolescent as a client first and is now meeting with both the suicidal adolescent and his or her family for the first time. In either case, I follow the same steps in joining mentioned in Chapter 5. I "dress down" to solidify my joining with the adolescent. I ask them to describe the "presenting problem" as each family member views it. I utilize client-centered (Rogers, 1957) techniques of warmth, empathy, and genuineness to lay the foundation for joining with each family member of the client family, including the suicidal adolescent. However, when the presenting problem is the suicidal ideation of an adolescent family member, there are other components to the joining process. When an adolescent has precipitated a suicide crisis or has verbalized suicidal thoughts, the family's established patterns of interaction are thrown into turmoil. Society sees suicide as being highly abnormal and is very judgmental about people who express suicidal desires by word or action. This is especially true when the suicidal person is an adolescent. Society's refrain is, "Something must really be wrong in that family if an adolescent wants to kill himself because he has so much to live for!" Such a rejection of life causes so much cognitive dissonance in members of our culture that people seek to diminish this dissonance by searching for explanations as to why this adolescent would be suicidal. Those explanations typically involve blame. "It could be the adolescent's fault because she was too screwed up." This is blaming the victim. "It must be the result of poor parenting." This is blaming the parents for their failure to parent adequately. "The teenager was okay until his parents got divorced," thereby blaming the parents for their failure as spouses. "That adolescent was just fine until her little sister was born," blaming a sibling for somehow causing the adolescent's suicidal ideation. Consequently, when the family comes into therapy, each family member, including the suicidal adolescent, understands the blame that members of society seek to place upon someone in the family. Family members tend not to question the legitimacy of placing blame; they just want to make sure that the blame isn't placed on them.

Families will often come into therapy with preconceived ideas of who is to blame for the suicidal adolescent. These are often initiated or exacerbated by their friends, extended family, or even well-meaning but misguided professionals in the community. I had a case in which the minister said that a suicidal teenage boy caused his suicidal ideation by not coming to church often enough. The father's boss said that his wife was not being a good enough mother. The mother's friends told her that her husband spent too much time at work to properly parent his son. Although any of these hypotheses may have had some legitimacy, they were not stated as speculations. They were stated as fact. Is it any wonder that, when the family came to the first therapy session, each family member felt like he or she was "walking on eggshells"? Nobody wanted to be blamed as the reason for the young man's suicide attempt.

The therapist must make the therapy room a safe haven from such societal scapegoating. Therapy is a place where we can talk about fear, shame, guilt, and blame, but it also is a place where we will talk about *all* possibilities without "rushing to judgment" in order to take the easy way out. Therapy is hard. It asks all family members to be honest about responsibilities for their actions. The therapist does not only have to teach this, but also model it.

In order to be honest about responsibility without blaming, I like to establish the following framework as a cornerstone for discussions of responsibility. I tell the family that when a person commits an act, he or she must take full responsibility for that act. The teenage boy who tries to kill himself is totally responsible for that act. Nobody made him do it. Even if others influenced him to commit suicide, the ultimate decision to act in a way that could or would end his life is *his* choice. No matter what anyone else said or did, even if they put the loaded gun in his hand, the young man could have chosen an alternative action. This may sound like a harsh message to communicate to a young suicidal teenager. I believe it is a necessary message to send everyone in the family for two reasons. First, if there is constant blaming and scapegoating, it slows the therapeutic process down to a crawl. Every discussion of responsibility becomes a struggle for locus of control. Responsibility becomes a therapeutic "hot potato" that each family member quickly throws to another family member in order to avoid being burned. This will slow the therapeutic process down significantly. Secondly, feelings of powerlessness are a crucial factor in the lives of suicidal adolescents (Jurich, 2002a). If suicidal adolescents are allowed to avoid responsibility for their actions, it reinforces the fact that they are truly powerless to do anything about their life or death. In order to empower adolescents who are having suicidal ideations, the therapist should be honest and straightforward about taking responsibility for their own actions. With power comes responsibility, but with responsibility comes power.

However, as the therapist, I also speak to the whole family about creating an atmosphere in which suicide would be more likely to happen. The suicidal adolescent woman, for example, still has to take entire responsibility for her suicidal actions but the rest of the family must ask themselves if they helped create an atmosphere or climate that would foster suicide as a maladaptive means of coping or that would promote alternatives to suicide as a coping strategy. The family members are not responsible for the suicidal action. That is the sole responsibility of the suicidal adolescent. However, they may have some responsibility for creating an atmosphere that supported dysfunctional coping strategies. This is a fine line of distinction but one which I have found to be very important to draw for suicidal adolescents and their family. If they understand this distinction, the lines of responsibility are clearer and everybody in the family will take some responsibility to change the family atmosphere. This empowers everyone to be able to do something that will help to break the present maladaptive recursive cycle.

In this way, the safety of the therapy room, in which nobody gets blamed for the adolescent's suicidal behavior, can be transferred to the home to reestablish a safe, trusting, and secure set of family relationships (Jurich, 1983a). The family learns to make distinctions about responsibility and can transfer that knowledge from one intimate environment (therapy) to another intimate environment (home). In addition, relational behavior in therapy can serve as a model for clients to use at home, as one suicidal teenage girl said to me:

> Damn it, Dr. J! We come to see you once a week but you follow us home. My mom talks and it's her voice but your words. What's worse is that sometimes I catch myself using "Tonyisms." Now that's scary!

When the therapist's behavior is transferred to the home, the family can establish or reestablish the family as a safe place in which to discuss difficult matters.

The other major issue that must be brought up in the first session is why the entire family should attend the therapy sessions. Using the logic and resources I discussed in the first section of this chapter, I try to explain to the rest of the family that the suicidal adolescent will benefit most if everyone in the family can attend. I typically use a baseball team metaphor. If, with one out, the pitcher has walked two batters, he is in trouble. He has also put his team in trouble. The object of the game is to get a victory for the team. If the batter hits a ground ball to the short-stop, the best thing to do is to try to turn a double play. The shortstop fields the ball and throws it to the second baseman, who catches the ball, spins around after he touches second base, and throws to the first baseman who steps on first base. That double play ends the inning and the threat to the pitcher and his team is over. This is a good outcome for both the pitcher and every member of the team. However, in order to accomplish this, the shortstop, second baseman, and first baseman all have to do their appointed jobs. If any one of them messes up and doesn't do his job, there is no double play and the threat of the opposing team scoring is still there. Likewise, even if the adolescent has created a threatening situation, the family needs to pull together as a team to get both the suicidal adolescent and his team (the family) out of this jam. This requires everyone's participation. If everybody plays, everybody wins. If just one person doesn't play, there is a good possibility that everybody loses. I use a sports analogy because it has been my experi-ence that females in our culture are typically more willing to actively participate in therapy than men. Therefore, I employ a metaphor which will be more "user-friendly" to the males in the family.

Once the family buys into the team approach of family therapy and the family feels as though therapy may be a safe place to express thoughts and feelings, the therapist can join with all members of the family. When the family first walks into the therapy room, I typically introduce myself and shake hands with every family member. I ask each what they would like me to call them in the therapy room and I try to respect their wishes. The only exception to that rule is if the adolescent has accepted a pejorative name, given by the family. If this occurs, I follow the course of action I described in Chapter 5 and try to suggest a more mature and functional name. Now that the family feels somewhat safe and welcomed, I ask the family to tell me what brought them into therapy. I don't really care who starts that discussion, just as long as I get every family member's viewpoint of why the family is in therapy, including the view of the suicidal adolescent. I want to hear how each family member defines the suicidal behavior and the role of the suicidal adolescent in the family. This will begin my analysis of the family dynamics. I also want the family to listen to the multiple views about the suicide behavior and the suicidal adolescent, and experience the therapist's acceptance of a multiplicity of views as all being valid. There is no attempt to change somebody's mind or arrive at the "right answer." All views are validated, even if they are contradictory. My ultimate goal is to have the family grapple with how the adolescent's behavior or ideation serves a particular family function and how this can be seen as a symbolic comment about the family system (Minuchin & Barcai, 1972).

In order to accomplish this, the therapist should ask each family member to discuss his or her perception of the sequence of events leading up to the suicidal ideation or suicidal crisis (Malouf & Alexander, 1974). The family is instructed to respectfully listen as each family member speaks without interruption. The family members not speaking are asked to hold their comments and responses until it is their turn to speak. Family members may struggle with this at first but they come to realize that the therapist will eventually give them a chance to speak without the interruption of the other family members while they speak. In this way, the therapist slows down the pace of the interaction. Instead of a staccato series of interruptions, the therapist allows each family member to voice their perceptions in a more relaxed atmosphere. The former barrage of questions and interruptions will accelerate the family into an emotional frenzy. Slowing down the conversation in the way described above slows down the tempo of the conversation to allow a less emotional discussion of the family situation. In that way the family can generate a clearer picture of the role that each family member plays in the genesis and maintenance of the suicidal family patterns. This will, in turn, lay the foundation for the idea that every family member is necessary for changing the maladaptive of the suicidal maladaptive recursive cycle (Jurich, 1983a).

In this manner, the ground rules are established for how communication will be structured during therapy sessions and fosters mutual respect for all family members. Most family members, including the suicidal adolescent, will address their comments to the therapist. This is to be expected, as the therapist is the authority figure in the therapy session. The therapist should accept this pattern as being normal for a family new to therapy, which is in the middle of a very difficult time. The therapist is their "security blanket." Over time, the family members should be instructed to talk directly to each other. In this way, the therapist changes the source of security from himself or herself to the other family members. The message is that the family is its own resource. The therapist is there on a temporary basis, but the family will always be there. I tell my clients in the first session that my purpose as a therapist is to help them out as well as I can and then put myself out of business as their therapist as fast as I can by helping them help themselves. Part of that process is to suggest that they speak to each other, because this is what they will be required to do after therapy is over. This will set the process in place for the directives that the therapist will give as therapy progresses.

The therapist can help the family discuss their feelings about each other in a nonaccusatory manner (Puryear, 1979). This will extract some of the venom from previous family communications. This will also lessen scapegoating and blame-avoidance patterns that are typical in such families. Although the therapist should try to keep the atmosphere as supportive as possible, he or she should not hinder the exchange of negative affects (Jurich, 1983a). As a matter of fact, disagreement and conflict should be encouraged as being normal and healthy, if discussed in a respectful way. Hiding negative affects from others in the family or from oneself is far more distracting than discussing them. This is especially true for families where negative emotions such as anger are not permitted to be expressed. The key to this communication in therapy is to grant each family member the right to feel negative without attacking him or her for having those feelings.

In many cases, I have helped families understand this process by offering to them some observation about emotions (Jurich, 1979). I believe that, to a degree, we *are* our emotions. We may modify our behavior that may be triggered by our emotions, but it is extremely difficult to turn our emotions on or off. For example, if we are angry at a friend for forgetting that he had a lunch appointment with us, we feel anger and frustration towards that person. If our friend says, "Please don't be angry with me," we may modify our behavior but we can't just turn off the emotion. Although we may answer that we are not angry with him, a more truthful response would be, "I'm not so angry with you as to damage our friendship. It will pass." Therefore, I try to tell my clients that I believe that we are entitled to have our emotions, without being criticized for having them.

Positive emotions (like love, happiness, and respect) are easy for a person to hear and validate. It is the negative emotions (e.g., anger, fear, and disappointment) that are much more difficult to hear, especially when they are directed at you. Therefore, it is my philosophical belief that a person is entitled to his or her emotions and that they should be validated by others, especially by his or her family. The behavioral expressions of these emotions, however, can be modified and changed. A person may be angry but that does not give him or her the right to hit another or call him or her names. In therapy, therefore, it is my task as a therapist to validate each family member and the emotions they express. However, it is also my job to help family members change their expressions of emotion and their behaviors so that they are not attacking or accusing another family member. I try to teach family members how to express their emotions in a way that will make them easier to hear and to be validated. This is crucial for families with suicidal adolescents. If the suicidal adolescent does not receive validation for his or her emotions, he or she will feel invalidated as a person. This will give the suicidal adolescent one more reason to end it all and commit suicide. However, if the adolescent's emotions are validated, especially by "significant others" such as parents and siblings, this will put them on the right road toward self-validation. Adolescents who can validate themselves are less likely to commit suicide (Henry et. al., 1993).

I also warn my client families about the dangers of not expressing feelings, both negative and positive. Feelings do not dissipate just because they are not expressed. The unexpressed feelings build up inside a person. I give the family the following metaphor:

> Surely we have all seen enough Westerns to know that when a person gets bitten by a rattlesnake, the wound needs to be cut open and the poison sucked out. This makes for a very dramatic scene in a lot of Western movies and television shows. However, the principle behind this drama is sound. If the poison is not extracted, the wound will fester and the person will lose a limb or his or her life. This is the way it is with emotions, especially negative emotions like anger and fear. If they are not expressed, they will remain inside and fester until the person's whole being is poisoned with the negative emotion.

William Blake (1956) wrote a poem, "A Poison Tree," in 1794. It is quite articulate in expressing this process:

> I was angry with my friend:
> I told my wrath, my wrath did end.
> I was angry with a foe:
> I told it not, my wrath did grow.
>
> And I water'd it in fears,
> Night and morning with my tears;
> And I sunn'ed it with smiles,
> And with soft deceitful wiles.

> And it grew both day and night,
>   Till it bore an apple bright;
> And my foe behold it shine,
> And he knew that it was mine.

> And into my garden stole
> When the night had veil'd the pole:
>   In the morning glad I see
> My foe outstretch'd beneath the tree.

William Blake (1956, p. 538)

To families who tend to repress negative feelings, especially anger, I often give a copy of Blake's poem. We then discuss the meaning of the poem in the context of their family. When the presenting complaint of the family is the suicidal ideation or behaviors of their adolescent, the expression of emotions, especially negative emotions, is especially important. A suicidal adolescent already has a reservoir of stored-up feelings that he or she feels cannot be expressed. If the family is unwilling to validate those feelings in therapy, that might be enough to push the suicidal adolescent over the edge of the metaphorical cliff to his or her death. If the therapist can encourage the expression of feelings, teach family members how to express those emotions in a way in which they will most likely be heard, and manage the affect in the family so that all family members feel safe with emotional expression, the therapist will set a strong foundation for the rest of therapy.

The discussion of goals for therapy is not as crucial to review in the first session or two of therapy because it is obvious that the overriding goal is to keep the suicidal adolescent alive. It is more important to achieve "buy-in" to the therapeutic process from the family members. The therapist has to sell the idea that therapy can work to lessen the suicide potential of the adolescent. Then the family, or at least certain key members of the family, have to buy therapy as a means of treatment. It would be nice if all of the client family members bought into therapy as a means of treatment but that is not always the case. The therapist has to have "buy-in" from at least two family members. One of these is obviously the suicidal adolescent. If he or she is not invested in therapy, any therapeutic work will be an uphill battle. The second person to sell on the therapeutic process is the person who has the most power in the family to either keep the family in therapy or pull them out. Sometimes, especially in male-dominated, authoritarian families, this is the father. Sometimes, especially when the mother is a strong expressive leader in the family, it is the mother. Sometimes, it is the suicidal adolescent, although often the adolescent is quite unaware of the extent of that power. I had a case in which the role of the most powerful person in keeping the family in therapy was played by an older sibling.

Once the suicidal adolescent and the most powerful person in keeping the family in therapy are sold, the family can begin to discuss goals for therapy. The goal of keeping the suicidal adolescent alive is a starting place but it is not enough. The therapist needs to push the family to discuss what type of future they would like to have. "Being alive" is good but what would that life look like. Toward this end, the therapist can use any of the techniques proposed by deShazer (1985) in Solution-Focused Therapy, where the family frames what they want their ideal future to be. This will help them develop goals for the suicidal adolescent and the rest of the family.

I had a case in which the suicidal teenage male seemed to be goalless. When I asked him what his goal is in his life he replied, "Make it to twenty-five. That's eight more years. I don't think it will happen." When I asked the other family members what were their goals for the future, nobody could articulate a goal more than five years down the line. Most of the goals the family stated were sketchy benchmarks given to them by the society. They included things like "have the kids graduate" and "keep my job." There was no further explanation. I asked them what they would like their life to look like in three years. No one could articulate a vision. They could express what they did not want it to look like but there were no expectations of what they would like it to be. This was a family without a sense of direction. They were sailing on a rudderless ship to destinations unknown. I used the Solutions-Focused Therapy miracle question technique (deShazer, 1988) to push the family to consider what they would like their lives to look like. I asked each family member what he or she would see if they woke up and everything was the way they wanted it. What would you see if a miracle occurred and you opened your eyes? How would that vision change if it were five years from now? I took notes on each person's answers and pointed out where all of their futures looked the same or could be compromised to be similar. I then suggested that those images of a desirable future could help us in formulating goals for therapy. Goals for the suicidal adolescent included graduating from high school, having a job, and getting a girlfriend. Goals for the family were being more open and cohesive. Articulating positive goals for the future is extremely important for the suicidal adolescent. The very act of articulating future goals is antithetical to the maladaptive recursive cycle in suicide where there is no future. If there is a future that the family can talk about sharing, suicide becomes less of an option.

If the therapist has seen the suicidal adolescent first in dealing with a suicidal crisis, the therapist can follow the same course of action outlined above. However, he or she must make several alterations to the process. Because the therapist has previously seen the suicidal adolescent under conditions which had to accelerate the therapeutic process, the relationship between the therapist and the suicidal adolescent is "out of sync" with therapist's relationship with the rest of the family. The therapist must shift roles from being the suicidal adolescent's therapist to being the family's therapist. If this is not done, both the family and the suicidal adolescent will become confused as to who has what role in the therapeutic process. Utilizing the Strategic Therapy principle of making the covert overt, I prefer to address this explicitly. I ask the suicidal adolescent, with whom I have previously worked, to introduce me to his family, one by one. I then overtly explain that this initial family therapy session marks the change in my role from being the adolescent's therapist to being the family's therapist. Therefore, I tell the family that I need to catch them up on the nature of the therapeutic role that their adolescent and I have already established and on the progress we've made. I then ask the suicidal adolescent if I can give his or her family a summary of what work we have previously done together? Before he or she answers, I ask if he or she will correct me if I misrepresent or forget what we did? I want to give the summary for two reasons:

1. I can summarize more appropriately than the adolescent client can. I've seen teenagers give a one-sentence summary that was totally inadequate and have seen adolescents drone on endlessly and leave out all of the important parts. The therapist is much better equipped to fill in the rest of the family.
2. As I summarize for the family, I can frame the previous encounter with the suicidal adolescent in such a way as to emphasize the adolescent's competence and sense of responsibility. This not only makes the adolescent look good in the eyes of his parents and siblings but it also sets up a set of expectations for the adolescent to follow for the rest of therapy. It also validates the therapeutic process as being useful to the adolescent.

Once the family is "caught-up," we can proceed to the joining process outlined above.

As I have mentioned in Chapter 5, I believe that a therapist must give a client family a gift with each session. If a therapist joins well with a suicidal adolescent and his or her family, the therapist can give the family three gifts:

1. By letting everyone in the family talk openly, the therapist has dragged the secret of the adolescent's suicidal thoughts and behavior out of the shadows and into the light.
2. The therapist has taken the responsibility of "fixing the problem" from any single family member and made it a "team effort" in which the family, the therapist, and the suicidal adolescent will all work on the problem together.
3. The therapist has given them hope. He or she has said that there is a "light at the end of the tunnel."

If the therapist can give the family these three gifts by the end of the joining phase of therapy, they will return to therapy with a sense of purpose, ready to work.

JOINING WITH CLIENTS WHEN SUICIDE IS NOT THE PRESENTING PROBLEM

In many cases, especially working with adolescents and their families, suicidal ideation or behavior will not be the presenting problem. Instead, there will be some other issue that brings the family or individual into therapy. What the specific diagnosis might be is not necessarily important to this discussion.

Once suicide is introduced into the ongoing therapeutic process, therapy must stop in order to address this topic. The therapist cannot go on with therapy as if nothing happened. The adolescent has put his life on the table by talking about suicide or engaging in suicidal behavior. To ignore suicide as an issue is to devalue the adolescent's life and, in essence, say it is worthless. This would leave the adolescent only one of two options: (1) to devalue his or her own life or (2) to follow through and commit suicide. The first response will set therapy back considerably or destroy the therapeutic relationship. The second results in a dead client. Neither outcome is acceptable. Therefore, the therapist must halt the therapy and deal with the suicide first.

There is a countervailing force which comes into play. Cases have been so disrupted by an adolescent's mention of suicide that the therapy has collapsed into a succession of emergency suicide interventions and have never gotten back to the issues that were being addressed in the original therapy. The therapeutic process has been shanghaied by the adolescent's suicidal ideation. This is also unacceptable. If the adolescent feels he or she can sabotage the therapy by mentioning the word "suicide," that will provide an irresistible temptation to disrupt the therapeutic process whenever the going gets tough in therapy. Therefore, I believe that the therapist has to "shift gears" when suicide becomes an issue during the course of therapy.

One way to accomplish this shifting of gears in therapy is to rejoin with the clients around the issue of suicide. Because suicidal ideas or threats make the therapy more volatile, I believe that the therapist must address suicide as a different type of issue than the rest of therapy and needs to rejoin with the family concerning this issue. If the therapist has an individual adolescent as a client, I feel that the therapist has to tell the adolescent that he or she will have to ask the client's parents to come into therapy to deal with this matter. If the adolescent protests that decision, I try to explain that I take the mention of suicide *very* seriously:

> Although your privacy is very important in therapy, your life is more important. If you are genuinely in danger of killing yourself, I believe it is my duty to help protect you. I am only with you for an hour a week. In order to protect you, I am either going to have you hospitalized or I have to set up a safety plan with your family. Either way, I'm going to have to contact your parents.

It is at this point that many adolescent will say, "Well, I didn't really mean it." At that point I tell the adolescent the following:

> If you are in a crowded movie theater and you pull the fire alarm what happens? Everybody will panic. People could get seriously hurt in the stampede to head for the doors. Fire trucks and police cars will race the rough streets to get to the theater. All of this is understandable if there really is a fire. However, if you pull the fire alarm as a joke or to get attention, you are in deep trouble, especially if someone gets hurt in the process. Saying that you're suicidal is like pulling a fire alarm. If you are seriously thinking about killing yourself, pull the alarm! If you are just musing about suicide as an option, bring it up and we'll talk about it. But if you're trying to get attention, let's talk about another way to get attention because trying to get attention by saying you're suicidal is *not* a good idea.

I then ask the adolescent to restate what his or her intention was by bringing up suicide. If he or she says that he or she was just trying to get attention, I will work with the adolescent on better, less destructive ways of getting attention. Most typically, I tell the adolescent that if he or she wants attention, overtly ask me for it. I ask them to say, "Tony, I need more attention right now." I tell them that I'll drop what I'm doing in therapy and we will deal with his or her need immediately. We may analyze why he or she needed attention then and we will talk about what to do if that need arises again. If the adolescent wants to discuss suicide in a more philosophical way, we will do so. If, however, the adolescent is seriously thinking about ending his or her own life, we need to have a plan in order to keep him or her safe until our next therapy session. This will require consulting with the adolescent's parents. I will tell the adolescent that we do not need to call them immediately because there is safety in the therapy room. We can talk it over and discuss his or her suicidal ideation but there is a good chance that we will be calling his or her parents. I take a skeptical stance and ask him or her to convince me that he or she is no longer actively suicidal.

If I have to call the parents, I typically briefly explain why I am calling and ask them to come into the therapy office as soon as possible. That may be later that night or that afternoon, if I have the time available, or the next day. If we have to wait a day and I feel that the adolescent is actively suicidal, I will hospitalize the adolescent for at least the night. Most parents make it in that night. Once they arrive, I join with them in a way that is similar to the way I would join them if I have seen their adolescent in a suicidal crisis, as mentioned earlier in this chapter. I try to convince them that it would be in the best interest of their adolescent if we switched to family therapy, at least for a while.

If the therapist was seeing the adolescent in family therapy when the issue of suicide arose, there is no issue of bringing in the parents; they are already there. However, I still tell the adolescent and the rest of the family about taking suicide very seriously, as outlined above. In some families the parents will try to convince me to do parent–adolescent therapy and leave the suicidal adolescent's siblings out of the discussion. I believe this would be counterproductive, and I explain to them the following:

> Silence is the ally of suicide. If you can talk about it, it loses its power. If your son [or daughter] is suicidal, the rest of his [her] siblings know that something is wrong. If we let them in on the discussion, they can voice their opinions. This meeting will also lay out the rules about discussing suicide for them as well as your teenage son [daughter]. It also lets your son [daughter] know that he [she] is not alone.

Many parents wish to protect their other children from the specter of suicide. They are afraid that a suicidal teen will give his or her younger siblings ideas about suicide as a viable option. However, it has been my experience that just the opposite is true. If siblings are allowed to stay in family therapy as suicide is discussed, they are more able to understand it all and will learn from therapy what to do if they should ever feel suicidal. In fact, as "preventative maintenance," I have had several siblings come in for a "check up" appointment at their request as they get older so that they would not get to the point of suicide. Furthermore, the presence of siblings in the therapy session can be very helpful in keeping the suicidal adolescent connected. I had a male client who was nineteen years old and had been "dumped" by his girlfriend. He was devastated and had entertained some suicidal thoughts. He told me that when he felt suicidal, he would hold his two-year-old brother, put on some blues music, and sing to the little boy about "having the blues." He said, "That was the best medicine to chase suicide away."

When suicide is brought up as a possibility, the suicidal adolescent and the family must be apprised by the therapist that the discussion is different than "regular therapy." The potential for a lethal decision by the adolescent heightens the sense of urgency to keep the adolescent safe. At that time, the therapist can follow the joining process outlined earlier in this chapter. However, as a therapist I also tell my family that, once the immediate suicide episode has been resolved, we will get back to the therapy where we had left off. I tell the family and the suicidal adolescent this "up front," so that they don't think that the ongoing therapy practice has been abandoned. The return to therapy at the point we "left off" signifies for the suicidal adolescent a return to "normality." If the adolescent admits to mentioning suicide as an attention-getting mechanism, I will try to "get back to therapy" by the end of the session or, at latest, during the next session. If the adolescent wanted to have more of a philosophical discussion about suicide, I will spend the rest of the session in discussion, if necessary; invite the adolescent to revisit the topic when he or she feels the need to do so, ask him or her if further discussion is needed at the beginning of the next session, and return to the "course of therapy" during the subsequent session. If the adolescent truly has suicidal ideation and behaviors, I will put our course of therapy on hold until the suicidal issues have been resolved. However, during the course of our therapy on suicide issues, I will frequently try to make the connection between suicide issues and our previous course of therapy.

For example, I had a case in which an eleven-year-old girl did not make the cheerleading squad. We were doing therapy around these issues and making some reasonable progress. In one session the young girl's fourteen-year-old brother had mentioned that one of the cheerleaders had her picture in the school newspaper. He described it as a "hot picture of her." That evening, after the session had ended, the young woman cried to her mother that she was having thoughts about killing herself. Mom called me and we set up an appointment for the family for the next day. We commenced on a course of therapy dealing with her suicidal issues. However, I never lost sight of where we were in therapy when she became suicidal. I frequently made reference back to the cheerleading disappointment while we were discussing suicide. It was obviously a major precipitating factor in her suicidal feelings. After about three sessions, I decided to use the brother's observation of the newspaper article as an intervention. I asked the young woman to imagine the school newspaper doing an article on her if she committed suicide and running a picture of her in her coffin as part of the story. I asked her what the caption would read. She answered, "Here is a picture of Carrie (not her real name) at her funeral; she had more problems than anyone realized." I asked her what the caption would read if they ran her picture next to that of the "hot cheerleader." She began to tear up and blurted out, "Here is what happens if you don't make cheerleader; they use you and throw you away!" By the end of that sentence, she was sobbing. She explained that her boyfriend had dumped her when she didn't make the cheerleading squad and started going out with one of the cheerleaders because she was "so hot." If I had not gone back to the session, which, unknown to me at the time, triggered her suicidal ideation, I would have missed a key factor in the therapeutic process. I would have been derailed from the issue that therapy was about to probe. Therapy became a process of working with both suicidal issues and boyfriend issues and, over time, bringing them back together as an integrated whole. Later in therapy, she revealed that, in fact, her boyfriend had sex with her before he dumped her and, at the time she was suicidal she believed it would be better to die than to have anybody find out about that, even in therapy.

If the issues surrounding the teenager's suicide have taken the therapy "off course," the therapist may have to slowly work therapy back to the original therapy process. Sometimes the best way to accomplish this is by dividing the time in the session between the two processes. For example, if the therapy session is fifty minutes long, do therapy around the suicide for forty minutes and save the last ten minutes for discussing how the things that were being discussed during the regular course of therapy relate to the discussions centering on suicide. After a few weeks, shift the ratio to thirty minutes for suicide as the central focus and twenty minutes on other therapeutic issues. Eventually, the therapist can shift to the first fifteen minutes on suicide and the other thirty-five minutes on other matters. Although this seems like an artificial mechanism to use, it has the effect of integrating the therapeutic process before suicidal ideation and behaviors became a problem and the therapeutic process centering around suicide. This therapeutic hybrid may never lose some focus on suicide but it will integrate it back into the main therapeutic process.

Eight

ANALYSIS

Understanding How the Adolescent Has Been Seduced

In strategic therapy, analysis is a continual process that begins with the phone call to set up the first therapy appointment and ends only after the family has terminated therapy. The therapist constantly is searching for the maladaptive recursive cycles imbedded in the client family's relationships and behaviors. Most of this is accomplished by listening to them tell their stories about past events. Throughout the joining process, the therapist needs to focus not only on the events which are reported but also the family members' meanings attached to these events. In Strategic Therapy, the therapist often takes on the role of the expert (Haley, 1976). The therapist, because of training, reading, and experience, has a greater knowledge base about the nature of suicide (Chapter 2) and the nature of adolescents and their families (Chapter 3 and Chapter 4).

The therapist also should have a greater degree of objectivity than do family members who have a history and live together. A therapist cannot be totally objective (Anderson & Goolishian, 1988), as he or she has joined the family in their efforts to cope with their suicidal adolescent. However, the therapist certainly has a more objective view than the family members in viewing the circumstances surrounding the suicidal adolescent. That more objective view of the family is only part of the picture. It must be coupled with an understanding of the way each family member, including the suicidal adolescent, interprets the events, thoughts, and feelings that comprise their family's stories (White & Epston, 1990). If the therapist is going to understand the family's "story," each family member's understanding of that story must be explored and understood. The analysis of the family must include those subjective views of the events brought forth by the family.

Strategic Therapy is a reactive therapy. It reacts to the information put forth by the family. Consequently, there is no specific prescribed pattern or path to take to analyze a family. The therapist must take the information the family discloses (including their interpretation of events), combine it with the knowledge base that he or she possesses and decide upon a course of action. There are, however, several key issues to focus upon which will bring the therapist into an understanding of the family situation that will allow him or her to target interventions for effectiveness and efficiency.

IDENTIFYING MALADAPTIVE RECURSIVE CYCLES

In exploring the family dynamics for maladaptive recursive cycles, the therapist needs to remember that family members do not typically think in terms of cycles and circular causality. Instead, they think of linear causality and will think in terms of "who started it" and blame. For example, a teenage male will complain that his parents are too strict and never let him do anything. His parents will complain that their teenager is irresponsible, can't be trusted, and constantly screws up. The teenager rebels against the rules of his parents because they are too strict. The parents restrict their son because he screws up. Consequently, each "side" (teen and his parents) simultaneously say, "Something is wrong with them (him), fix them (him)!" The reality of the situation is that they are now trapped in a cycle. The false belief that "the other side caused it" only serves to mask the cycle and perpetuate the circular causality. As an intervention, I typically say, "I don't care who caused it, our job is to stop it!" The point of this discussion is that the therapist must recognize the cycles present in the family without the family's cognitive awareness that there is a cycle present. Therefore, the therapist has to listen to the family members' linear ideas of causality presented by a family member. The therapist should always ask, "What did another family member or the family as a whole do to trigger this supposedly independent action?" In most cases, with very little probing, the therapist will be able to discover something that triggered the response. The cycle is then unveiled.

Just because the cycle is clear to the therapist does not mean that it is very clear to the family members. Circular causality and systemic concepts are often foreign to members of Western society. Even if the family members do understand the logic of circular causality, they may have a vested interest in maintaining the linear causality idea that it is "the other side's fault" so that each side feels less responsibility for the current problem. The logic flows as follows:

> If suicidal thoughts are not entirely my teenage son's fault, then they must be totally my fault and my son's suicidal ideas are there because I am a horrible parent.

The adolescent's thought pattern follows the same logic in the opposite direction:

> If my parents didn't make me suicidal, then it is all my fault. I must be a totally incompetent teenager and will become a totally incompetent adult.

Either of those two streams of logic are fatally flawed. Nobody is totally responsible. It is not a situation that is "all or none." In circular causality, responsibility for the continuance of the cycle is shared. However, many families don't understand that and are, therefore, very reluctant to give up "total linear causality" as a description of what is happening. This should not deter the therapist from identifying cycles in his analysis.

The cycles are typically maladaptive. They don't work. The question that is logical to ask is, "If the cycles don't work, why does the family keep them up?" There are typically one of four answers to that question. First, the family does not know that what they are doing is not working. For example, a child, who has been physically abused all of his or her life, has experienced violence on such a daily basis that he or she expects that violence is simply a part of life. Maladaptive cycles surrounding violence are not questioned or analyzed. They are simply accepted as the way life is. Secondly, maladaptive cycles may be tied to what Nagy has labeled as "invisible loyalties" (Boszormenyi-Nagy & Spark, 1973). These are patterns of behavior that are learned in one's family of origin. The family reproduces the same patterns of behavior—despite the fact that they don't work—because of loyalty to their parents' or their family's traditions. Family members may be aware of these loyalties or they may be so imbedded in their past family history as to be invisible even to the family members who are now acting them out as a maladaptive cycle. Thirdly, although the cycle may be maladaptive, one family member may actually be benefiting from it to the detriment of the others in the family or the family as a whole. In fact, the maladaptive cycle may ultimately harm the person who thinks that he or she is benefiting also. For instance, in our previous example of the rebellion-restriction cycle, the parents may get temporary compliance from their adolescent. Therefore, the parents continue their part of the cycle because they feel that they have "won the battle." If the adolescent, however, gives in because his parents hold the keys to greater resources (for example, the car keys), but he resents his parents as being unreasonable and too restrictive, the teenager will build up his resentment over time and may become suicidal as a consequence of the continuation of the maladaptive cycle. The parents may have won the battle but ultimately lost the war. Lastly, the family may keep engaging in a maladaptive cycle because they are too afraid to try anything else. The old adage of "better the devil you know than the devil you don't" applies here. They are simply too scared about the unknown to try something new. Hopefully, the safety of the therapy room will be able to help them see other alternatives.

The maladaptive cycle is also recursive. It keeps on occurring over and over again. Many times the family is quite aware of this and feels a tremendous amount of frustration with the situation. Other families will be oblivious to the continuation of the pattern. Still other families will attempt to change but, despite some differences, they will still engage, in essence, in the same pattern. Going back to our example of the young man and his parents, the parents may try to change the recursive maladaptive cycle by altering his restriction from "house arrest" to doing chores. This may be a significant change to them. However, it may be the "same old thing" to the adolescent. He still feels restricted and still rebels. The parents saw their change of consequences to be an attempt to break the cycle. The teenager saw their attempt as simply "a variation on a theme."

In all of these cases, the therapist needs to point out the maladaptive recursive cycles, even if the family is not aware of them or disagrees that they are either cycles, maladaptive, or recursive. Suicidal ideation and behaviors are themselves maladaptive recursive cycles. They are often an extension of the maladaptive recursive cycles that have been already present in the home. I had a case in which the father often said, "You're going to give me a heart attack" to both his wife and his children when they would do something that would displease or hurt him. As problematic as this may have been, it was effective, as no family member wanted to literally cause Dad to have a heart attack. What made it even more effective was that Dad's own father had died of a heart attack at age 55. The father held himself hostage to gain compliance from the rest of the family members. When the family's oldest daughter turned seventeen years old, she wanted to date a young man whom her parents found objectionable. Dad said that "he was blue collar and has an attitude problem." When the daughter wanted to discuss the point further, her father said the old standby, "Are you trying to give me a heart attack?" The daughter shouted back, "Are you trying to push me to commit suicide?" Everyone was silent. For the first time in the history of the family someone had responded to dad's standard question and used the same dynamic to trump his ploy. The daughter held herself hostage with a threat of suicide. It was an escalation of the same logic that had dominated the family for years. It was a variation of the same maladaptive recursive cycle.

At other times, suicidal ideation of actions may be the attempt of a family member—for the sake of this book, an adolescent—to break the already existing maladaptive recursive cycles. I consulted on a case in which the adolescent daughter had been sexually abused by her father over a number of years. Now, as a seventeen-year-old, she had "made herself as unavailable to him as possible," although she still felt threatened when she was around him. She tried to see her family only as a group and avoided being in the same room with him alone. However, she was now worried about her thirteen-year-old sister, who had recently begun to wet the bed at night. This was something she did when her father began to sexually abuse her. Not for her own sake but for the sake of her sister, the seventeen-year-old told her mother of her father's abuse. She was called a liar and ignored. Desperate to disrupt this maladaptive recursive cycle which had haunted her for years and was now being visited upon her sister, the seventeen-year-old wrote a suicide note detailing her father's incest, went into the girl's bathroom at school, and took an overdose of sleeping pills. Her dramatic suicide attempt, in a place where school authorities would find her note, was an attempt on the part of the young woman to disrupt her family's maladaptive recursive cycle by unveiling it to the world. The fact that it was a suicide attempt further validated her "selfless sincerity" that her family was in need of outside help. Whether the suicidal ideation or behavior is an extension of an already existent maladaptive recursive cycle or an attempt to disrupt a maladaptive recursive cycle already in place in the family, suicide is often tied to such cycles.

A third reason for looking at maladaptive recursive cycles is that these cycles, learned in the family of origin, may be transferred to relationships outside of the family. I had a case in which an eighteen-year-old girl was feeling suicidal because her boyfriend of fifteen months recently had broken up with her. He told her the reason why he wanted to break up was that she was too jealous and bossy. When her parents took her to me for therapy, her father said little but her mother told me that she was making her go to therapy so that I "would stop this suicidal nonsense." In other words, Mom was going to make her daughter stop being suicidal, and I, the therapist, was her instrument. I thought to myself that Mom sounded controlling and bossy. As the family spoke about the events leading up to the daughter's suicidal ideation, it was obvious that Mom was in charge of the family and that Dad deferred to his wife in family matters. The daughter had witnessed this relationship for years, growing up in the family, and had modeled her own hetero-sexual behavior after her parents' example of male–female relationships. In her family of origin, the father had been very passive-aggressive in response to his wife's control but the daughter had not overtly made that connection as being her fathers' response to her mother's controlling behavior. When her boyfriend was challenging her own control of their relationship, she redoubled her efforts to control him. When he said he wanted to break off their relationship, she tried to control him by saying that she had suicidal thoughts. The maladaptive recursive cycle of the parents (control versus passive-aggressive behavior) was mirrored in the young womans' participation in her own relationship. Her suicidal ideation was a logical extension of the pattern she experienced in her family between her mother and her father.

Maladaptive recursive cycles are a key element in understanding much of adolescents' suicidal ideas and behavior. They need to be iden-tified and cataloged for use during the intervention stages of therapy.

FOCUSING ON INCONGRUITIES

As the suicidal adolescent and his or her family tell their therapist the stories of family life and their perceptions of what led up to the suicidal thoughts and actions, special attention should be paid to the incon-gruities that the therapist hears. Incongruities may tell the therapist more than incidents that seem consistent with known information, because incongruities give the therapist messages about the process of the individuals and family as a unit. There are often incongruities within people. Family members may give conflicting messages between the verbal and nonverbal message of their communication. The lexi-cal verbal message (the typescript of what is said) is the content of the communication (Watzlawick et al., 1967). The nonverbal aspects of the communication (such as facial expression) and nonlexical parts of the verbal message (such as tone, meter, and volume) comprise the metamessage of the communication. The metamessage is the part of the message that tells the receiver of the message how to interpret the content of the message. If these parts of the message are congruent, the message is easy to understand. For example, a compliment said in a melodic tone with a smile on the speaker's face is easy to understand. So is an angry criticism, said loudly and with a stern facial expression. The latter message may not be pleasant to hear but the congruence makes it easy to comprehend. If a message is incongruent, the listener is confused as to how to interpret what is being said. If the words of a message are harsh but they are delivered in a melodic voice and with a smile on the speaker's face, the listener will be confused as to what is really being said. Does the listener believe the message or the metamessage, as they seem to be in conflict? Families who give such incongruent messages to each other can greatly confuse the adolescent living in their home.

Adolescents are at a developmental stage where interpersonal relationships are very important to them, but they have limited skills to draw upon in trying to navigate the waters of interpersonal interactions. It is hard enough for them to comprehend congruent messages. When the messages are incongruent, adolescents can find it very difficult to function. I had a case in which sarcasm was a major form of family communication. Most of the parents' positive messages, to either each other or their children, were said with at least a twinge of sarcasm. It was my speculation that this was a way to keep distance in intimate relationships so that each parent could be protected from possible rejection. From this parental model, the children learned that all relationships, especially intimate male–female relationships should be laced with sarcasm if things "got too mushy." When the oldest daughter turned fourteen, she had a boyfriend who became frustrated with her sarcasm, got angry with her, and asked her, "Why do you have to be such a bitch when I try to get close?" As she tried to tone down the sarcasm in her relationship with her boyfriend, she also began to question the messages she got from her parents. In therapy she said that she had never gotten a positive message from her parents that was not discounted by the way that they said it. Consequently, she felt unloved and unappreciated by her parents. Some parents' messages may, on the surface, sound positive but they are cloaked in a negative metamessage. A suicidal adolescent male told me that his parents had said that they would accept him no matter what his grades were but they said it in a way which let him know that bad grades were unacceptable. In school, he had forgotten that there was a test in math and was so panicked that he might let his parents down that he cheated. He got caught and was told that he would flunk his course. That night he went home and tried to slit his wrists. His parents were puzzled at his behavior, as they said that they would accept whatever grades he got. That message was overridden by their metamessage that it was unacceptable to get bad grades. Suicidal adolescents often take incongruent messages in a negative way by focusing on the metamessage and not the message.

Sometimes incongruities occur within a person because they are ambivalent. "Ambivalence" does not mean that the person has no feelings about something. It means that the person has equal and opposite feelings about something. Those feelings may be quite strong. However, because they are opposing each other, the individual may be immobilized. Adolescents frequently feel this ambivalence because they "want it all" and do not have enough perspective on life to realize that it is simply impossible to "have it all." Therefore, adolescents often give incongruent messages to others because they do not have the ability to make a choice that will satisfy their conflicting desires. Adolescents of both genders have a hard time deciding which of two different boyfriends or girlfriends they would like to date. For many adolescents, the difficulty over this choice fills up hours of conversations with their friends. I had a fifteen-year-old male come in to see me who was very troubled by his ambivalence over his sexual identity. He was an attractive young man who was pursued by many of the girls in his class. He knew that he would have much better acceptance from his parents, his peers, and society if he dated women. However, he felt no attraction to women. He did feel attracted to men, but he well knew that there was a tremendous social stigma attached to homosexuality. Although he was not suicidal when he first came into therapy, he did come back into therapy two years later with suicidal ideations because he felt such tremendous incongruity between his feelings about his own identity and his family's expectations for him. Such personal incongruities put a young person at war with himself. To this young man, suicide seemed like the only solution.

There are also incongruities between and among people. Two people might see the same experience quite differently. For one teenage boy, making the football team may be a tremendous accomplishment. For another, it may mean that he is stuck, trying to fulfill his father's dream. Although it is the same event, it will be looked upon quite differently by these two young men. When family members give incongruent accounts of the same event, it may tell the therapist a lot about the relationship between those two people. If dad is overjoyed that his son made the football team and his son is ambivalent, this could indicate a father–son conflict over playing football. Such incongruent messages from two family members could fester if unresolved and, consequently, could result in suicidal ideation from the adolescent. Such interpersonal incongruities should be a "red flag" for the therapist.

In families with a suicidal adolescent there are often incongruities between the perceptions of all or at least some of the family members and reality. I had an eighteen-year-old female client whose single-parent mother had pushed her to enter the local beauty pageant. The daughter felt that she could not "measure up" to the other girls in their appearance.

Her mother kept telling her how beautiful she was. Although there was certainly nothing wrong with the young woman's appearance, by most objective criteria, her view of her "beauty" was probably more accurate than her mother's opinion. When she did not gain acceptance into the pageant, the girl actually felt a sense of relief from the pressure of being something that she was not. However, when her mother heard of her daughter's being cut from the pool of entrants, she was devastated. The daughter felt like she was a failure and let her mom down by not getting into the pageant. Suicidal ideas began to take over her thoughts. When she told a friend about these thoughts, her friend brought her in to see me. Later in therapy, her mother was shocked that her daughter would feel suicidal over the pageant and felt terrible that her disappointment had pushed her daughter to consider suicide. Any time the therapist detects an incongruence between a client family member's perception and reality, it should be a red flag to explore. Such distortions of reality are the breeding grounds for suicidal ideation.

Finally, therapists should explore incongruities between the way things are and the way that a client would like them to be. Because of their adolescent intellectual growth spurt (as discussed in chapter 3), adolescents have an intellectual capacity to think like they never have before and consider abstractions and the hypothetical, for the first time. However, because of their lack of world experience, they do not have a good handle on what is truly possible. Consequently, adolescents are often naively idealistic. They simply do not understand why things can't be perfect. As they get older, they will make concessions to reality but, during adolescence, they will complain often and vigorously that "things are not as they should be." On one hand, this can be a breeding ground for the emergence of suicidal thoughts and behavior. In the early 1970s, two teenagers, Craig and Joan, had felt that there should be an end to all war, but to the Vietnam War in particular. They wrote a manifesto of their beliefs and decided to commit suicide to emphasize their point. They went into the young woman's parents' garage, closed the door, and started the car engine. They were found the next day. Such idealism and an expression of incongruity between the way things are and the way they should be can precipitate a suicide, especially in adolescents. On the other hand, if a therapist can look for discrepancies between a suicidal adolescent's perceptions of the way things are and his or her thoughts about the way things could or should be, the therapist can utilize this incongruity to increase the adolescent's cognitive dissonance to change the way things are. In this case, emphasizing the suicidal adolescent's incongruences is a good way to motivate the adolescent to change from a consideration of suicide to another course of action.

LOOKING FOR THE COVERT OR INDIRECT

Families who have a suicidal adolescent are often indirect in their methods of communication. As explored in the previous section, some messages may be covert because they are contained in the metamessages of their communication. Sometimes the messages themselves may have covert or hidden messages. The therapist must recognize that the suicidal adolescent may face covert communication from the rest of his family on a regular basis. It is difficult for the therapist to make sense of some of these covert messages because he or she isn't privileged to the insider information upon which the covert message is based. I had a fifteen-year-old male client, with suicidal ideations, who felt trapped at times by anxiety. He was not aware of the origins of his anxiety, and these anxiety attacks seemed to occur almost anywhere and at almost anytime. I even witnessed one of these anxiety attacks in the middle of a family therapy session. The fifteen-year-old suddenly seemed to get very quiet and appeared to be under quite a degree of stress. I saw nothing in the session that seemed to indicate a reason for an elevation of stress for the young man. We were, however speaking about his father's disciplinary techniques at the time of the son's anxiety episode. I began to wonder if the father had abused his son or if the son was trying to protect his father in some way. In a later session, one of my fifteen-year-old's younger siblings stepped on one of the play toys I had provided and broke it. It was nothing but a little plastic truck. One of the younger siblings said, in a very serious voice, "Sam, you better apologize or the gypsies will come and get you." At that utterance, the whole family fell into silence. To say the least, I was puzzled. It seemed incongruous that such a simple but strange remark would pull the entire family into silence. I asked the family what the youngster's remark meant and nobody answered. Finally, the father said, "It's just an expression." The family quickly switched topics.

I told the family that I wanted to see the fifteen-year-old by himself the following week. This is something which is somewhat unusual for me to do, as I would rather work with the entire family. However, in this case, I felt that I would get nowhere pursuing this line of inquiry with the entire family. At the next week's session, I asked my adolescent client what his sister's comment about the gypsies meant. He said:

> It's nothing. It's just something my father used to say when we were little kids. If we did something bad, he would tell us that he and my mom were going to give us away to the gypsies.

I noticed his getting more and more anxious as he spoke. I asked him if he took his father's remarks as being serious. He replied that he did as a little kid, but that he now knew that it was just a lot of foolishness. I pointed out the increase in his anxiety as he spoke about this topic. He seemed surprised by my observation. I asked him to observe how often references to gypsies or a gypsy lifestyle came up in family conversation and if his anxiety increased when they did. Over the next few weeks he said that he was surprised at how many times references to gypsies came up in his Kansas farm family's conversations.

Through weeks of his observations and my analysis of the family interactions we came to the following conclusion. What started out as a foolish little saying by Dad that he had borrowed from his own father was, on some level, believed by the children. Once the image of "being given to the gypsies if they were bad" was set in the mind of the children, the father kept on using it to help control his children's behavior. He did not have to mention the specific phrase again. He would use short-hand by, for example, asking the child who was disobedient if he or she wanted a "babushka" (a scarf worn by Eastern European peasants) to wear. This reference to gypsies became a shorthand for the father to use when he wanted to control his children or when his own anxiety started to rise.

During one family discussion session about the father's need for control, I noticed that everybody, including the mother, gradually fell into silence. The father had never said a word but he was softly humming. He was humming the melody from the song "Green Tambourine" by The Lemon Pipers. The family associated tambourines with dancing gypsies. In this elaborate, covert language that he had created, he was conveying to his family that he did not want the present conversation to continue. As long as these covert messages remained hidden, they had tremendous power to control the family members. The fifteen-year-old son realized that much of his anxiety, which he thought was random, was actually connected to this covert communication system. Once we made this covert pattern of communication overt to the family, not only did the adolescent's anxiety attacks become fewer but his suicidal ideation diminished as well. Most covert messages will not be quite as elaborate as this example was but they may have a powerful hold on the suicidal adolescent and contribute to his or her feelings of being out of control. This will exacerbate the adolescent's suicidal ideation.

Sometimes the covert messages may be channeled indirectly. Murray Bowen's concept of "triangulation" is a good example of this (Bowen, 1976). I consulted on a case in which the standard form of husband–wife communication was to talk to each other through the daughter. This was so prevalent that nobody in the family (mother, father, or daughter) questioned this pattern, and they considered it to be "normal." The mother and father reduced their anxiety by channeling their conversations through their daughter. The daughter felt that she has been given a very important role in the family by her parents and felt responsible for the maintenance of her parents' marriage. All three were happy with this arrangement until the mother and father began fighting. This occurred when the daughter was thirteen years old. She became very distressed at her parents' fighting and felt as if she was failing in her job of maintaining her parents' marriage. She became suicidal in response to her feelings of failure. A secondary gain was that her parents stopped fighting when she spoke of committing suicide. Once the therapist exposed this pattern and worked with the husband and wife to speak directly to each other, this extracted the daughter from the middle of her parents' marriage. Subsequently, the teenager's suicidal ideation decreased significantly.

Covert and indirect patterns of communication and interaction can be a powerful force in driving an adolescent to suicide. The adolescent feels strangled by these covert interactions, in part, because he or she doesn't know they exist. If the therapist is going to help the suicidal adolescent and his or her family, the therapist must look for these patterns and analyze how they are affecting the adolescent's suicidal ideation and behavior.

LOOK FOR FEARS

Much of the behavior surrounding thoughts and acts of suicide is generated by fear. For the suicidal adolescent, fear is often the immediate cause of suicidal actions. The young woman who fails to make the basketball team fears rejection by her peer group and a lifetime of failure. Although her fear of peer humiliation and rejection may be quite real, it is hard for an adult to fully understand her fear of "a lifetime of failure." Because adolescents have the newly acquired intellectual capabilities to reason abstractly, they are capable of projecting into the future as they have never been able to do before. However, they lack the experience to fine-tune this projection in order to distinguish which projections will be probable and which ones will fall outside the lines of probability. Because the young woman feels rejected by the coach and the team, she is feeling both pain and helplessness. The combination of these two feelings can easily lead to a feeling of hopelessness. With her recently acquired intellectual abilities to project into the future, she assumes that this "failure" will be the story of her future life as well. She has no life experience of overcoming difficulties to draw upon to counteract these feelings of hopelessness. Hence, she assumes her present feelings and the failure that triggered them will be with her for the rest of her life. With these thoughts in her mind, her adolescent impulsiveness kicks in and she reasons, "If this is the way it will be for the rest of my life, it may be better to end it all now." Suicide becomes an option.

A sixteen-year-old male, who is in the ecstasy of his first romantic relationship, feels invulnerable to the slings and arrows of the world as he sits on "Cloud Nine" in the heavens. However, if his "true love" should reject him by ending the relationship, he will quickly descend into the throes of despair. It is not only the immediate pain of a love lost that overwhelms him but it is the fear that he will never be loved again. Like the girl's rejection by the basketball team, he will feel the immediate pain but he will also incorporate the fear that he is unlovable by any-one else. Our cultural myth of relationships is that we must search for our perfect mate through the stormy and tempestuous seas of life. The myth goes on to say that the quest for this perfect partner is the hard part of the journey. Once we have found that special, perfect person, the rest of life will be easy. Notice that every fairytale ends with: "And they got married and lived happily ever after." As children, we believe that fairytale. That belief still exists in adolescence. This young man thought that he found the perfect mate, and it took him sixteen years to come to that point (an eternity in the adolescent's mind). Everything from that point was supposed to be easy. The break-up wasn't in the "happily ever after" script. The young teenager is devastated. Not only does he feel a pain about which he can do nothing but he feels that he has lost his "one true love" and will never find another. Through my experience as a therapist, I believe that, although adolescent males and females feel this devastation, in our culture the male may feel it worse than the female. Adolescent females are more likely to have shared more intimacy (not sex, but intimacy) with others (e.g., their mothers or girlfriends) than the adolescent males. Sharing one's innermost thoughts and feelings (which is true intimacy) is much more the cultural role for females than males. For many males, the first intimate exchange with anyone is that first romantic relationship, be it heterosexual or homosexual. That is the reason why so many men say that that first girlfriend will always have a special place in their heart, which no subsequent girlfriend or spouse can touch. For a sixteen-year-old male, having such an important part of his young life stripped away from him and, according to the culture, irreplaceable for the rest of his life is devastating. He is so afraid of never having intimacy again that suicide becomes an option.

Once the adolescent has mentioned suicidal thoughts or feelings to his family or friends, their fears over his or her possible death take over those people who would be the suicidal adolescent's potential resources. If their fear immobilizes them or causes them to spring in to "overprotective modality," they may lose their ability to be effective resources for the suicidal adolescent. They begin to act in ways that will quell their own fears, rather than help the adolescent to cope with his suicidal ideations. Furthermore, when a young person "with so much to live for" talks about choosing death over life, it often throws both peers and adults into an existential predicament. Both adults and peers begin to fear their own ability to choose life over death. For some, this is so troublesome that they will avoid the suicidal adolescent at a time when he or she needs them the most. Others will take over responsibility for keeping the suicidal adolescent alive. Unfortunately, because of the fact that they are being driven by their own fear of death, they may not be very effective at helping the suicidal adolescent cope with his or her own situation.

Because of the primary role fear plays in the circumstances surrounding adolescent suicide, the therapist needs to pay special attention to the fears of all involved. If nobody in therapy mentions their fears, the therapist may need to probe for them to express their fears. This may be especially difficult for male clients who have been told, either explicitly or implicitly, never to admit that they have any fears. They have been told that acknowledging fears is a sign of weakness. If clients shy away from talking about their fears, the therapist can ask them about their anger. Often people, especially males, are much more comfortable talking about their anger than they are talking about their fears. After having an extended conversation about their anger, the therapist can state the aphorism that "anger is almost always a secondary emotion which serves as a proxy for an underlying emotion." The therapist can then ask, "What is the emotion under your anger?" If the client can speculate on that underlying emotion, the therapist can explore that emotion. If the client cannot tell the therapist what emotion underlies his or her anger, the therapist might ask if fear is the underlying emotion. With that tentative hypothesis in mind, the therapist can explore the fears of the suicidal adolescent and his or her family.

CONTROL ISSUES

A study by Jurich (2002a) of accidental survivors of lethal suicide attempts indicated that these suicide survivors thought that control issues dominated their thoughts as they weighed the decision of life or death. They felt that helplessness, feeling little or no control over their lives, played a larger role in their decision to commit suicide than their level of pain or suffering. Therefore, the therapist should focus on the control issues of both the suicidal adolescent and the family members.

Adolescents, as reviewed in chapter 3, have the central developmental task of trying to establish their own independent ego identity. They are trying to develop and define who they are. They try to test the waters by demanding more autonomy over their lives. However, they often lack the skills to accomplish what they ask for the freedom to do. Their demands overreach their competencies. Because of the ambiguity of society in providing any benchmarks for autonomy during adolescence, it is hard for them to judge whether they are "ahead of the curve" in their burgeoning autonomy or whether they are behind their peers in this important task of adolescence. Consequently, even if adolescence are given a lot of control over their lives, they do not feel that it is enough and will ask for more, even if it stretches them beyond their capabilities. How many parents have heard the phrase, "Mother (Father), you're treating me like a child!" To some degree, these struggles are quite normal when dealing with adolescents.

There are several circumstances where these struggles for control go beyond the label of "normal." In "enmeshed, rigid families" (Olsen et al., 1979), for example, adolescents may feel their autonomy stunted because their family rigidly demands that things are done in a family-prescribed way. Adolescents may feel stifled by their family's rules and strongly desire to have control over their own lives, but they may lack the skills to handle that control if they were to get it. Suicidal ideation could arise as an adolescent runs out of options to control life. The adolescent looks upon suicide as the last effort to wrest control from an enmeshed family. Likewise, suicide may become a last option of an adolescent who demands control over his or her life and doesn't have the competence and skills to manage life. That adolescent may get into so much trouble that he or she feels helpless to handle life. What makes it worse is that the adolescent asked for this. The adolescent's predicament is made worse by the fear of a chorus of "I told you so's" from the very people who could be resources to the adolescent. Suicide may seem like a logical way out.

Other adolescents may actually have a lot of control over their lives. However, because of their over-idealism and a lack of benchmarks from society, they think that they should have even more control over their lives. Their unrealistic expectations give rise to dissatisfaction with the amount of control they have over their lives. The therapist may have to give the adolescent a "reality check" to pull their expectations back to developmentally appropriate levels.

When an adolescent is struggling with control over his or her life, the therapist needs to explore how helpless the adolescent feels in controlling his or her own life. If the adolescent feels helpless to control his or her life to a realistic degree, the helplessness can turn into hopelessness. Once that occurs, suicide is more likely to be considered as a possible course of action. When the level of pain, expressed by the adolescent, is high and the adolescent is also feeling hopeless to do anything about it, the adolescent is much more vulnerable to suicide.

In some families, the adolescent may show no specific signs of distress about his or her autonomy or control over life. This may be especially true of preadolescents or early adolescents. However, the therapist may detect serious control issues in the adolescent's family, especially with the parents. This may not be a problem in the family at the present time but it may grow into a problem as the adolescent matures and requests or demands greater autonomy. Especially if the parents have relied on a close and compliant relationship from their child, as the child grows into an adolescent and emerges into an incipient adult, a parent may experience a great deal of difficulty with their child's growing independence (Jurich, 1983b). If the parent reacts by trying to restrict the adolescent's quest for autonomy, the adolescent could feel overcontrolled and consider suicide as a means of setting himself or herself free of parental controls. If the parent were to give up this close parent-child bond and retreat from the adolescent, the adolescent could feel abandoned and overwhelmed by the responsibility of sudden autonomy. He or she may create such a mess by trying to be independent but not having the capability to do so that suicide may be considered as an option out of this difficult situation. Therefore, the therapist needs to be aware of the power and control struggles of both the adolescent and the family.

SEMISUICIDAL BEHAVIOR

The therapist should explore any adolescent behavior that seems to be self-destructive. This would include drug-use, self-mutilation, and extreme risk-taking behavior. I had a drug-dependent male adolescent whose drug of choice was barbiturates. I asked him why "downers" were his drug of choice, instead of "uppers" or hallucinogens. He answered me by saying that, "Downers were a piece of suicide, only not so absolute." An adolescent with that attitude about his drug of choice is only one step from suicide. Self-mutilating adolescents often feel such pain that they feel the need to let it out by cutting on themselves. Some adolescents who self-mutilate are trying to punish themselves as a retribution or penance for some previous transgression, either real or imagined. I had a female adolescent who had cut the labia of her genitals as a way to punish herself for seducing her father to have sex with her. She was seven years old when it happened. A seven-year-old obviously does not seduce an adult who is her father. The father had told her that he was having sex with her because she seduced him. He was her father and good little girls believe their daddies.

Extreme risk-taking behavior includes anything that would put an adolescent at risk of death or harm. This could include reckless driving for the thrill of it, unprotected promiscuous sex, drug-taking, strangulation to heighten masturbation, or a number of behaviors which could have lethal consequences. The treatment of these issues is beyond the scope of this book. Mathew Selekman (2002) has an excellent book on treating these types of cases. Their importance for the present discussion is that any of these behaviors can quickly escalate into suicidal ideas and actions. For the adolescent who runs away from problems by taking drugs, suicide is the ultimate runaway. For the self-harming adolescent, suicide is the ultimate self-harming. For the risk-taking adolescent, is there any more extreme risk-taking than flirting with ending his or her own life through suicide? Consequently, all self-harming behaviors of any kind should be a red flag to the therapist. These behaviors are best discussed with the adolescent and his or her family to see if the path down the road of self-harm could lead to suicide.

PRESSURE POINTS

As the therapist explores all of these issues with the suicidal adolescent and his or her family, the therapist should always be aware of pressure points within the individual and within the family system. A pressure point is a point of leverage within the adolescent or the family at which the therapist can apply pressure to help bring about change (Jurich, 1990). Some of these pressure points are typical of most adolescents, such as the need for autonomy and the desire to engage in adult behavior. These can be extracted from Chapter 3 and Chapter 4 in this book. Some pressure points can be found in the family dynamics, such as the family's struggles with power and control. Some pressure points may be found in the peer group and their desire to provide the adolescent with a morality that is different from that of the adolescent's parents. Pressure points may be typical of adolescents who are on the brink of suicide, as described in Chapter 2. Many pressure points are idiosyncratic of the specific adolescent and/or family in therapy. As described above in this chapter, how many fathers would try to gain control of their children in a therapy session by humming "Green Tambourine"? Regardless of their origin, the therapist needs to search for pressure points to make the therapy maximally effective. Insight-oriented, behavioral, and strategic interventions can all work in therapy. However, if they can be linked to specific pressure points within the adolescent or the family, the interventions will have a greater power to bring about change.

TESTING

Although the majority of the analysis of a case, involving a suicidal adolescent, is often done though interviews with the adolescent and the family, there are occasions where the use of assessment instruments may be useful for the therapist. Many of the pencil-and-paper tests to determine suicidal ideation are established personality inventories which measure psychological traits which have been associated with suicidal behaviors (Jurich, 2001). For example, Johnson, Lall, Bongar, and Nordlund (1999) used scales from the Minnesota Multiphasic Personality Inventory (MMPI) to predict individuals who would be prone to suicidal behavior.

One of the most widely used scales in both clinical and research settings is the Beck Depression Index (BDI) (Beck, Steer, & Brown 1996). Because of the well-founded close association between depression and suicidal ideation in the literature, this twenty-one-item scale with four choices per item is the choice of many clinicians to assess suicidal ideation. As a therapist, I have often used the Beck Depression Index to assess the degree of the adolescent's depression. This instrument is especially useful when I am unsure as to the degree of pain the adolescent feels. I have also found it very useful to suggest to students and supervisees who have a case they are worried about regarding the client's potential for suicide. I also use the Hopelessness Scale (HS) (Beck et al., 1974) to assess an adolescent client's potential for suicide. As hopelessness is a trait that has been closely linked to predicting suicide, the use of the Hopelessness Scale, which is a twenty-item true/false scale, is very useful to assess the degree to which the adolescent has run out of resources and options to cope with his or her stressful situation. In fact, the Hopelessness Scale has demonstrated one of the highest degrees of accuracy in predicting which people will ultimately commit suicide. The main problem with these personality inventories is that they do not actually measure suicidal ideation or potential for suicide. They measure personality traits and states that are closely associated with suicidal ideation and behavior, which is useful but not the primary purpose of the instrument (Jurich, 2001). However, the advantage of these scales is that they provide a more objective indication of suicidal ideation and potential for suicide, based on a tested, psychometrically sound instrument with established validity and reliability. The other advantage is that, because these instruments do not measure suicide ideation or behavior directly, the adolescent who is seeking to get attention by threatening suicide is less likely to be able to "fake sick" than on an instrument which directly asks about suicidal behavior. Her or she can still "fake sick" on both the BDI and the HS but there are more indications that the therapist can use to see if the client is projecting a "false positive."

Beck, Kovacs, and Weissman (1979) have a scale that specifically is designed to measure suicidal ideation. The Scale for Suicidal Ideation (SSI) requires the therapist to read nineteen items to the client with three possible responses: "strong," "weak," or "none." This scale yields three factors: (1) active suicidal desire, (2) passive suicidal desire, and (3) preparation for suicide. The method of administration is one that may be more suited to preadolescent or early adolescents, adolescents who are oppositional-defiant and will not fill out a written questionnaire, or adolescents who have poor reading or thinking skills. Beck, Steer, and Ranieri (1988) have constructed a self-administered written version of the SSI, the Self-Rated Scale for Suicidal Ideation (SSI-SR), which can be completed by the client on paper or on a computer. The SSI-SR highly correlates with the original SSI. As these instruments measure suicidal ideation explicitly, they get to the heart of the matter and do not rely on "proxy variables" such as "depression" or "hopelessness." However, they are also somewhat transparent, and answers can be manipulated by an adolescent who is seeking attention. They may be highly misleading, for instance, if administered to an adolescent with a borderline personality disorder. There are also instruments to specifically measure suicidal behavior, such as the Suicide Behaviors Questionnaire (SBQ) by Cole (1988), which has nicely established reliability and validity (Cotton, Peters, Range, 1995). Such questionnaires have the same assets and liabilities as instruments measuring suicidal ideation directly.

An instrument that I have found to be interesting is the Reasons for Living Inventory (RFL) (Ivanoff et al., 1994; Linehan, Goodstein, Neilsen, and Chiles, 1983). Instead of focusing upon the demand and stressor side of suicide, it focuses upon the positive side of the equation. This forty-eight-item six-point scale asks the client to rate the forty-eight reasons why a person who had the thought of suicide cross his or her mind would not kill himself or herself, despite those recent suicidal thoughts. In this way, instead of focusing upon the reasons why an adolescent may want to commit suicide, the authors focus upon the client's resources and barriers that would prevent suicide. The advantages to this approach are the same as those for employing solution-focused therapy. Accentuating the positive reasons not to commit suicide may disrupt adolescents' maladaptive recursive cycle in which suicidal adolescents feel hopelessly trapped in their suicidal ideation. This also affords the therapist some ideas about the suicidal adolescent's strengths and resources. In therapy, the therapist can then build upon these strengths.

Once any test or assessment instrument is given to the suicidal adolescent, I believe that it is imperative for the therapist to sit down with the adolescent and discuss the results. The numbers on the page are important but so is the adolescent's reactions to them, explanations of them, and feelings about them. The clinical assessment instruments are not an end in and of themselves. They are part of the process of assessment, and a discussion with the adolescent about the results will flesh out a more complete picture of the adolescent's suicide dynamics. As a family therapist, I will also try to discuss the test results with the rest of the family after I have discussed them with the adolescent. Again, this is a powerful piece of the assessment process. However, a therapist needs to make some therapeutic judgment as to what to share with the rest of the family and when to share it. For example, if the adolescent presents with suicidal ideation, which the Self-Rated Scale for Suicidal Ideation rates as moderate and scores on both the Beck Depression Index and Hopelessness Scale are relatively low, that needs to be discussed with the adolescent, and the discrepancy between the adolescent's self-report and test scores needs to be discussed. If those scores were shared with the family immediately, the family might interpret them as saying that there really is not a problem. The family might not come to therapy or pull the adolescent out of therapy. This would ignore the problem that the adolescent still claims to have suicidal thoughts and is exhibiting some distress, even though it may not be highly suicidal at this point in time. Discussion with the family needs to occur, but the therapist must be careful of when it should occur and what topics would be best to discuss.

There are times when the therapist will find the suicidal adolescent or the adolescent's family reluctant to speak about key issues in therapy, such as death or suicide. They may be unresponsive in an interview or may minimize the importance of a conversation about suicide. Some clients may complete a questionnaire, whereas others may refuse to fill one out. If they do fill out a questionnaire, they may answer the questions in a socially desirable way. In cases like this, I have found the use of projective techniques to be valuable in helping the suicidal adolescent and his or her family talk about suicide and death indirectly. For example, in Henry Murray's Thematic Apperception Test (TAT) (1943), there are several cards that have been found to elicit stories about suicide or death from subjects who have been tested. Picture 3BM depicts a figure of a person on the floor, huddled against a couch, with his or her head bowed on the right arm. Next to this figure is an object most often interpreted to be a pistol. I use this picture as a stimulus to elicit a story about what is happening in the picture (including feelings), what led up to the picture, and what will be the outcome of the story. Among suicidal adolescents, I have often received stories, triggered by this picture, that describe the person as suicidal and contemplating suicide or even having already committed suicide. The adolescent will project himself or herself into the story and often will give me facts or ideas about his or her own suicidal ideation. In this way the adolescent can talk about his or her own suicidal ideation without talking directly about himself or herself.

Other TAT pictures that I have found useful stimuli for eliciting stories from suicidal adolescents are Picture 12M, which depicts a young man lying on a couch with his eyes closed, with a gaunt elderly man leaning over him with his hand outstretched over the young man's face. Suicidal adolescents often describe this scene as death coming to get the young man. In Picture 15 there is a gaunt man with his hands clenched standing in a cemetery among the gravestones. Suicidal adolescents often describe this picture as the "Grim Reaper." Picture 17GF depicts a woman leaning over the railing of a bridge over water. Suicidal adolescents often describe this woman as a person ready to jump off the bridge to drown herself. With each of these four pictures as a stimulus, the suicidal adolescent can tell a story concerning death or suicide without talking about himself or herself. However, it is the hypothesis of Murray that the adolescent will project himself or herself into the story. In this manner the therapist can gain valuable information about how the adolescent views death and suicide. I have had some success with giving the pictures to the adolescent and his family and asking them to construct a story about the picture as a group project. In this manner, I not only can analyze the outcome of the group story but can also watch the family interaction as they construct the story. All of these observations can help "prime the pump" so that the suicidal adolescent and his or her family can better tell their story.

DIAGNOSIS

Although there is no specific diagnosis for suicide in the *Diagnostic and Statistical Manual of Mental Disorders* (Fourth Edition [DSM-IV]; American Psychiatric Association, 1994), both suicidal behavior and suicidal ideation are listed as a criteria for a number of diagnoses. Most mood disorders list suicidal acts and thoughts as a primary criteria for diagnosis. The diagnosis most often cited as being linked to suicide is the diagnosis of major clinical depression (Ladame, 1992). Suicidal ideation has also been linked to affective disorders, conduct disorders, schizophrenia, and organic mental disorders (Blumenthal & Kupter, 1986; Wekstein, 1979). Other authors have linked suicidal thoughts and behaviors to some personality disorders (Jacobs et al., 1999).

Although the research allows for a wide range of diagnoses to be linked to suicidal ideation and behavior, the therapist should choose the diagnosis carefully. Most of the literature on the link between depression, especially major clinical depression, and suicide has focused upon the type of case where the depressed client considers suicide as a means of ending the depression or believes that suicide is the natural end of severe clinical depression. Many of the intervention strategies for suicidal ideation or behavior are based upon this causal relationship. It is important for the clinician to at least explore other potential diagnoses if they present a more accurate picture of a specific client. If suicidal ideation is presented in an adolescent diagnosed with a conduct disorder, the treatment will have to focus upon suicidal thoughts as a rebellion against authority, rather than as the ultimate escape from the pain of depression. An adolescent diagnosed with schizophrenia who is engaging in suicidal behavior will have to be treated with anti-psychotic medications in order to participate in a therapeutic process without the therapy's being thrown off course by delusional thought patterns. For most cases, some diagnosis of depression will tell the therapist that the case is a good fit to the types of therapeutic interventions presented in this book. However, if the suicidal ideation and behavior are linked in a specific client to another DSM-IV diagnosis, the unique aspects of that diagnosis will need to be focused upon as being primary in therapy. The therapist will still have to focus on suicidal ideation and behavior in order to keep the client alive. However, the main focus of therapy will shift to the treatment of the client's primary diagnosis (e.g., schizophrenia or organic mental disorders).

MEDICATION

Finally, a key aspect of treating suicidal adolescents is the therapist's need to consider if the client or anyone in the client's family needs medication. A discussion of the various types of medication and their indications and contraindications is beyond the scope of this book. However, an overview of medication protocol was well presented by Denton, Walsh, and

Daniels in 2002. It is also beyond the scope of practice for most mental health clinicians outside the field of psychiatry. However, the therapist must consider if his or her suicidal adolescent client would benefit from some medication being administered by a medical professional. This is especially true if the therapist suspects that there is a significant organic component to the suicidal ideation or behavior (Bluementhal & Kupfer, 1986). Medication may prove to be helpful in the crisis intervention stage of therapy as well as the long-term clinical work. Both the therapist and the client need to be aware that many psychoactive medications may take some time to take full effect and that, in may cases, medication levels may have to be adjusted for maximum effectiveness. Consequently, the medication may not have the immediate effect that the client is so desperately seeking (Jurich, 2001). In addition, great care must be taken that the helping professional does not give the client a means to commit suicide by providing the client with medications that often have a lethal overdose potential. Because of these aspects of using psychoactive medications, the therapist is cautioned to remain in close contact with any physician who prescribed medication for the purpose of monitoring the medication and its effects. As the therapist often has more frequent contacts with the client in therapy, he or she becomes the "eyes and ears" of the prescribing physician to more accurately judge the effects of the medication. The National Institute of Mental Health (2004) is an excellent resource for information about medications used in the treatment of children and adolescents.

Clinicians and physicians often get dragged into a battle over whether to do therapy or administer medication. This should not be an argument which occupies our time. It should not be a question of "either or" but instead be a matter of "both and." We need to put an end to petty turf battles and, for the sake of our clients, ask what treatment regimen works best. Increasingly, clinical trials and outcome studies of severe mental illness have indicated that medication, together with some therapy in which the client talks, is the best combination for treating clients with depression. A recent NIMH study, reported in the New York Times by Gardiner Harris (2004), reported that the most effective treatment protocol for treating adolescent depression is medication (in this study, Prozac) together with psychotherapy. Although the type of psychotherapy was not delineated, I would argue that, especially in the case of suicidal adolescents, family therapy should be the psychotherapy of choice for reasons that were covered in previous chapters. As mental health practitioners, we need to unite in our treatment of suicidal adolescents to provide the best and most efficient care possible.

Nine

COGNITIVE INTERVENTIONS

Freeing the Mind from Destructive Ways of Thinking

Because the decision to commit suicide has a strong cognitive component attached to it, even though that cognitive may be severely clouded by the adolescent's emotions, some form of cognitive or insight-oriented therapy is often useful in treating suicidal adolescents and their families. In fact, cognitive therapy is one of the most widely used types of therapy with all types of both depressed (Beevers & Miller, 2005; Kaufman et al., 2005) and suicidal clients (Westfeld et al., 2000). It stands to reason that, if a client has suicidal thoughts and if our society has such a strong taboo against suicide, a therapy that either clarifies the assumptions upon which these self-destructive thoughts are based or challenges the "distorted thinking" of the client would have great appeal for the clinician. Cognitive therapy strikes at the heart of the suicidal ideation. If the therapist can alter the suicidal client's thoughts about suicide, it stands to reason that suicidal behaviors will decrease. A similar line of logic applies to family therapy with suicidal adolescents and their families. My first strategy of intervention is to employ cognitive family therapy techniques.

INSIGHT INTO THE WORLD OF THE ADOLESCENT

Many adolescents lack insight into the adolescent experience because they are in the middle of it. This may sound contradictory but adolescents who are in the middle of experiencing their own adolescence have no perspective about being an adolescent. They are so bombarded with their own unique experience that they have no idea about what is abnormal or normal. They are so engulfed in their own thoughts and experiences that they cannot perceive anything to which they can compare themselves. To this extent, adolescence is truly an egocentric experience. Many adolescents feel as if they are going through an experience that nobody before or after them has ever or will ever experience. If their life is progressing to their satisfaction, the adolescent will feel unique and even "special." However, if the adolescent is having a difficult time with life, he or she may feel singled out by God or the fates to have a uniquely miserable adolescence. Telling a young person that he or she is going through a period of adolescence that is typical of many other adolescents gives the adolescent the perspective that he or she is not alone in these trials and tribulations. Such a "normalization" by the therapist will help the adolescent feel less isolated and give him or her the message that "Other adolescents, just like you, have gone through similar stuff and have done so successfully. So can you!" Events that had been labeled as uniquely tragic by the adolescent can instead be seen as a normal developmental task of adolescence. Consequently, the anxiety of the adolescent is reduced, and his or her confidence is enhanced.

I had a male client, age thirteen, who was greatly disturbed that everybody seemed to be growing up, especially the girls. He had not gone through his adolescent growth spurt yet. Consequently, he looked less mature than his peers did, and he retained many physical childlike qualities. The rapid growth of the girls particularly disturbed him. He worried that he would never grow up and that he would "have to stand up on my tip-toes to kiss my girlfriend goodnight" in the future. "What self-respecting girl would want to go out with me?" The way he sought to cope with this "humiliating condition" was to work out his muscles to build a "buff body." As he couldn't afford weights, he purchased a second-hand set of Charles Atlas springs to enhance his physique. He tired to work out twice a day, every day. Despite all of his efforts, he built up very little muscle mass and still looked like a "skinny kid." Although he said that he was not suicidal, he did mention that he had occasional thoughts that it would be better to die now, rather than suffer a lifetime of humiliation.

In the first therapy session, I mentioned to him that he was probably a "late maturer" who would go through his adolescent growth spurt soon. I told him that it was not unusual for a young man to go through puberty late, compared to his peers. I also told him that the girls typically went through puberty one-and-a-half to two years earlier than the boys did. I asked his parents to schedule an appointment with their family physician so that he could offer his medical opinion. He concurred with my normalization of the adolescent and concurred that he was well within the normal range of development. I also told him that, although his work ethic in exercising was laudable, he would not see any major results of his exercise until his body went through puberty. I told him that, at puberty, girls increase their muscle mass by five percent, whereas boys increase their muscle mass by fifty percent. Consequently, it would not be until he was into puberty that he would see a marked increase in his muscle mass. These normalizations eased his anxieties and he reported no further suicidal ideation. Within seven months of that session, my client went through puberty. He not only grew in size and stature but, because he continued to exercise, he built up quite a physique to match.

Sometimes adolescents may not experience a "normal" progression of development because of some childhood trauma. I had a young adult woman, age twenty-one, who came to me for therapy because she was bothered by conflicting feelings about her sexuality. Sometimes, she felt sexually adventurous and had had dreams of being promiscuous. At other times, she said that she would have liked to "take a big eraser and erase my genitals so that they would never enter my mind again!" This war within herself concerning her sexuality exhausted her to the point of wondering if death would be preferable to this constant battle. After two sessions of exploration about this internal battle, the client mentioned to me that she had been sexually molested by her stepfather at the time of her puberty. This lasted fifteen months. She went on to report that nobody would believe her when she told them what had happened. Therefore, she stopped telling anyone. The metamessage she delivered as she told me of her childhood molestation was that this piece of information was only mentioned "in passing" and that it was of only minimal interest in our therapy. She was puzzled when I wanted to go back and visit with her feelings about her molestation. I explained the following:

When a child at the age of puberty is introduced to sex by someone who is not supposed to be sexual with her, that child gets two conflicting messages:

1. Sex is very important and the perpetrator says that it's supposed to be fun.
2. This sexual experience is awkward, weird, and shameful (since the perpetrator tells me not to tell anyone).

This causes the child to feel ambivalent toward her sexuality. Because the child feels helpless to do anything about her abuse, these extreme feelings intensify and feel more extreme over time. This is a typical reaction to a very atypical situation for a young girl. Does this sound like some of the "stuff" you're going through?

The young woman was flabbergasted! She said:

> You mean that other girls went through the same shit as I did, and they feel the same way I do? So, in a strange way, I'm normal?

This greatly reduced her anxiety and we were able to link her childhood sexual abuse to her present war of sexual desires. This is not "normalizing" in the traditional sense but is, instead, labeling her feelings as a normal response to an abnormal situation from her past.

There are times when the suicidal adolescent's family members need to know that their adolescent's feelings and behaviors are not pathologically abnormal. This is especially true for parents. For example, parents may "knock themselves out" trying to talk to their adolescent son about the dangers of illegal drug use. The adolescent seems to comprehend what they say. Then he goes out to a party and smokes marijuana. I have heard parents ask their adolescent if he heard them and, if he did, why the hell did he go and smoke pot anyway? The parents may easily come to the conclusion that their son is either mentally deficient or delinquent. In all probability, neither is the case. I will explain to the parents that, in our culture, parents try to socialize their adolescents by giving them good rules by which to live life. However, the number one task of adolescence is for their adolescent to establish his own independent ego identity. Peers help this process by offering to the adolescent an alternative to his parents' set of rules and code of ethics. Therefore, even though they told him not to do drugs, the peers at the party offered him a "joint" to smoke as a symbol of his budding independence. I tell the parents that this is fairly typical behavior for a teenager who is their son's age. By stating this, I am trying to defuse the potential for the parents to feel that the adolescent "did this to spite his parents." Instead, if I can present the adolescent's behavior as typical for his age, I can engage the parents in a rational discussion of the consequence that should be imposed upon the adolescent for making a poor choice. If this can be done with fewer emotions exhibited by the parents, it is easier to negotiate a behavioral contract with the adolescent for future behavior.

This section of this chapter contained three examples in which the therapist, in some way, normalized some aspect of adolescence to either the suicidal adolescent or the parents. Applying the developmental scheme outlined in Chapter 3 and the etiological factors outlined in Chapter 4, the reader can draw upon the research to teach both the suicidal adolescent and his family (especially parents) about the typical world of the adolescent.

INSIGHT INTO FAMILY DYNAMICS

Many families are aware of the ways that their family interacts, but each family member may see it only from his or her own individual perspective. Consequently, family members are often unaware of the systemic dynamics at work in their own family. There has been some supporting evidence to show that psychoeducative models have some empirical validation in helping parents understand the psychosocial problems of their adolescents (Mattejat, 2005). Using an example from the previous chapter of the family caught in a rebellion-restriction maladaptive recursive cycle, each family member is more likely to recognize this pattern, using linear logic, rather than circular causality. The adolescent will admit that he or she rebels but claims to do so only when the parents are "unreasonably restrictive." The parents admit to being restrictive, but they claim to do this only when the adolescent is unreasonably rebellious. Each of these oppositional "sides" clams that "the other side started it." The parents claim that they were "perfectly reasonable" until the adolescent "lost control." The adolescent counters that he or she rebelled (not "lost control") because of some previous "unfair restriction" imposed by the parents. The parents counter that the previous restriction was set in motion by previous "out of control" behavior by the adolescent. This cycle goes on and on. Of course, the truth is that, regardless of what started this cycle of rebellion and restriction, it now is mutually stimulating the problematic behavior and is mutually reinforcing these responses of rebellion and restriction. The family is now stuck in a circular causality. The purpose of therapy is to "unstick them." The reason why the family can't unstick themselves is that their paradigm is linear. It assumes ultimate causality and, therefore, assigns guilt to the "one that started it." As each party thinks that the "other side" started it, they have a vested interest in holding onto that belief because it exonerates them of all responsibility for the problem. Teaching the entire family about the systemic concept of circular causality takes guilt out of the equation and places responsibility upon all family members to halt what they are doing to keep the maladaptive recursive cycle alive. Each of the family members is then invited to engage in a different set of behaviors that may result in better outcomes. With the therapist's guidance, these are planned by the entire family. As the therapist helps the family negotiate a different way of interacting, he or she invites the voices of all family members to be expressed and makes sure that every voice is heard and taken into account in the negotiations. If there is some success in altering the maladaptive recursive cycle into something which is more constructive, the family will experience a feeling of success *as a team*, striving for mutual family goals, instead of competing individual goals.

Creating a "win–win" outcome, instead of being trapped in "win–lose" situations is especially important for disrupting maladaptive recursive cycles that lead to suicide. In speaking to the subjects in my study of accidental survivors of lethal suicide attempts (Jurich, 2002a), they all spoke about trying to gain control over what they perceived to be a hopeless "win–lose" situation in which they felt that they were bound to lose. They either felt that their suicide would "snatch victory from the jaws of defeat" or their suicide was an attempt "not to play the game." In the former scenario, the participants felt that their suicide was a triumph over losing because they were going to demonstrate that they would exercise some control over their life, even if the only control they felt they possessed was to end their life. This resulted in a very deadly game of "you can't fire me; I quit!" In the latter scenario, the participants said that they were in a hopeless situation that they were helpless to alter. To them, their suicide was an attempt to opt out of the situation that they felt could not be changed. To borrow a phrase from the 1983 movie *War Games*, "The only way to win is not to play the game." If the therapist can create the possibility of a "win–win" outcome by teaching the family about circular causality, he or she can open up a new avenue of thinking and behavior for the entire family. Suicide does not have to be a consideration for an adolescent if everyone in the family can win, even him or her.

There are times when teaching the family about one of the principles of Systems Theory can reduce the power of a maladaptive coping technique. For example, I supervised a case in which the presenting problem was the sixteen-year-old daughter's suicidal behavior of cutting her wrists. The cuts were horizontal and were superficial. Therefore, the attending physician made the determination that this was probably more of a suicidal gesture than it was a true suicidal attempt. Because of the parents' bickering in the emergency room, he referred the family to the University Family Center. The family consisted of mother, father, sixteen-year-old daughter (the "identified patient"), and her fourteen-year-old sister. The student therapist found it hard to speak or get either daughter to speak because the mother and father monopolized the time by bickering between themselves. Neither parent could say a sentence without the other parent's challenging what was said. Each blamed the other for their daughter's suicide attempt. The luxury of supervising behind the two-way mirror is that the supervisor does not have to manage the moment-to-moment flow of the session like the therapist does. Consequently, he or she can focus upon the more subtle aspects of family interaction that the therapist may miss because he or she is juggling the clients in the room. This was particularly difficult because of the parents' constant bickering. However, from behind the mirror, I could see how anxious both daughters were getting as the session wore on. Forty-five minutes into the session, the therapist took a break and came behind the mirror for supervision. I suggested that the therapist should make sure to end the session "on time" and to give the sixteen-year-old daughter the choice of whom she would like to come to the next therapy session. I wanted to give her some sense of control over her own therapy. She seemed pleased to be given this choice and chose to have her and her sister come into the next session without their parents. Despite the parents' protests, the family eventually agreed.

At the next session, both girls spoke very freely. The atmosphere was much calmer, freed from the staccato quarreling of the parents. Both girls agreed that, in their home, Mom and Dad never talked about anything calmly. They either argued or were silent. The therapist said that she had seen how their parents were when they were bickering. She asked how the family interacted when they were silent. The fourteen-year-old said:

> Well, they really aren't silent. They just don't talk to each other! They both talk to my sister. Mom tells her what a louse Dad is, and Dad tells her what a bitch Mom is. They send messages through her (the sixteen-year-old) to each other. No matter what the problem is, my sister gets dragged into the middle of it. I just try to stay out of it.

At our mid-session break, the therapist and I agreed to teach both daughters about the Bowen concept of "triangulation" (Bowen, 1976). The therapist labeled their parents as "triangulating" the sixteen-year-old into their relationship. She explained that, in relationships where there is tension and anxiety between spouses, mothers and fathers often try to enlist one or more of their children as a "buffer" in order to reduce their anxiety. The therapist labeled this "triangulation" as a manipulation on the part of the parents to reduce their own anxiety at the expense of the daughter. In this situation, the daughter was carrying her parents' marital anxiety on her shoulders. The sixteen-year-old responded by saying:

> Shit! I thought they really needed me to keep them together. All the while, they were using me. No wonder I've got an ulcer!

The therapist asked the sixteen-year-old if she would like to teach her parents about "triangulation" in the next session or if she would like the therapist to do so. The young woman answered that, if the therapist would help her "get a word in edgewise," she would teach her parents. The therapist agreed and gave the young woman the extra homework assignment of thinking about how to tell her parents how she intended to deal with their triangulation in the future. She agreed.

The following week, the entire family met with the therapist. The therapist introduced the idea that she had taught the daughters something about family dynamics that seemed to resonate with both daughters and that their sixteen-year-old would like to tell her parents what she learned. For the rest of the session, the therapist's job was to validate the daughters and to remind the parents that, for this session, their primary job was to show respect to their daughters by listening to them. The daughters did an excellent job of explaining "triangulation" to their parents and giving them examples of how each of them had used it. This was very difficult for both parents to hear. They typically blamed each other for any family problems. Now they were being asked to share responsibility for their daughter's suicide attempt. Even though neither daughter ever mentioned the suicide attempt, it was obvious that that was the ultimate result of the triangulation. The daughter ended her "lesson" by telling her parents that she was not going to let them put her in the middle of their fights and was returning to the business of being a sixteen-year-old. She went on to say that she would like to alternate weeks of therapy between seeing the family in therapy and having her parents come into therapy to work on their marriage. In this way she was making the therapist responsible for improving her parents' marriage so she wouldn't have to do so. I was pleased that, despite some protests, the parents agreed to this plan of action. I asked the therapist to thank the parents profusely for taking such a courageous stance. She did so.

In the following months, the therapist (who took on a co-therapist) worked with both the family and marital therapy. The parents worked hard on their own issues and tried to detriangulate both daughters from their relationship issues. They terminated after five months of therapy. By teaching the family about the systemic concept of triangulation, the therapist created a paradigmatic shift in thinking. The parents went from blaming each other for their daughter's suicide attempt to recognizing a maladaptive recursive cycle in which they were stuck. Upon that lesson turned the entire course of therapy. Ironically, in this case, which was initiated by a trip to the emergency room for a suicide attempt, very little mention of suicide occurred after the first two or three sessions.

CHANGING COGNITIVE DISTORTIONS

One of the most frequent forms of therapy for treating suicide is the cognitive therapy put forth by Aaron Beck (Westfeld et al., 2000). There have been some evidence-based studies which have demonstrated the effectiveness of cognitive behavioral therapy in working with depressed adolescents (Klomek & Mufson, 2006) and with adolescents experiencing traumatic grief (Dowling, 2005). Beck (1976) purported that cognitive distortions can occur when people experience problems. Instead of helping people to cope with these problems, such cognitions can maintain or even exacerbate those problems. This rationale dovetails nicely with strategic therapy's concept of maladaptive recursive cycles. These distortions include:

1. Arbitrary inference—Drawing conclusions based on little or no evidence
2. Dichotomous thinking—Thinking things must be black or white, right or wrong, etc.
3. Magnification/minimization—Making things of much greater importance or much less importance than logic would dictate, based upon the person's emotional needs
4. Overgeneralization—Taking one incident and assuming that all subsequent incidents will be the same
5. Personalization—Assuming everyone's actions will be directly tied to the person as a stimulus or response to that person
6. Selective abstraction—Not seeing the forest for the trees

Beck's Cognitive Therapy is based upon the principle of "collaborative empiricism." In this type of therapy, the therapist asks the client to empirically test the client's beliefs by examining relevant data. If the data supports the belief, the therapist encourages the client to embrace that belief. However, if the data refute the belief, the client is asked to reconsider the belief and to construct an alternative belief that is more in keeping with the data. For a suicidal adolescent, many of the cognitive distortions listed above are typical of a young person who has the cognitive capacity for abstract and hypothetical thought but little experience in which to ground those ideas.

For example, in the previous chapter, a case was presented in which a young adolescent male was crushed by being rejected by his first true love. This young man experienced all of the cognitive distortions outlined by Beck (1978). He experienced "overgeneralization" and "arbitrary inference" in that he assumed that, because one woman rejected him, all other women would also reject him. He magnified this failure in his love life so much that he could not function in any of the other areas in his life (selective abstraction). He exhibited dichotomous thinking by believing that he would only find one true love in his life and that love had rejected him. Therefore, he was unlovable. Lastly, he began to personalize all of the negatives in his life as a punishment for having screwed up the one true love in his life. His thought processes bordered on paranoid delusional. A large part of his treatment was to challenge these beliefs by collecting data and processing the veracity of those assumptions.

In this respect, having this suicidal young man in the family therapy was very helpful. His family would often provide evidence of his beliefs. A key family member in this process was his little eight-year-old sister. Although she was eight years his junior, he tended to believe what she said. When his parents told him that their data demonstrated that he was worthwhile, he dismissed it by saying, "You have to say that, you're my parents." To some degree this was true, as his parents were desperate to help him out of his suicidal depression. However, his sister was more believable. As the therapist, I asked him to set up meetings with his family and friends to collect data on his worth as a person. I asked both his family and friends to suggest other people to whom he should talk in order to gather data about himself.

Sometimes these "data collection interviews" were given as homework assignments. At other times, especially when the client requested it, we would hold a data collection interview in the therapy room with the therapist present. The mountain of evidence contradicting his distorted beliefs began to cause cracks in his belief system. This form of therapy also elicited a serendipitous result. One of the people a friend had selected as a person from whom to collect data was a fifteen-year-old woman who, unbeknownst to anyone, had a crush on the client for the past year. She was soft-spoken and too shy to let the client know of her feelings. She took the opportunity of the "data collection interview" to tell him that he was a good enough human being that she would like to go out with him. The client waited a week, talked over that possibility in therapy, and asked her out. They began dating; needless to say, this helped the therapeutic process immensely! The data collection method of Aaron Beck (1976) was utilized with great effect in this case. However, we, as therapists, must recognize that sometimes events happen serendipitously which are far more powerful than anything we have the power to do. As a good family therapist who knows and understands the power of relationships, I'll take the help anywhere I can get it. There is therapeutic magic in the eyes of a fifteen-year-old girl.

IMMEDIACY

Because suicide is such a taboo act in Western society, suicidal adolescents and their families often experience a lot of shame for having suicidal thoughts or committing suicidal actions. Phrases like "I am suicidal" or "my son has thoughts about killing himself" may be very difficult for an adolescent or parent to utter. Such phrases may produce anxiety that is overwhelming. The therapist may find a concept put forth by Weiner and Mehrabian (1968) to be useful in these situations. Weiner and

Mehrabian elaborated upon a concept they termed "immediacy." Their idea was that people are most vulnerable when they are speaking, in person, about themselves, in the present tense, about a real-life concern that has a major impact upon them. This is a situation of high "immediacy" to them. The risks are high in this situation, with an intensified possibility of either great success or great failure. For example, therapy is an endeavor that is often filled with high immediacy. There is a potential for great rewards, such as improved mental health or improved family relationships. However, highly immediate situations in therapy can also be very dangerous. Clients often worry that they will appear "foolish" or "stupid." They worry that the therapist or the rest of the family will be judgmental about their attitudes, feelings, or actions and either ridicule or condemn them. Because, during the course of therapy, therapists ask clients to disclose their innermost thoughts and feelings, the therapist is asking them to be very vulnerable about very crucial aspects of the core of who they are as a person. Therefore, therapy by nature is an anxiety-provoking endeavor. When the therapist asks the client to provide this self-disclosure "here-and-now," face-to-face with the therapist and the rest of the family, the client's anxiety increases even more. Despite the care the therapist takes in joining with the clients and in creating a safe environment, the process of the therapy is still, of its nature, anxiety-provoking to the clients.

Weiner and Mehrabian (1968) make the observation that individuals reduce their anxiety over what they are saying by reducing the immediacy of what they are saying. Everyone is familiar with the friend who comes to ask for advice by saying that the advice isn't really for them but for a friend of his or hers. As our friend describes his or her friend's situation it is often transparent that our friend is talking about himself or herself. However, if we ask our friend if this question really pertains to another person, our friend will "swear on a stack of Bibles" that it really is for another friend. We might ask ourselves why our friend has gone through all that trouble. Weiner and Mehrabian (1968) would answer that our friend sought to manage the anxiety of asking for help by doing it in a way that was less immediate. "I'm not asking for me but for someone else" is less immediate than "I need your advice for the mess I got myself into."

An adolescent might pose a question to his or her parents by proposing a hypothetical situation. "What if someone asked me to a party at which there will be beer available?" The hypothetical is certainly less immediate than the adolescent's admitting that he or she was, in fact, asked to go to such a party. Bringing it up as a hypothetical is less immediate. Speaking of past events is less immediate than speaking of present events. Lots of adults will speak openly of foolish things they did when they were children or adolescents. The past makes it less immediate and, therefore, safer to talk about. These same adults would be far less willing to discuss the foolish things they did last weekend. That conversation would be much more immediate. Sometimes a person's manipulation of the immediacy of his or her communication may be very subtle. One person who is speaking of giving money to a homeless shelter may say, "We have to help these people." Another, giving money to the same cause may say, "We have to help those people." Both are giving money to the same cause but the word "these" implies more immediacy than does the word, "those."

Wiener and Mehrabian (1968) posed that immediacy was a subtle channel of interpersonal communication similar to nonverbal cues. They posed that the immediacy of a person's communication transmitted a metamessage about the content of the communication. It is a lexical cue on how to interpret the content. I have found the concept of immediacy to be a useful indicant of anxiety in the client. To that degree, the concept of immediacy is a good assessment tool. However, I believe that immediacy has even more utility in conducting therapy. Because suicide is considered to be such a taboo by Western society, the anxiety of talking about one's own suicidal ideation with a high degree of immediacy, even in the safety of the therapy room, will be elevated. A typical client response to this situation is to "shut down and shut up." There is simply too much anxiety generated by communications of self-disclosure. Therefore, the clients withdraw from the process of therapy by refusing to contribute any intimate information to the discussion.

The parents may do this by declaring that their adolescent's suicide attempt or ideation was "situation specific" and, since that situation is now in the past, the situation is over and, therefore, so are all suicidal thoughts and actions. Sweeping the adolescent's suicidal ideation and behaviors "under the rug" is perceived by the parents as being safer than discussions about the intimate details of the family's life, especially if there have been secrets in the family. The suicidal adolescent's family may declare that they were totally surprised by the adolescent's claims of suicidal thoughts or actions. Although this actually might be the case, the stance taken by the family that they knew nothing about the adolescent's struggle with suicide serves to distance them from the adolescent's suicidal thoughts and behaviors. It makes them less immediate for the family who claims to have no pertinent information to add to the discussion. Even the suicidal adolescent may refuse to contribute to the discussions in therapy for fear of being judged by the family or by the therapist. This is most likely to occur if the adolescent's suicidal ideation or thoughts have been dismissed as being "stupid" or "silly" by significant others in the adolescent's life. Such reactions to discussing suicidal thoughts or behaviors and what led up to them shut down the therapeutic process by cutting off its lifeblood, the exchange of pertinent information.

In this situation, the therapist is left "high and dry." There are a number of strategic ways of handling this situation. These will be discussed in Chapter 11. However, Weiner and Mehrabian's concept of Immediacy is a useful cognitive tool for moving the therapy through the anxiety which is triggered by adolescent suicidal ideation and behavior. Once the therapist had joined with the family and tried to make the therapy room as safe as possible, the therapist must pursue the circumstances surrounding the adolescent's suicide. As stated above, the therapist knows that this will create anxiety. If the therapist can make the discussion less immediate, it may reduce the anxiety enough to enable the suicidal adolescent or the rest of the family members to join the conversation in therapy. For example, the therapist might use a hypothetical situation instead of the actual suicidal behavior. When families take the stance that "the incident is over—we don't need to talk about it," the therapist would increase the anxiety if he or she pushed the family to talk about it anyway. What the therapist could do is to ask the family a hypothetical question:

> I understand that the suicidal incident is over and probably won't happen again. What would happen if your son (or daughter) did start to have suicidal thoughts? I'm not saying that this is going to happen but, if it did, how would you feel and what would you do to help them?

In this way the therapist is not asking anyone in the family to disclose what happened in reality. Instead, the therapist is asking the parents how they would feel and act if a hypothetical situation were to arise? This reduces the immediacy of the conversation and changes the focus of the therapeutic conversation from "what went wrong" to "what would you do that would help" that hypothetical situation. This would be an intentional effort to shift the cognitive framework from being defensive about what occurs to discussing a hypothetical situation. This reduces immediacy and turns the focus of therapy to a more solution-focused therapy paradigm (deShazer, 1985).

Instead of asking the suicidal seventeen-year-old adolescent male to focus on his suicidal thoughts last week, the therapist might ask him to describe his feelings about life when he was fourteen years old. As the therapist has asked him to comment on the person he was three years ago, the therapist has lessened the immediacy of the situation. To an adolescent, talking about himself when he was fourteen is almost like talking about a completely different person. If the adolescent can describe what his thoughts, feelings, and actions were like when he was fourteen and have those descriptions accepted without judgment by the therapist, he will feel validated and may feel as if he can be more immediate about his self-disclosure. The therapist can then ask the question, "What's changed from the time you were fourteen to the present?" Since the therapist has demonstrated to the suicidal adolescent that the less immediate situation (discussing the remote past) was safe, the therapist can then invite the adolescent to participate in a more immediate discussion of the "near past" (what led up to the suicide attempt). This technique also introduces to the suicidal adolescent a method by which he can gain "perspective" on his life. As perspective is a rare commodity among adolescents, in general, and even more rare in suicidal adolescents, in particular, this opens up a new cognitive paradigm to the adolescent. This gives the adolescent a new resource and changes the perspective the adolescent may have on his stressors.

If a sixteen-year-old adolescent female is reluctant to talk about her own suicide, the therapist might ask her how she might help others:

> As you have been to the brink of suicide and back again, how would you use your own experience to help a classmate who is suicidal?

Talking to a suicidal classmate is certainly less immediate than speaking about herself and her own suicide. In addition, this strategy shifts the client out of the role of being "helpless victim" to being in the role of "helpful expert." This empowers the adolescent and gives her a greater feeling of control over her life. If the therapist can vary the immediacy of the therapeutic conversation, he or she can help to reduce client anxiety and free up both the adolescent and the family to disclose their thoughts and feelings surrounding the suicidal episode.

DRAWING UPON PAST SUCCESS

Because helplessness plays such a crucial role in adolescent suicidal ideation, the therapist might find it useful to devise a plan of action to reduce the adolescent's feelings of helplessness. Arguing with the adolescent will not help the situation. The adolescent will only escalate the perception of helplessness in order to justify why the adolescent became suicidal. Furthermore, if the adolescent believes that he or she is truly helpless, he or she does not have to take any responsibility for changing the situation. This reinforces the adolescent's external locus of control and makes the whole situation seem even more hopeless. If the situation is genuinely hopeless, why continue therapy? If this is the adolescent's attitude, therapy will stall out.

Doing family therapy with such a client is helpful because the therapist can enlist the family to counter the adolescent's extreme external locus of control. The family knows the adolescent better than the therapist does. In addition, the members of the adolescent's family are significant others who have always been in the adolescent's life and will probably be there until death pulls them apart. The therapist is only a significant other to the adolescent for a specific purpose (getting better) and for a specific length of time. Therefore, if the parents can testify to the adolescent's competence and share stories of past successes, it will have a greater impact upon the adolescent than if the therapist speculates about past successes and or pulls them out of the adolescent's "memory bank." These don't have to be great successes. Even small successes can be drawn upon to challenge the "helpless–hopeless" ideation held by the suicidal adolescent. This strategy is similar to the Solution-Focused Therapy strategy of "looking for exceptions to the rule that contradict the problematic behavior" (deShazer, 1985). These past "victories," both large and small, serve as evidence to contradict the adolescent's "cognitive distortion" (Beck, 1976) that he or she is helpless and, therefore, the situation is hopeless. The seventeen-year-old male who has just been dumped by his first true love may feel helpless to do anything to ease his own pain anyway, other than committing suicide. If the therapist can get him to describe previous successes and triumphs or can get the family to do the same, the therapist can use this as evidence of his competence. The therapist can then ask the client to employ the same technique that he utilized before to help his present situation. This reawakens the suicidal adolescent to recognize skills and resources that may have become dormant and, therefore, were forgotten in dealing with the present suicidal episode.

THE CULTURAL MYTH OF THE HERO

Joseph Campbell, in a book called *The Hero with a Thousand Faces* (1956), postulates that there is an archetypical hero who serves as the blueprint for all of our epic heroes and, subsequently, for all of the heroes who are the descendants of those epic figures. The hero is typically a relatively average person who receives a "call to adventure." Even if that call goes unheeded, circumstances will converge so that the hero is reissued the call. The hero begins a perilous journey, a "road of trials," culminating in the hero's becoming prisoner in the "belly of the whale." He is swallowed into the unknown and appears to have died. Through his courage, fortitude, and sometimes supernatural aid, the hero returns from his journey. In many cases he may need to be "rescued from without," requiring external assistance to make the return. Because of this journey, the hero ascends to new heights and has won the "freedom to live" a superior life. This is the adventure of the epic hero that Campbell postulates is the same journey of heroes through the ages.

Examples of this heroic journey are numerous. The mythological story of the Battle of Troy spawned many heroes (Hamilton, 1940). Odysseus of the House of Athens helps win the Battle of Troy but is called by the gods to undergo a perilous journey, wandering around the Aegean Sea and being tormented by mythical beasts (such as the Cyclops), until he can return home triumphantly to Athens. On the losing side of the Battle of Troy, Aeneas, of The House of Troy, must wander the Mediterranean Sea and face many trials and tribulations at sea, on land, and even a descent into the "Lower World" before he can journey to the western shores of Italy and found Rome. The legend of El Cid, the eleventh-century Spanish national hero, tells us that, on the eve of the greatest battle against the Moors, El Cid is assassinated. Fearing that without him the Castilian Army would not ride into battle, his closest soldiers strap his dead body on his horse to ride into battle, leading his troops to victory. Campbell points out that even religious leaders such as Jesus Christ follow the journey of the epic hero. Jesus is called by his Father in heaven to begin the "road of trials," which is his public life. This reaches a crescendo in Jerusalem with his crucifixion. He is buried in the tomb (the "belly of the whale"). He rises from the dead and eventually ascends into heaven. Campbell's point is that this heroic journey is so much a part of human culture that it permeates the legends of all epic heroes—mythological, historical, and religious.

Because this epic journey is so embedded in our culture, I would postulate that, on some level of consciousness, we all see ourselves walking in the footsteps of these heroes along that road. One of those times where this heroic journey is most applicable is when a person enters into therapy. The therapeutic journey is, to my way of thinking, very much an epic hero's journey. Using the example of a suicidal adolescent male, this young man finds himself on a perilous journey. Most therapy clients will tell the therapist that they have endured a "road of trials." To the suicidal adolescent male, he feels as if his depression has "swallowed him whole." At the beginning of therapy he feels that he is held prisoner in the "belly of the whale" (i.e., his depression). He feels that he had been swallowed into the unknown and is on the brink of death. This is the point at which the suicidal adolescent enters into therapy. The adolescent is feeling helpless and hopeless. The promise of therapy is to return him from his "journey into the pit." If he can summon his courage, his fortitude, and sometimes supernatural aid, he can, with the external assistance of the therapist and his family, ascend to new heights of mental health and functional relationships to achieve the "freedom to live" the life he desires, with the new wisdom he has acquired by going through this heroic journey.

I believe that, at some level, every therapy client feels this connection to Campbell's "Hero with a Thousand Faces." Often in therapy, I believe that clients, especially suicidal adolescents, lose their way along that journey. They feel like a failure who has been forsaken by all. They feel isolated and disconnected. They feel hopeless.

It is at this time that the therapist can remind the client that he or she is connected to this tradition of epic heroes. As a therapist, I teach my clients about Campbell's formulation about heroes and their archetypal journey. I give them examples like the ones I provided above. I ask the clients to provide examples of their own heroes and we analyze them to see if they fit the heroic pattern. I can use Odysseus or Aeneas as examples but, for suicidal adolescents, Batman, Spiderman, and Wonder Woman may be more fitting models. I agree with Campbell; I've never seen a hero who didn't fit the archetypal pattern, for the most part. The therapist has to show the client how that hero is one of the faces in the "Hero with a Thousand Faces." The therapist can then point out to the client the similarities between all those heroes' epic journeys and the client's journey in the therapy room. The therapist can then invite the client to complete the journey though therapy with the hope of achieving the "freedom to live" the life he or she desires. To suicidal adolescents, their own life-or-death struggle with the option of suicide and death fits well into this presentation that they are on an epic journey. On some level I believe that they already feel connected to this archetypal cultural pattern. The therapist has to bring this connection to a higher level of consciousness. Suicidal adolescents who have felt isolated can begin to feel a connection to a story which has been part of human culture dating back to ancient times. This also engenders hope in the hopeless client that he or she, too, may complete this epic journey and achieve the "freedom to live" his or her own life as he or she seems fit to do. Therapy becomes the completion of that heroic journey. It still may be hard, fraught with the demons and Cyclopses of modern life. However, there is a promise of hope of the eventual completion of the epic journey. Lastly, if the client is walking in the footsteps of such epic heroes as Odysseus, Jesus, and Batman, doesn't that make him or her a hero, also? Most people, especially suicidal adolescents, do not see themselves as heroes. However, I have found that they will embrace the idea of being a hero if it is presented to them in the way I described above. If the therapist can sell this idea of being a hero to a suicidal adolescent, it is amazing how therapy can turn around for the better. As a person and as a therapist, I truly believe that my clients are heroes on an epic journey society calls "therapy." They might not be heroes who are "larger than life" but they are what Steve Seskin calls "Everyday Heroes" in a song by that title with the lyrics "Everyday heroes are heroes everyday." I teach my suicidal adolescents that, as they are in the middle of an epic journey, they are heroes if they make the rest of the journey. I challenge them to be a hero in their lives. This appeals to the idealistic adolescent, especially when faced with an existential crisis like suicide. This can be a very powerful intervention.

VICTIM ➞ SURVIVOR

Many adolescents who have been victimized in their lives find themselves on the doorstep of suicide. Adolescents who have been neglected, emotionally or physically abused, sexually abused, or abused by some societal plight (e.g., racism, poverty) often seek suicide as a way to end the suffering caused by their victimization. For most of these adolescents, they have taken on the identity of a victim and cannot move beyond the victim role in their lives. They feel trapped in the maladaptive recursive cycle of being a victim. They feel helpless to break out of this cycle. Therefore, they feel hopeless and suicide begins to look like the only way to break out of the victim role, ironically by becoming the ultimate victim, one who dies by one's own hand.

In such cases, the suicidal adolescent is immobilized by his or her perceptions of the stressors as being insurmountable, the resources as being minimal or nonexistent, and, most of all, himself or herself as being destined for further victimization. Because this self-definition is so powerful, the therapist may want to challenge this perception and replace it with a cognitive framework that is more conducive to therapy. Therefore, a cognitive intervention may be singularly appropriate.

I had a case of a twenty-one-year-old woman who had been sexually molested by her father for two years from the ages of twelve to fourteen years of age. When she told her mother of her father's abuse, her mother divorced her husband and formed a single-parent family with her daughter. Two years later, one of mom's boyfriends sexually abused her. At the age of eighteen, she attended a party, got drunk, and was raped by one of the boys at the party. She was date-raped at age twenty. She was now in a dead-end job where her boss "gives her all of the shit work" and tells her that, if she doesn't like it, she can get another job. She described herself as being "born under a bad sign." Her initial complaint centered around the job situation. She felt so bad about her job that she started having dreams about committing suicide. This scared her and she sought out therapy. Over the first two sessions, we spoke about her life, and it became clear to me that she defined herself as a victim who was helpless to change her lot in life. At the beginning of the third session, I went up to the white board in the therapy room and wrote the word "victim" in the upper left hand corner. I asked her to give me a definition of "victim." She responded that "a victim is a person who bad stuff happens to." I thanked her for her definition and asked her if I could alter her definition slightly. She nodded her head affirmatively. I told her the following definition:

> A victim is a person to whom, through no fault of her own, bad things have happened. Those bad things hurt her so much that she tries not to look at them or remember them. The victim finds herself being revictimized frequently.

The 21-year-old said that, in essence, our definitions were the same but mine was "more specific."

I then picked up the marker and wrote the word "survivor" on the upper right-hand portion of the white board. I asked the young woman to define that word. She replied, " I don't know. I guess a survivor is somebody who survives, you know, gets by." Again I thanked her for her definition and asked her if I could, once again, alter it. She said, "OK." I told her the following definition:

> A survivor is a person to whom, through no fault of her own, bad things have happened. Those bad things hurt her very much but she summons the courage to look them in the eye and conquer her hurt and her fear. She learns from her past and constructs strategies of how to avoid being hurt again in the same way. She is on her guard against being victimized again and has a solid plan for how to act if someone ever tries to do bad things to her again.

The young woman looked at the two words and said, "I see there's a big difference." I agreed.

I asked her if she knew of anyone who was a pure victim all of the time, twenty-four hours a day, seven days a week. She thought hard about that. She finally said, "I know some people who come pretty close but not 24/7." I then asked her if she knew anyone who was a survivor all of the time? She answered, "No way!" I replied:

> I guess that no one is that extreme. So this isn't an "either/or" kind of situation where someone is either a victim or a survivor.

She agreed. I drew a line between "victim" and "survivor" and said:

> So there's a continuum between "victim" and "survivor." Nobody probably fits on either extreme 24/7. We probably all fall somewhere in between. Where would you put yourself on this line? Closer to "victim" or closer to "survivor"?

She thought about that question for a while, lowered her head, and, with an embarrassed smile, said "closer to victim." I told her that it took a lot of guts to admit that, and I told her that it also demonstrated great insight. I asked her to get up and put an "X" on the spot on the line that would indicate where she was on that scale. She got up and put her "X" about one-fifth of the way from "victim" to "survivor," indicating that she was much closer to "victim" than she was to "survivor." I thanked her for her honesty. I then got up, took the marker, and put a little arrowhead on the end of the line by "survivor," pointing to the right. This created an arrow pointing from "victim" to "survivor." As I did this, I explained:

> This is the course of therapy for us. Our job in our sessions is to try to move you from victim to survivor. We may do a lot of other things in this room but this will be the core of our therapy.

She smiled and nodded her head affirmatively.

What this intervention is designed to do is to create a cognitive shift in role definition from victim to survivor. By teaching the young woman two different definitions, creating a continuum between them, and using that model as the cornerstone for therapy, I concretely demonstrated a new way of thinking about herself. I wanted to teach the client some information but I wanted to make it personal by involving her participation and using feminine pronouns in the definition. From that moment on, I put my little diagram "victim → survivor" at the top of the white board at the beginning of every session. Not only did this continually reinforce the cognition shift I was promoting but it became a shorthand for the definitional shift for the rest of therapy. The client and I would be talking about anything, from past abuse to what happened in the office today. When the client would describe her ideas, feelings, or behaviors, I would ask her, "Where would you put that thought (feeling or behavior) on our chart on the board?" After a while she needed no prompting but would put herself up on the chart without my asking her to do so. I told her that our goal was to have her marks on the continuum keep moving to the right toward "survivor." This was a good indication of her progress and was very reinforcing to her. About twelve sessions into therapy, she told me that my "victim →" survivor scale" had been permanently etched in her head, even when she was not in the therapy room. She said:

> A little voice is inside of me saying, "Dr. J will want to know if that was more of a victim response or a survivor response? I keep thinking, Slide right."

I specifically asked her to tell me where "suicide" was on our scale? She responded, "As left as you can get!" After eighteen sessions, we went to meeting every other week and then once a month. We completed therapy in about fifteen months with the young woman proudly saying, "Most of my thoughts, feelings, and actions are on the survivor side of the scale." We discussed many matters over the course of therapy, but this intervention remained the cornerstone around which our therapy was built.

SELF-DISCLOSURE

Since Sydney Jourad published *The Transparent Self* in 1964, most clinicians, theorists, and researchers have agreed that "people self-disclose to those who self-disclose to them." However, what has been much more debatable has been how much therapist self-disclosure is good therapy. Some forms of therapy, such as Freudian psychoanalysis (Freud, 1955), would suggest that any self-disclosure would be counter-productive to the client's transference, a core mechanism of psychoanalytic treatment. Therefore, therapist self-disclosure should be avoided. Other clinicians have suggested self-disclosure to be an integral part of therapy, as the client's self-disclosure plays such an integral part of the therapeutic process (Jourad, 1964). In dealing with suicidal adolescents and their families, I have found that some self-disclosure is useful for joining with the adolescent and establishing a meaningful relationship with him or her. If the therapist asks the clients to self-disclose very intimate information about themselves and the important relationships in their lives, many clients will be reluctant to do so unless the therapist is willing to reciprocate with some self-disclosure, also. They simply feel too vulnerable. In this case self-disclosure by the therapist "primes the pump" to help the client self-disclose. It also models how to self-disclose for the client and creates an atmosphere in therapy where it is typical to disclose intimate information.

However, it is important to restrict the therapist's self-disclosure. I have found that the best self-disclosure is that in which I tell the client that I have been personally familiar with some of the feelings in his or her life and have been involved in similar circumstances. It also helps if my self-disclosure emphasizes my vulnerability. In this way the therapist makes a personal connection with the client and demonstrates that he or she is vulnerable and human, like the client. This encourages the client to be more self-disclosing and builds that client–therapist relationship that is at the core of the treatment process (Duncan et al.,1997).

However, the use of self-disclosure should be done very judiciously. If the therapist self-discloses too frequently, the client will feel that the therapist is narcissistic and therapy is really "all about him or her," instead of the client. Similarly, the therapist's examples of self-disclosure cannot "top" the client's own problems. For example, if an adolescent female is distraught over the death of a friend, the therapist cannot say, "I know what death is. I've lost my mother, my father, my spouse, one of my children, my cat, and a parakeet!" By doing so, the therapist has just trumped the client's presenting problem. The client will wonder why the therapist isn't a client instead of a therapist. Furthermore, nothing is to be gained from such a self-disclosure, except for the narcissistic self-aggrandizement of the therapist. If anything, such a self-disclosure will shut down future self-disclosure from the adolescent client because she will feel inadequate when she compares herself to her therapist. Likewise, the therapist should avoid saying, "I know exactly what you mean." To a client, especially an adolescent client, it sounds arrogant. When confronted with such a remark, most adolescents will argue back, "You're not me! How can you know exactly how I feel?" Once again the therapist's response will shut off any further adolescent self-disclosure.

If the therapist is judicious with his or her self-disclosures, a lot can be gained to profit therapy. If the therapist were to respond to the adolescent female whose friend had died with the following, there is much to be gained:

> It's tough when one of your friends dies, especially at your age when she had so much of her life ahead of her. When I was your age, I knew a couple of people my age who had died. I felt terrible for them and it also scared me that I could die, too. But these were not close friends to me like your friend was to you. It's got to be a lot harder for you to go through! Why don't you tell me about it so that I can better understand?

The therapist has respected the client's pain as unique and, although the therapist knows something about what it is like to experience death at that age, the therapist admits that it is not the same level of grief experienced by the young woman with her friend's death. The therapist also "primes the pump" for the adolescent to further explore her feelings by reporting that he or she knew that the dead adolescent had so much to live for and that his or her own mortality was called into question. From studying the adolescent research literature, these were educated guesses as to how the adolescent might feel. If the young woman agrees with these feelings, it will move her along in her explanation of her own thoughts and feelings. If she does not agree, the therapist can respond:

> Well, that's what I felt. But that was long ago and you and I are different people. Tell me how *you* feel?

When the therapist invites the adolescent to further self-disclose, it moves the therapeutic process along. When the adolescent can have this type of conversation with an adult who is willing to listen to her, it is highly unusual and very validating. When this conversation can take place in front of the adolescent's entire family, that validation is witnessed by some very important "significant others" in her life. By listening to this conversation, without interrupting, the family also validates the adolescent and the importance of her words and feelings. This changes the adolescent's perceptions of herself and her family as a resource. A validated adolescent is one step further from the edge of the cliff of suicide.

Ten

BEHAVIORAL INTERVENTIONS
When Actions Speak Louder Than Words

Some families do not process cognitive interventions well. They may be a family of concrete thinkers who feel that cognitive insights do not connect with their primary method of functioning. Concrete thinkers work far better with behaviors than concepts. Behaviors are tangible. They can be seen and counted. Instructions surrounding these behaviors can be explicit. Outcomes can be seen and measured. All of these qualities of behavioral therapy appeal to concrete thinkers. In addition, behavioral therapy has been found to bring about change with problem adolescents (McGovern et al., 2004).

Some families may be overwhelmed by the severity or scope of a suicidal problem. Suicide is multifaceted. The sheer number of influences upon an adolescent's life that could push him or her to the brink of suicide is exhausting for an adolescent or a family to consider. Behavioral therapy allows both the adolescent and the family to narrow the focus down to a set of specific behaviors and proceeds to deal with them one at a time. To an individual or family overwhelmed with possibilities, behavioral therapy is manageable. Being manageable is a comforting feeling to a suicidal adolescent and his or her family, all of whom feel out of control. Most families do not have to face a situation where the life of one of their own is on the line. Most adolescents are not in a situation where his or her life is on the line. The severity of the situation can also overwhelm both the adolescent and the family. Once again, behavioral interventions help to break a problem down into more manageable steps. When the stakes are as high as a family member's death, a therapy that makes progress more manageable may be much more closely embraced by both the suicidal adolescent and his or her family.

Some suicidal adolescents and their families may desperately need to see concrete, measurable progress in therapy in order to reduce their fears and anxieties that their adolescent is on an inexorable path to suicide. Many insight-oriented interventions may work quite well but the outcome of that insight will only be evident "down the road." Both the adolescent and his or her family may need to see progress in therapy more quickly. Behavioral therapy gives the clients more immediate feedback than many more cognitive approaches. Even if the steps are small, they are measurable and can be rewarded. In the world of a suicidal adolescent, where the pain is high and communication is low, such an immediate and concrete feedback system is very important to the clients.

Finally, some problems or aspects of treatment lend themselves better to behavioral formulations for treatment. For a suicidal adolescent who has severe control issues, working within a framework that is both concrete and immediate can give both the adolescent and his or her family a greater sense of control of their lives. If a behavioral intervention can create a formula for success, the suicidal adolescent will feel more in control of his or her life. If the adolescent will feel more in control of life, the family will feel more control over the suicidal crisis. For example, bed-wetting has been found to be very responsive to behavioral therapies. At some time in the future, the therapist and child may focus on underlying issues. However, since bed-wetting is so responsive to behavioral techniques, a wise therapist might initially turn to behavioral interventions in order to give both the child and the parents some feelings of success and accomplishment first. Once the family has made progress in overcoming the immediate crisis, they will be more willing to participate in a therapeutic process that is more cognitive and insight-oriented. In this way behavioral interventions can "prime the pump" for other kinds of therapeutic interventions.

SAFETY PLAN

One of the first behavioral interventions that is needed in cases of suicidal adolescents is the development of a safety plan. Both the suicidal adolescent and his or her family need a concrete plan in case the suicidal ideation gives rise to lethal suicidal behavior. Therefore, unless there is a reason to suspect some underlying abuse in the home, the safety plan should be constructed with the help of the whole family. Even the school-age children should participate in the safety plan.

Being good observers of the family dynamics, they may have crucial information to include in the plan. Furthermore, their participation in carrying out the plan has several advantages. It gives the family an extra set of eyes and ears to monitor the suicidal adolescent. It keeps them from being triangulated by other family members, including the suicidal adolescent. It keeps them informed as to both the dangers and the progress of the suicidal situation. If they are kept "out of the loop" of information, they will still be aware of the tension in the family. Without any knowledge of what is going on, these siblings will fall in that vacuum of knowledge with all of the irrational fears which the child's mind can manufacture. I had a case in which a seven-year-old sister of the suicidal adolescent had been kept in the dark about her teenage brother's suicidal struggles. She knew something was wrong but she did not know what it was. Therefore, she filled this knowledge gap with her own fears that her brother had killed his girlfriend, had hidden her body, and Mom and Dad were protecting him from the police. Of course, none of this was true, but it was easier for her to understand than it was to comprehend her brother's wanting to kill himself because his girlfriend had dumped him.

It is very affirming to the suicidal adolescent that the entire family participates in insuring his or her safety. Needless to say, the participation of younger siblings requires that the therapist help the family explain what is going on in a language that the younger siblings can grasp. This is not an easy task but it is well worth the effort. The therapist also needs to be mindful that some discussions are simply beyond the scope of the younger children's understanding. If the younger siblings are excused from the therapy room for a session or part of a session, they should be reassured that the safety of their suicidal sibling and the parents are in the therapist's good hands. Lastly, I have found that, when the whole family participates in making and carrying out a safety plan, it serves to guard the nonsuicidal family members from becoming suicidal as they grow older. I have had several siblings of suicidal adolescents with whom I have done therapy contact me about problems when they became teenagers. Although they had a variety of typical adolescent problems, none of them thought suicide was a viable option. As one young man reported, "I still remember how my whole family met when my sister tried to commit suicide. That taught me that suicide is simply not an option."

I believe that there are five aspects of creating and carrying out a safety plan that must be discussed. The therapist needs to lead the discussion of these aspects and encourage the participation of all family members.

Antecedents. The first step to setting up a good safety plan is to open up a family discussion about the antecedents of both suicidal thoughts and suicidal behaviors. The therapist should begin with the suicidal adolescent's ideas about what in his or her life triggers the thoughts about suicide. As mentioned in Chapter 6, both the therapist and the family need to let the adolescent tell his or her story his or her way. Giving the suicidal adolescent the initial chance to discuss the antecedents of his or her suicidal ideation demonstrates respect for the adolescent and his or her ability to demonstrate introspection into his or her own thought processes. The main things that the therapist has to do is encourage the adolescent to speak and to stop other family members from interrupting. My general rule for this conversation is that the person who is speaking has the floor. Anyone else in the family and the therapist needs to listen. A family member or the therapist may ask a question of clarification but all other questions and comments should be saved for that person's turn to speak. If the adolescent refuses to talk about the antecedents to his or her suicidal ideation, the therapist should ask the family to help the therapist look at antecedents of suicidal ideation. After each family member has given his or her thoughts, the therapist should return to the suicidal adolescent and ask him or her if what the family member said seems to hold validity for him or her. If the adolescent has speculated upon the antecedents to his or her suicidal ideation, the therapist can open up the discussion to the other members of the family by soliciting their opinions on the adolescent's speculations. By involving the entire family to speculate as to the situations that trigger the adolescent's suicidal thoughts, the therapist leads the family in creating the landscape which prompts the adolescent's suicidal ideation.

Once the therapist has a picture of the antecedents that trigger the adolescent's suicidal thoughts, he or she repeats the process to determine the antecedents of the adolescent's suicidal actions, if the adolescent has indeed taken his or her thoughts into behaviors. If the suicidal thoughts have not given rise to suicidal behaviors, the adolescent may be asked to speculate what it would take to trigger suicidal actions in his life. The content of these discussions could cover a multitude of topics, many of which are described in Chapter 3 and Chapter 4. From a behavioral standpoint, the object of these discussions is to identify the antecedents or stimuli that result in the adolescent's suicidal ideas and behavior. Many feelings and family dynamics may also surface during these discussions. These should be validated and cataloged for use in further therapy sessions but, when constructing a safety plan, the primary objective is to identify the triggers of suicidal ideation and behavior. They will serve as the foundation for the safety plan.

Accelerators. Once the antecedents have been identified, the therapist should inquire as to the existence of any conditions that may accelerate any of the antecedents triggering suicidal thoughts or actions. These accelerators do not have the power to trigger suicidal ideas or behaviors, in and of themselves. However, they do have the power to quicken the process. Accelerators could be the adolescent's affective state or the time of day or day of the week.

Deterrents. Once the therapist and the adolescent and his or her family have agreed upon the stimuli (both antecedents and accelerators) that trigger suicidal thoughts and behaviors, it is time to create deterrents which will slow down or stop that process from occurring. Each deterrent should block the stimulus from one or more antecedents or dampen the effect of one of more accelerators. The first deterrent has already been accomplished. Working with the suicidal adolescent and his or her family on defining antecedents and accelerators, and recognizing when they occur, is the first deterrent. In this case, knowledge deters these conditions from resulting in suicide ideas and actions because, once they are understood by the adolescent and his or her family, they can be identified early in the process when they are manageable. They provide an early warning system.

Using the Double ABC → X model (McCubbin & Patterson, 1982), a deterrent may perform its function in several ways. A deterrent may reduce the stress of an antecedent. An adolescent violinist may be taught relaxation techniques to ease preperformance stress, which often has resulted in suicidal ideation. A deterrent may alter the way that the adolescent or the family may view the stressor. For example, wetting the bed may still be highly embarrassing for the seventeen-year-old girl and, therefore, may be highly stressful for her. However, if the therapist can reframe the bedwetting as her subconscious' trying to help her cope with her previous sexual abuse, it may reduce the level of stress caused by that event. A deterrent may give the adolescent more resources to balance out the stressors on the other end of the Teeter-Totter Model (Jurich & Collins, 1996). For example, having the parents agree to provide the adolescent with a nonjudgmental sounding board gives the adolescent a resource that he or she did not know was available. Of course, one resource, which the adolescent now has that he or she did not have before, is therapy.

Once these deterrents have been identified, the therapist needs to develop a behavioral plan to follow when the adolescent perceives the confluence of antecedents and accelerators is strong enough to precipitate suicidal ideation or behavior. This plan needs to be specific and yet contain enough options to be put into operation, even if one or more deterrents are not available to the adolescent and the family.

Alternatives. Once the deterrents are in place, the therapist needs to designate alternative courses of behavior that will be different from the adolescent's previous maladaptive recursive cycle. For example, most adolescents tend to isolate themselves when the antecedents of suicide begin to gather. An alternative course of action may be to design a set of activities for the adolescent to begin at the first signs of suicide antecedents. These activities may be interpersonal interactions with a group of people (family or friends) who will keep the adolescent from being alone.

Follow-up. Once the safety plan has been designed, the therapist has to follow up on how it is working. Both the adolescent and the family need to report on the viability of the safety plan every session. Adjustments to the plan need to be made as needed. The safety plan, even if written down for clarity, needs to be a living document which should be reshaped as the adolescent and his or her family change and grow.

Case Example. As formulaic as the process, as outlined above, may be, there are so many permutations and combinations of factors that are possible we can't cover them all in a single book. To demonstrate how this safety plan process works, let's take a look at a case study as an example. Let us look at the case of an adolescent female, age sixteen, who had been dumped by her boyfriend. This triggered suicidal ideation in this girl and had even pushed her to take an overdose of her mother's sleeping pills (a mild sedative). It was this episode that brought her and her family (mother, father, younger brother (age twelve)) into therapy. There was an older brother (age twenty-one) who was away at college and did not plan on coming to therapy.

In the first session, I joined with the young woman and her family in the way outlined in Chapter 7. Although I assessed that the young woman was not actively suicidal, she was so distraught over the end of her intimate relationship with her boyfriend that I was not sure that she wouldn't become suicidal again fairly rapidly if the situation shifted even slightly. Therefore, I wanted to design at least a temporary safety plan in that first session. From listening to her tell her story her way, it was clear to me that the primary antecedent for triggering her suicidal ideation was when she thought about her boyfriend or was "struck" by some event that reminded her of him. For example, if she heard their favorite song, it would bring back a flood of memories that would trigger suicidal thoughts. Her main accelerator was isolation. Any antecedent became much more powerful when she was alone. The main antecedent for her suicidal behavior was seeing her boyfriend with another girl in his car. Based upon these quick observations, I suggested that we needed to develop a temporary safety plan and put it into place so that the suicidal adolescent would be safe between sessions and be able to come to the next therapy session.

The first deterrent I suggested was to get the suicidal adolescent to sign a "No-Suicide Contract." This contract is a form we have at the Kansas State University Family Center. It is basically a contract that the suicidal client signs, pledging not to engage in any suicidal behavior without first calling the therapist (or other designated person) to discuss the matter. The reason for designating the therapist as the primary person to contact is that, after one session, the therapist cannot be sure of anybody else to provide an "active listening ear" to the suicidal person if they were called instead. This can be changed subsequently if a competent person emerges over the course of therapy. It is standard operating procedure at the KSU Family Center to require any client who has said that he or she is or has recently been suicidal to sign a "No Suicide Contract." Although this contract is required, in part, to help legally protect the clinic, the primary reason is because it has a deterrent effect upon the suicidal client. This may seem a little bit crazy to the reader. The reader may ask, "If the client is really intent on committing suicide, will a piece of paper stop them from doing so?" The question is a valid concern. The interesting point, however, is that our experience at the KSU Clinic over the last 30 years is that it *does* work. Clients have told us that this little slip of paper with everybody's signature on it is taken seriously and does form an effective barrier to keep them from suicidal behavior. If a client refuses to sign the contract, I tell them that they are telling me that they are actively suicidal and need to be hospitalized.

The next deterrent I suggested was an attempt to lower the stress caused by the antecedent event. As the young woman could not avoid all of the things that reminded her of her ex-boyfriend, I struggled to find an alternative behavior for her to do when confronted by an "ex-boyfriend stimulus." Heretofore, her response to such stimuli was to fall into silence and even to begin to weep. Borrowing from strategic therapy, I tried to suggest something which would break the maladaptive recursive cycle. As songs were very powerful in evoking emotions in her, I asked if there was a song that she did not associate with her boyfriend which calmed her. She had to think a while. Finally, she said that she remembered a song her mother sang to her as a child which would calm her down and make her think of a sunny spring day. She said that she didn't remember the name but the chorus repeated the words, "Feelin' Groovy." Her mother said, "My God, that's the '59th Street Bridge Song' by Simon and Garfunkle. I haven't thought of that for years." I asked Mom to write down the words for her daughter and, if she couldn't remember them, to go on the computer to the Internet and dial up www.leoslyrics.com to get the words. She said she would. I then instructed the daughter to sing or hum that song whenever she received an "ex-boyfriend stimulus." She said that she thought I was crazy but agreed to try to do so.

As this suicidal adolescent had stated that she was sure that she would never fall in love again, I told her that I wanted to help her change her perception of this terrible event (getting dumped). I told her that, when faced with an "ex-boyfriend stimulus," I wanted her to pick another young man whom she thought would be a desirable dating partner, and analytically compare that young man with her ex-boyfriend. I was attempting to change two things in her maladaptive recursive cycle. I wanted her to challenge the idea that she would never fall in love again. I also wanted her to engage in a cognitive task (the comparisons) to short-circuit the emotional feelings she typically had.

I also wanted to give her at least two resources, one in the family and one outside the family. Within the family, she was unsure of whom to choose. She was afraid of hurting somebody else's feelings. She simply could not make that decision. I suggested that, as she was using Mom's song in a previous intervention, that, for the time being, Mom would act as her family resource. Mom asked what that entailed. I told her that if her daughter felt that she was slipping away into suicidal ideation or behavior, she was to tell Mom that she was in trouble and that, for at least the next week, Mom would make her daughter the number one priority. Mom agreed. I then asked the suicidal daughter to choose a designated non-family resource. She answered that she and her best three girlfriends were inseparable. She said she couldn't choose just one of them but would chose all three. I labeled them as the "Three Wise Women" and asked her to ask them if they would be her non-family resource. I found out the next week that they said yes. The suicidal adolescent agreed that, if the going got tough, she would ask her designated resources for help.

At the next week's session, the suicidal adolescent said that the week had gone much better, thanks in large part, to the temporary safety plan. The adolescent, her family, and I proceeded to work at making the temporary safety plan more permanent. We explored new antecedents. For example, the adolescent said that she also had suicidal thoughts when she did poorly at some task, such as a test at school. With this antecedent, she was most helped by giving her added academic resource people, someone who could help her in her academic parsuits. One of those resource people was her big brother who was away at college. She admitted that she really missed him and used to talk a lot about "life" with him.

Especially when she was stressed by academic issues, he was a calming influence on her. I suggested that she start to e-mail him regularly and to ask him if he would be a resource. He not only agreed to do this but also came to therapy when he was on vacation from school or could get away for a quick visit. A highlight for her during our seven months of therapy was the weekend he asked her to come to his college for a weekend. He was a great resource person! We added new deterrents and alternatives and adjusted the old plan. For example, the young woman told me that singing or humming the "59th Street Bridge Song" was good for her to do but she couldn't carry that tune if a song reminding her of her ex-boyfriend was also playing. The whole family discussed what she could do in that circumstance. We finally agreed that she would not sing or hum the "59th Street Bridge Song" but, instead, would sing or hum the song that was causing her difficulty "through clenched teeth." The client explained that the clenched teeth would allow her to "take the song back from her ex-boyfriend" and reclaim it for herself.

Once we had fine-tuned the safety plan, we got it typed up and gave everyone in the family, including the suicidal adolescent, a copy. I kept one copy for the client's file. The client never engaged in any subsequent suicidal behavior. After seven months of therapy, the suicidal adolescent was free of intrusive suicidal thoughts. She reported feeling much better about both herself and her family. She even got a new boyfriend. Ironically, he was one of the guys she used as a comparator with her boyfriend as part of the safety plan. She told me that the safety plan and therapy had given her a "whole new style of evaluating men." Not only is a behavioral safety plan good for keeping the suicidal client safe, but it is also an excellent behavioral intervention.

BEHAVIORAL CONTRACTING

There are many forms of behavioral contracts. For example, a therapist can create a specific behavioral contract to lessen the tension between a parent and an adolescent having conflict over a specific aspect of their relationship, such as establishing a curfew. The therapist asks the parent what he or she would like the adolescent to contribute to one side of the contract. The adolescent is then asked to voice what he or she would like the parent to give to the other side of the contract. The therapist then negotiates a contract that attempts to bring about both desired behaviors by making the behaviors of the adolescent rewarded by the behaviors of the parent. Likewise, the contract should be constructed so that the behavior of the parent is rewarded by the behavior of the adolescent. Around the issue of curfew, for instance, the parent may want a greater compliance to the curfew by the adolescent. The adolescent wants to extend the curfew. With the therapist acting as the moderator, each side (parent vs. teenager) tries to argue his or her side. The therapist, from a more objective position, can bring up the elements of the contract: (1) an official clock, (2) the time of the curfew, and (3) consequences for missing curfew which are differential, depending on how late the adolescent is beyond the curfew. I typically ask clients to create consequences for the adolescent for being (1) one to fifteen minutes late, (2) sixteen to sixty minutes late, and (3) over sixty minutes late. The therapist helps both the parent and the adolescent negotiate a middle ground on each issue. If done effectively, the final contract will give the adolescent a later curfew (not what he or she wanted but still later than he or she had) and a differential consequence that is dependent upon how fast (after curfew) he or she can get home, which is a factor that he or she can control. The parent gets compliance to the new curfew and a system of consequences that will encourage the adolescent to be "a little bit late," rather than "very late." In addition, both parties have discussed their differences openly and directly, instead of with covert hinting and indirect inference. With the help of the therapist, they have agreed upon a course of compromise to the mutual benefit of each. They are given a copy of the contract (one copy is kept in the client's file) signed by all parties. It is amazing how arguments are truncated when a contract, signed by both the parent and the adolescent, is produced. This type of behavioral contracting is very useful when working with adolescents and is covered in much greater detail elsewhere (e.g., DeRisi & Butz, 1975; Patterson, 1971; Stuart & Lott, 1972).

One of the specific advantages of this type of behaviors contracting is that the therapist can choose a family problem and narrow the focus to that one specific problem. The problem with suicidal adolescents is that seldom is the suicidal ideation or behavior confined to just one area of conflict. Consequently, I would suggest that the contractual model of conflict negotiation proposed by Harrell and Guerney (1976) is a better fit for working with suicidal adolescents and their families. The purpose of this method is to use behavioral contracting as a method for resolving interpersonal conflicts that will be new to the family. Because of the novelty of this technique to the family, it also holds the strategic promise of interrupting the maladaptive recursive cycles that the family has created and that have produced the suicidal situation in which the family now finds itself. This model also has the added advantage of stressing the importance of teaching empathy to all of the family members. Several clinicians (Hill, 1970; Richman, 1979) have found an absence of empathy in the families of suicidal individuals. The lack of empathy among family members greatly contributes to the isolation of the suicidal adolescent. Richman (1979) even goes so far as to suggest that abetting the development of empathy in families where there is a suicidal person is essential for positive outcomes in therapy. Therefore, this type of behavioral contracting holds many advantages for working with suicidal adolescents and their families.

During this process of developing contracts, as with all forms of behavioral contracting, the therapist should attempt to focus the family's discussion on concrete behavioral aspects of the problem identified by the clients. Families typically, especially in highly stressful situations, discuss their problems in sweeping statements that have very little specificity. Although this may give another family member a broad and even dramatic view of the problem, it does not let the other family members know what exact behaviors exist so that they might know explicitly what needs to be changed. A family member might say to another family member that he or she needs to "be loved more." That statement is simply too broad for the listener to fully comprehend. Is the speaker asking for more hugs or more words of encouragement? If the speaker wants more hugs and the listener thinks that the speaker wants more encouragement, the speaker will still be unhappy and unfulfilled, despite the best intentions of the listener to comply with the speaker's wishes. In my experience, the primary reason why most behavioral contracts are not successful is that they are not specific enough.

Once this specificity has been accomplished, the therapist can help the family develop alternative response patterns to the maladaptive recursive cycles that already exist. The therapist encourages the family to create new solutions to the problems that are different from those already employed by the family. These alternative solutions should be discussed by the family with the therapist's help in guiding the conversation and supporting all family members for contributing to the discussion. The discussion should evaluate the capability and efficiency of those new alternatives to meet the needs of the suicidal adolescent and the rest of the family. This "in-depth" discussion should allow for all viewpoints of the family members, including the suicidal adolescent. As every family member has a unique perspective of the present suicidal situation, the therapist should encourage all family members to participate in order to create the richest view of the family's predicament.

Each family member is asked to institute a behavioral change that would support an alternative solution to the family's identified problem. Everyone in the family is asked to identify a behavioral change that can be instituted in response to the reciprocal changes in behavior identified by the other family members. Each family member agrees to change a behavior because the other family members have agreed to change their behaviors. Once each family member's behavioral change is identified, the therapist helps the family negotiate how to link these changes into a behavioral contract. Each person should have to give something up for the sake of the family while understanding that every other family member is also giving up something else. All of these behavioral changes are contingent upon the entire family's participating in the creation of an equitable behavioral exchange contract. In this situation, if everybody participates, everybody wins. If one person does not follow up on the behavioral change he or she has agreed to do, the entire contract begins to shake and falter. However, if all family members participate, they all contribute to the resolution of the family's problem to the natural benefit of all concerned.

It is the therapist's goal to help the suicidal adolescent and his or her family learn to use more direct and functional behavioral change strategies than they have employed in the past. As many families of suicidal adolescents tend to use manipulative or coercive strategies of problem-solving (Jurich, 1983a), this type of behavioral contracting is valuable in disrupting those former maladaptive recursive cycles. Because this type of behavioral contract will produce observable outcomes that will serve as concrete examples of the family's ability to work together in good faith in order to accomplish a goal which is mutually beneficial to all parties, it will reward the family members to continue the process to make other changes. The family with the suicidal adolescent, who originally thought the situation was both painful and hopeless, has now received concrete evidence that they are able to exert power and control over that pain and hopelessness.

Once the behavioral contract has been agreed upon by the entire family, the therapist should have it typed up and signed by all family members. This not only increases the clarity of the contract but each person's signature is tangible proof of that family member's pledge to work on behalf of the family in service of all family members. In addition, as mentioned above, since everybody gets a copy of the contract, it forces family members to abide by the terms of the contract. Once the behavioral contract is implemented, the therapist always asks for the family members' feedback. This will allow the therapist and the family to evaluate their progress and, if necessary, to renegotiate the contract in order to achieve maximum efficiency. Some families need to completely break down the problem into manageable behavioral components. Likewise, these families benefit by being able to tangibly see and experience the results of the contract.

Let us look at a case example of the use of a behavioral contract with a family who had a suicidal adolescent. In Chapter 8, I presented the case of the father who asked his family "Are you trying to give me a heart attack?" until his daughter asked him "Are you trying to push me to commit suicide?" In that case, I worked to have the family set up a behavioral contract. The family discussed the suicide threat of the daughter, and it was clear that her threat had really "shook up" the entire family. I began with the seventeen-year-old who had threatened suicide. I explained to her that her question about being pushed to suicide was very similar to her father's question about being pushed into a heart attack. I asked her if she liked it when her dad did that to her. She replied that she did not and that her dad's question felt to her like manipulation. She said, "If he wants us to 'back off' or 'tone down,' why can't he just come out and say it?" I asked the seventeen-year-old if she would be willing to strip her question about being pushed into suicide from her behavioral repertoire of phrases. The alternative we agreed upon was that she would take a moment to think about what she was feeling and express that feeling directly.

I turned to the father and asked if he would like to see his daughter put her alternative strategy into practice. He said, "Yes, definitely!" I asked him what behavioral alternative he would volunteer to change to reciprocate his daughter's behavioral change. He told us that he would remove his heart attack question from his stock of phrases. For his alternative behavior, he said that he would think about and express his feelings. Furthermore, he said that he would ask another family member for help if he needed it and not hold himself hostage to manipulate a family response. The mother said that, instead of "going to pieces" when either phrase was uttered, she would ask her husband or her seventeen-year-old what she could do to help and try to comply to their wishes. The fourteen-year-old son said that he wouldn't laugh at other family members when they asked "stupid questions." He explained that he laughed when he didn't know what else to do or when he felt threatened by what someone said. He said laughter makes him feel superior. Instead, he said that his behavioral change would be to listen to other family member, so that he could better understand them. The 9-year-old daughter and baby of the family said that, instead of being scared and retreating back into her room, when there was interpersonal tension in the family, she would hug the person who was expressing those scary feelings. As a family and their therapist, we discussed the assets and liabilities of their behavioral changes. After we "fine tuned" contributions to the behavioral contract, we finalized the contract, had the secretary type it up, had everybody sign (including the therapist), made copies, and sent them on their way. The next week, I asked them how the contract went. They reported no threats of suicide or heart attacks, less derisive laughter, more mutual understanding, and a lot more hugs. They described their family life as being less filled with stress, even though they were talking more, as an entire family. Their total cycle of interaction had slowed down because they were listening to each other in a manner they had never done before. This positive feedback encouraged them to fine-tune their process and they were eager to try their hands at another behavioral contract. They felt closer, more empathic, and better understood by the family. This was not a family who could have handled insight very well but the concrete nature of the behavioral contract fit well for their style of interaction.

INTEGRATING BEHAVIORAL THERAPY WITH OTHER INTERVENTIONS

Many therapists will not use behavioral therapy alone but instead use a behavioral approach in combination with other types of therapy. Combining behavioral therapy with cognitive therapy has long been recognized as a worthwhile endeavor that has produced good outcomes in therapy (Compton, March, Brent, Albano, Weersing & Curry, 2004; Klomek & Mufson, 2006; Meichenbaum, 1977). In fact, cognitive behavioral therapy has been suggested to be the treatment of choice for many cases of depression (Klein, Santiago, Vivian, Arnow, Blalock, Dunner, Kocsis, Markowitz, Manber, McCullough, Jr., Rothbaum, Rush, Trivedi, Thase, Borian, Keitner, Miller & Keller, 2004). Often in my behavioral therapy, I still focus on such cognitive intervention techniques as pointing out the incompatibility between a client's thoughts and behavior. In the above example, when setting up the suicidal adolescent's alternative behavior, I compared her "question about suicide" to her dad's "question about a heart attack." I then asked how she felt when her dad asked his question of her. When she answered, "manipulated," I was trying to bring her to the cognitive realization that her own behavior would produce feelings in others that she did not like when they were produced in her. Therefore, there was an incompatibility between her behavior and her thoughts about what she was trying to accomplish. I believe that this focus on incongruities enhances the client's motivation to work on the behavioral contract and subsequently to follow through in doing his or her part to make the contact work. I have found this to be especially effective with adolescent clients.

A more recent style of therapy combines cognitive behavioral therapy with a humanistic orientation which recognizes the importance of the therapist's interpersonal relationship with the client (Linehan, 1987). In this treatment, there is a group format used to teach the client the principles of humanistic psychology and some life skills that flow from those principles (i.e., interpersonal effectiveness, regulation of emotions, tolerance of distress, and being mindful of others). There is also a component of the treatment that focuses on a cognitive-behavioral approach. Grounded in a framework of behavioral change, this therapy combines skills training in problem solving and managing contingencies to shape behavior with validation-based humanistic techniques. This model of therapy has been found to be very successful when treating suicidal clients (Linehan, Armstrong, Suarez, Allmon, & Heurd, 1991). Because of the emphasis of this dialectic behavioral therapy upon the interpersonal aspects of the client's life, it holds much promise for use in family therapy as well.

PROSCRIBING BEHAVIORAL TASKS

There are moments in therapy, even if the therapist is not specifically following a behavioral model, where a behavioral task may be very useful to move the therapy forward. These tasks may take the form of in-session or homework assignments. The task is a direct behavioral prescription designed to produce insight in the client or help the client behaviorally practice a difficult task.

A behavioral task that would help to produce insight typically attempts to change the client's perspective. For example, a simple behavioral task, usually given to produce new insight, is a proscribed shifting of roles in a family. In a case where a suicidal adolescent female is in conflict with her father, the father may express an attitude towards his daughter's suicidal ideas that sounds clueless, cavalier, and unfeeling. To his daughter's expression about her suicidal thoughts he may say:

> What's she got to feel bad about? She has no responsibilities and has her whole life ahead of her. This suicide stuff is nonsense! Just say "no" to feeling bad.

The daughter will feel as he is just blowing off her concerns and feelings. She says:

> This is just what I expected. Dad doesn't have any worries. He controls everything! He can do anything he wants because he controls the purse strings. What's he got to bitch about?

Both the daughter and her father have unrealistic views of each other's lives. Each thinks the other has a life that is easy. Neither is willing to listen to the other because it would upset their preconceived assumptions of each other. They speak but they don't listen. In this situation, prescribing a role reversal for each of them is a behavioral task that should give each of them new insights to each other's lives. Perhaps the daughter may learn that, with all of that freedom and power she envies her dad for having, comes a burden of responsibility that shackles him far more than she ever imagined. Maybe the father would learn that being a teenage girl is not all freedom from responsibility and "fun and games" because the lack of power and dearth of polished social skills make every day a threat to who you are. If they do learn these things by role reversal, the experiential learning will bring these lessons home to them far better than listening to each other complain about his or her lot in life.

Sometimes a client may feel trapped in a maladaptive recursive cycle and find it impossible to get out. I had a case in which a suicidal adolescent seventeen-year-old was estranged from her father for years. Her parents were divorced when she was fourteen because he had had an affair. The seventeen-year-old blamed her father for the breakup of her parents' marriage. They argued bitterly whenever they tried to have a conversation. When the father found out that his daughter had tried to overdose on sleeping pills, he drove back into town to try to help her. However, as soon as he arrived in the hospital where she was in recovery from having her stomach flushed, they fell into their old patterns and started to argue. She later expressed in therapy:

> Even the sight of my father sets me off. The sound of his voice still grates on me! We just can't talk.

I asked her what she wanted to say to him? She replied, "Nothing!" Then she paused, smiled a crooked smile and said, "Actually, lots!" I gave her the behavioral task of constructing a letter to send to her father. I told her that we may never actually send it and assured her that she would have control over whether we sent it or not.

The next week, the young woman had not completed the task and said that she was having trouble thinking about what to say. I gave her an additional task for homework. I asked her to keep a journal in a notebook and jot down feelings and thoughts that she might have about her father. I then asked her to construct her letter from the pages of her journal. She agreed. Her first journal entries were very angry. Her first letter was filled with venom. As her mother, the suicidal adolescent, and I proceeded in family therapy and her anger (and Mom's) were expressed, it was clear to me that the adolescent had been scapegoating her father for years, blaming him for all of the pain in her life. This was fueled by her mother's own anger at her ex-husband for his betrayal. We revised the letter but never sent it. I archived it in her therapy file.

One day in therapy, the young woman said that she would like to bring her journal for me to read. Over the course of time, her journal had transitioned from anger to questioning her father about "why?" to expressing that she missed him and wanted him to be part of her life. She also wrote that she felt terribly guilty for feeling that because she felt that it was as if she were taking sides against Mom. To her surprise, her mom was not threatened by her wanting to be closer to her ex-husband. Mom said that she understood her feelings and shared that part of her still loved her dad as well. Mom said that that frightened her, but she did have to admit it to herself.

We began working on a second letter to Dad. This one was much more balanced between good and bad feelings. This one we sent. For a while the suicidal adolescent and her father exchanged letters. Then they exchanged emails. My client admitted that she still did not want to see her dad. His facial expressions and his tone of voice still "set her off." However, by sending letters and emails, she did not have to look at him or hear him. After nine months of therapy, the formerly suicidal adolescent said that she would visit with her father but only if she could see him in therapy, where it was safe. Eventually, the father and daughter could visit without the presence of the therapist. The young woman had to journal about her father and practice writing letters before she was "centered" enough to see him in person. The behavioral task acted as a cast around a broken leg, holding the leg together artificially until the relationship could heal and stand on its own.

Sometimes a behavioral task can allow a person to progress in therapy because it provides the structure needed to make progress. I had a fifteen-year-old female client who was depressed and had a lot of suicidal ideation. Her five-year-old half-sister was tragically killed by a car as she ran into the street to get ice cream from the ice cream truck in front of the neighbor's house. The fifteen-year-old was distraught at her sister's death and felt guilty that she couldn't do anything to keep her from running into the street. She would stare for hours, thinking of her dead sister. After seeing two therapists with little progress, she was referred to me. I told the family that I would see her only if we could do family therapy with everyone in the room. They agreed. Doing family therapy worked better than individual therapy because family members could be questioned as to how they thought the fifteen-year-old would answer questions. This was often at the beginning of therapy.

Eventually, the young woman began to affirm or disagree with her family's speculations about her thoughts and feelings. This was a very beneficial strategic intervention.

Despite her eventual participation in therapy, the fifteen-year-old could not seem to let go of her sister's death. She said:

> If I don't keep on thinking of my sister, I'll never think of her again. It's painful, but I'm keeping her alive.

I asked the parents to bring in a photograph of their deceased daughter. I placed the picture (eight by ten inches) on an empty chair and asked the fifteen-year-old to talk to her sister and look at the photograph, rather than talking *about* her sister. At first this was awkward but the 15-year-old began to do this task and eventually grew to like to do this behavioral task. I reasoned that because she had a desire to keep her sister alive, I would let her do this in a more overt fashion. The first time she really opened up, she spoke to her sister's picture for almost thirty minutes. I encouraged the other family members to talk to the deceased child, also. I reserved the last fifteen minutes of the therapy hour for those "conversations with the baby."

In one session the sister said, "I would like to keep on talking to you but we have to go away now." I took the opportunity to say, "She has to go away, too." Soon the fifteen-year-old picked up my phraseology and would say good-bye to her sister at the end of each session by saying, "I'm sorry but I know you have to go." In therapy, we began to discuss that the fifteen-year-old was a victim of an "incomplete mourning process." She needed to talk to her sister and eventually say good-bye to her. After several more weeks the fifteen-year-old said at the end of therapy to her sister's picture:

> I'm sorry but I know you have to go. I'd like you to stay but you can't. I have to go, too. I'll always remember you. You'll always be in my heart but I have to say good-bye. I don't need to see you next week. I can still talk to you in my heart.

Instead of letting her mother take the picture home, she picked up the picture and told her parents:

> I'll take her home and put her up on the mantle where she belongs. I've said good-bye.

The behavioral task became the centerpiece of the therapy. The young woman needed a consistent behavioral task, in the presence of her family, to help her complete the mourning process.

I used a variation on this task with an eighteen-year-old male client who was depressed and had suicidal thoughts when his girlfriend of two years dumped him. He said that he tried not to think about her and tried to "put her out of my head." This did not work. Thoughts about her would creep into his head at the most inopportune times (e.g., taking a test). A song would come on the radio and it reminded him of her. He would pass by a park bench where they had sat and his mind would be flooded with her image. He described himself as being "haunted by her."

I told him that he was suffering from an incomplete mourning process. I explained that the reason why he was having intrusive thoughts about her was that he was not spending any time thinking about her. He told me that he was afraid that, if he started to think about her, he couldn't shut it off. I asked him if he had an alarm clock. He explained that he did. I gave him the following behavioral task. I told him that each day he needed to arrange to have a half-hour of time in his house (he lived in a house with his family) where he was home alone with nobody else in the house. At that time he should set the alarm clock for fifteen minutes. He should then get pictures of his former girlfriend and CD's of songs that he associated with her. I told him to play the music and look at the pictures and think of her. I told him that until the alarm clock rang (after fifteen minutes), he had his therapist's permission to act any way he needed to act. If he needed to cry, he should cry. If he needed to scream and yell, he should do so. If he needed to cuss up a storm, he should spend the time cussing. Once the alarm rang, he should shut it off, stop playing the CD, and put the pictures away. I told him that he needed to do that every day without fail. He asked me, "Why should I do that?" I explained that if he couldn't get her out of his system, she would always be there. If he did this every day, when he had an intrusive thought about her, he could say to her, "I can't think about you now but I will tonight at seven o'clock." "You can make a date with her in your mind for later." He asked me, "How long do I have to do this?" I answered, "Until you don't have to do it anymore."

He tried doing this task for a week and decided that it was more trouble than it was worth. She still invaded his thoughts and he lost another half-hour of time. However, by the second week, the intrusive thoughts started to diminish. So did his suicidal ideation. By the third week the suicidal ideation was gone and the intrusive thoughts greatly diminished. By the fifth week he set his alarm clock for "old girlfriend time" every other day. In another two weeks, he sat the alarm only once a week. After eight weeks, the young man declared that he didn't have to have any more "alarm clock talks" with her. While this task was being carried out, we still did therapy. The therapy assisted him in diminishing his necessity to mourn. However, the task cleared his mind of intrusive thoughts so that therapy could progress forward. In this way, behavioral tasks can allow the therapy to progress and the suicidal threat to diminish.

Whether it is the core of the therapeutic process or if it is used to augment another form of therapy, behavioral contracts and tasks can be useful to the therapist. In the middle of a very complicated psychosocial process, behavioral interventions bring the suicidal adolescent's attention down to a more simplistic, concrete focus. When life has become so complex that it has immobilized the adolescent from being able to act, behavioral interventions give the adolescent a set of recipes to move forward. In a world where the act of taking one's own life seems the only clear choice to tame and harness life's vicissitudes, behavioral therapy gives the suicidal adolescent other concrete choices which can clarify other choices for the adolescent to exercise. These choices don't have the finality and permanence of death.

Eleven

STRATEGIC INTERVENTIONS
The Art of Overcoming the Fear of Change

There are times when, despite the therapist's best efforts and the clients' hard work, direct interventions, either cognitive or behavioral, simply do not work. In some cases, the clients are not feeling enough pain to motivate them to change. In cases in which an adolescent is suicidal, this is seldom the case. If the adolescent is to the point of seriously considering taking his or her own life, there is typically a large amount of pain experienced by both the adolescent and the entire family. In fact, if the therapist does not sense any pain in one or more members of the family, the therapist needs to explore that dynamic immediately. Flat affect in the face of a loved one's imminent death is a sign that there are strong covert forces at work in the family. These need to be identified and discussed by the clients and the therapist.

It is more likely that therapy has stalled out because the suicidal adolescent, some members of his or her family, or both have become frightened at the prospect of change and have, therefore, become resistant to the prime objective of therapy to bring about change. Remember, resistance is expected in strategic therapy. If the clients become resistant to more direct methods of change, as put forth in the previous two chapters, the strategic therapist must shift to more indirect means of intervention. Even though the cognitive and behavioral interventions of the previous two chapters have strategic overtones to them, the client's resistance may force the therapist to use more indirect means of interventions to disrupt the maladaptive recursive cycles that have trapped the family into immobility. In these situations, strategic interventions can be extremely helpful. The research evidence on empirically-based strategic therapy is almost nonexistent. The only evidence-based research on the use of strategic family therapy with suicidal adolescents was the study reported by Jurich (1983a), in which strategic family therapy was shown to be very effective in remediating adolescent suicidal ideation. It is the strategic family therapy model that was employed in the study forming the basis for this chapter.

SLOWING THE PROCESS DOWN

In any therapeutic endeavor, one of the benefits to therapy is that it slows down the process surrounding the presenting problem. This is especially true when suicide becomes an issue in therapy. Suicidal clients will often refer to their life as "spinning out of control." When stressors pile up (McCubbin & Patterson, 1982), there is a feeling of acceleration of events surrounding those stressors. With suicidal clients, for whom control is such an issue, this feeling of acceleration is highly troublesome. As the client's life has been laid on the line with the threat of suicide, the potential for lethal consequences of "spinning out of control" makes this acceleration even more dangerous. Therefore, when the client and his or her family come into therapy, part of a good therapeutic process is to slow the process down. In doing so, the client and family are able to step out of the spinning vortex of the maladaptive recursive cycle and begin a more measured and less hurried look at the dynamics of the situation. I would label this as a strategic therapeutic maneuver because it creates a counterpoint to the panicked acceleration of the maladaptive recursive cycle that is spinning out of control outside the therapy room. However, almost any school of therapy utilizes this mechanism to assist in therapy.

With suicidal clients, especially adolescents, and their families, there is also a potential for a secondary acceleration of events, this time within the therapeutic process. In most cases of therapy, after the initial joining and assessment, the clients and the therapist begin to develop a rhythm for therapy. For some clients, this may be fairly slow. For others, it may be paced much faster. Family therapists must negotiate a rhythm for family therapy that respects and takes into account the rhythms of all the family members. With a suicidal adolescent and his or her family in family therapy, there are often some major discrepancies in the rhythms of the suicidal adolescent and the rest of the family. In these cases, two patterns often emerge.

The first pattern is one in which the suicidal adolescent wants to accelerate the pace of therapy much faster than his or her family wants to. In these cases, most typically, the suicidal adolescent comes to the realization that his or her suicidal ideation and actions were more extreme then they needed to be. He or she will typically say, "I can't believe that I was willing do die over this!" The adolescent is understandably embarrassed that he or she was so "out of control." Every time the adolescent feels more embarrassed at discussion of the events surrounding the suicidal thoughts, feelings, and actions and the treatment to remedy the situation with both the therapist and his or her family, the adolescent wants to accelerate the therapy so that he or she can put an end to the embarrassment. At the same time, the family wants to slow things down so that they can be sure that their adolescent will never become suicidal again. Some families may slow therapy down to a snail's pace in the hopes that obsessively exploring every detail will insulate the adolescent from ever feeling suicidal again. Needless to say, this situation will be stressful for both the suicidal adolescent and the family.

I believe that the therapist needs to make the covert overt, and normalize the feelings. The therapist can tell the suicidal adolescent that everyone feels embarrassed about how they act when they feel stressed out and scared. The therapist puts the feelings of embarrassment overtly "on the table" and normalizes feeling embarrassed as being typical for most people, including the therapist if he or she was in the adolescent's shoes. The therapist also needs to normalize the family members' caution as being generated by their fear that it could happen again. I tell the family that I know that they would like a guarantee that their adolescent will never again feel suicidal but that there are no guarantees in life. However, I also pledge to them that I will not only help all of them cope with the present situation but also with future situations so that suicide is not an option. I ask the adolescent to slow down his or her therapeutic process so that the gains he or she has made in therapy will have time to sink in and become part of a new behavioral pattern, a new way of looking at things, making suicide not a viable option in the future. I also ask the adolescent to work with me and the family through therapy so that none of his or her siblings will have to consider suicide as an option in their lives, either. I then define this as a heroic task. It is surprising how many suicidal adolescents are willing to slow their process down, not for their own sake, but for the sake of their siblings. Likewise, I ask him or her to slow down his or her process to demonstrate to his or her parents that he or she is, in fact, getting better and no longer considers suicide to be an option. Once again, adolescents who would like to rush through therapy will often be willing to help their parents calm down and stop worrying about them. This is especially true if they feel guilty about putting their parents through a lot of grief by having suicidal thoughts and feelings. This is a way to gain some control over their lives, paying back their parents by helping quell their anxiety. Lastly, I tell the adolescent that suicidal adolescents will often rush the therapeutic process if they are "blowing therapy off" and still are actively suicidal. The best way to demonstrate to me that they are no longer suicidal is to continue to progress through therapy at a measured pace. I tell them that, if he or she can't agree to slow down the pace of therapy, I may have no alternative except to consider him or her to be actively suicidal and reconsider hospitalization. This is an option that most adolescents would like to avoid. It is easier to slow down the process and cope with the normalized embarrassment of working in therapy. Once I get the suicidal adolescent to agree to slow down his or her pace, I ask the family to accelerate their pace slightly to match the adolescent's pace. My rationale is that, as he or she is the person who has been suicidal, that is the pace which will be most important in therapy for the family therapy to follow. Although they may have some reservations, most family members will agree to this.

The second pattern is more complicated. This occurs when the family would like to rush therapy and the suicidal adolescent begins to feel accelerated beyond his or her comfort level. Sometimes the family wants to quicken the pace of therapy because they feel a sense of stigma for having an adolescent who has felt suicidal. Although this is not the norm for families who have a suicidal adolescent, this group is important to recognize because they can be very counterproductive to successful therapy for the suicidal adolescent. When the family—even one family member—is more concerned with their own embarrassment than they are with the proper therapeutic treatment of their suicidal adolescent, it is doubtful that they will be much of a resource for the suicidal adolescent. As the therapist, if I thought that this was the case, I would confront the family members with the metamessage that their attempt to speed up therapy gives to the suicidal adolescent: his or her life is not worth their embarrassment. I would orchestrate this confrontation without the suicidal adolescent's being present because I want the family members to be honest with me about their feelings, and I am afraid to let a suicidal adolescent hear what they say. I did have a mother of a suicidal adolescent daughter say to me that she wished her daughter would "just stop dilly-dallying with her treatment and just get cured." The mother said that she was afraid that her friends would talk about her not being a good mother. I obviously did not want my adolescent client to hear her mother's remarks. If the family will agree to tolerate their embarrassment for the sake of their adolescent's treatment, family therapy can resume. If, however, they continue to place their feelings ahead of their suicidal adolescent's treatment, family therapy is contraindicated, at least for the moment, and the therapist should continue individual treatment. Although this has been very rare in my practice, it has occurred.

The much more typical reason for the suicidal adolescent's family's escalation of the pace of therapy is that they do not understand the nature of therapeutic treatment. Family members often compare psychotherapy to the only other treatment experience with which they are familiar, medical treatment for a physical injury. With most medical treatment the family has experienced, there is a specific diagnosis, a standard treatment protocol, and a predictable limited course of treatment. In psychotherapy, diagnoses are complicated and much less certain, treatment protocols differ from therapist to therapist—and sometimes differ within the course of therapy by one therapist—and the course of treatment is much less predictable. Because of the family's expectations, derived from their experience with the medical model, family members often have expectations of the course of therapy that are in conflict with their son's or daughter's course of therapy. These expectations are sometimes exacerbated by the unrealistic expectations imposed upon the therapy by some health maintenance organizations (HMOs). The therapist must explain to the family the nature of his or her therapeutic process with their adolescent and help them to readjust their expectations. I try to explain to them that, if it took 15 years (or whatever the age of the adolescent is) to get to this point of suicide, it will take some time to help their child move away from considering suicide as an option.

Once confronted with their unrealistic expectations for therapy, the vast majority of families will readjust their expectations. If it will help, I will break up the therapeutic process into six-week segments. At the end of each five weeks, the family, the suicidal adolescent, and I will reassess the therapeutic process in order to determine if the sixth session will be the beginning of a new six-week segment or will be our termination session. This gives the suicidal adolescent and the family a greater feeling of direction to and control over the therapy. It also gives them a structure within which they can allow the therapeutic process to slow down.

When a suicidal adolescent first comes into treatment, they typically feel that things are mounting so fast that life is unmanagable. The slower pacing of therapy works to decelerate the pace of the events swirling around them. However, after initial deceleration, most adolescents who embrace therapy begin to accelerate their therapy as they learn new cognitive perceptions and behaviors to use in their lives. They quicken their pace as they meet with success and feel more in control of their lives. This is typical of a lot of suicidal adolescents in therapy. However, some of these adolescents begin to move so fast that they become frightened at the pace of their process. They describe themselves as feeling "out on a limb." Adolescents who have previously described themselves as "being on an uncontrolable roller-coaster ride, travelling" toward suicide may begin to feel the same feelings of uneasiness and lack of control over their lives. The therapist needs to keep his or her finger on the "pulse" of the adolescent in order to discern when the adolescent is beginning to feel anxiety that the pace of therapy is going too fast for his or her comfort. When the therapist feels this begin to happen (the therapist may very well feel the beginning of that anxiety before the adolescent client becomes aware of that feeling), the therapist needs to counter an acceleration back into the maladaptive recursive cycle by slowing the pace of therapy down. The suicidal adolescent may not even be aware of the slowing pace but his or her ease with the process will assist him or her to benefit most from therapy.

ADJUSTING IMMEDIACY

Previously, I have mentioned the utility of using Weiner and Mehrabian's concept of Immediacy (1968) to understand clients' behavior during their progression toward suicidal ideation and behavior during therapy. The concept of immediacy can also be used in Strategic Therapy in order to help the client progress in bringing about change in therapy. In Chapter 8, I gave an example of a case I had in which the fifteen-year-old female client had been dumped by her old boyfriend because she was too jealous and bossy. This event triggered suicidal feelings in the young woman and her parents brought her into therapy. Her mother demonstrated the same bossy attitude of which her daughter had been accused. This case was used as an example of the transgenerational transference of maladaptive recursive cycles, in this case from the mother to the daughter.

The therapy in this case proved to be a challenge because neither the mother nor the daughter would admit to being bossy or jealous, even though their behaviors could easily be labeled as such. Each woman saw the bossiness and jealousy in each other but not in themselves. My therapeutic efforts to work with insight-oriented explanations of their need to control their environments in order to maintain predictability and safety in their lives were met with denial and resistance. Each thought that my insight about needing control was "on-target" for the other woman but not for herself. Faced with this resistance I shifted gears to Strategic Therapy.

I gave them the hypothetical example of a six-year-old girl who did not know how to cope with a group of girls at school who were unpredictable in their behavior towards her. Sometimes they got along well and they were very nice to her. At other times, they ignored her or seemed to prefer the company of the other kids. I asked the mother and her fifteen-year-old daughter what they thought the little girl should do? They both agreed that the little girl should take a leadership role in the group and initiate things to do. If the other girls tried to ignore her, she should pursue them and "make them understand" what a good time they would all have if they followed her suggestions. Both the mother and the daughter agreed that this would be an excellent strategy for the six-year-old to employ.

I then asked them what the little girl in the example should do if, as a result, the other girls called her "bossy"? At first, neither the mother nor daughter felt that the other girls had any reason to call her bossy. After further discussion, both the mother and daughter admitted that some of this little girl's behavior could be viewed as bossy, but that was because they didn't understand that the little girl was not trying to control them but, instead, felt scared and was trying to simply "be safe." The fifteen-year-old daughter said that the little girl's first impulse might be to run away but she should stay and "talk things out" with the other girls and try not to be jealous. The mother said that the little girl should confront the other girls with the fact that she was not, in fact, bossy and tell them that they were all going to play together and be happy!

What the mother and daughter could not discuss for themselves in their own situation could be discussed in terms of giving advice to a six-year-old girl about how to handle her playmates. The dynamics were identical. I framed them in a hypothetical situation with a child. They could discuss the less immediate situation and carry on a reasonable and fruitful discussion about it. In fact, after further discussion, both the mother and her teenage daughter agreed that the little girl should try to calmly talk with her friends, even if she had to get a teacher to moderate. These clients were very pleased with their mutual conclusion in this case. I told them that I was proud that they could have such a fruitful discussion about their *own* problems. They both looked at me like I had lobsters crawling out of my ears. I pointed out that they were both like the little girl, trying to control a dangerous and anxiety-provoking situation by trying to take a leadership role. They had both been accused of being "bossy" and both of them rejected that label, yet they both gave the hypothetical little girl advice to handle the situation as they had done.

In her own situation, the daughter had tried to run away by feeling suicidal, then thought that it would be better to talk to her boyfriend, but felt too jealous to do that successfully. The mother tried to deal with the anxiety of therapy by trying to take over the therapy process. However, they both agreed that it would be best to rationally discuss the situation (therapy), even if they had to have a teacher (therapist) moderate it. Once I congratulated them on the wisdom of their logic and their choices, it was much easier for them to carry on future discussions in therapy in the "here and now" (high immediacy), rather than discussing hypothetically about 6-year-olds (low immediacy). Temporarily shifting to a less immediate venue, the imaginary school yard, for our discussions, however, had effectively disrupted their resistance, which had become a maladaptive recursive cycle that kept them from moving forward in therapy. Once the cycle had been disrupted, both the mother and the daughter became less anxious and therefore more able to recognize their own roles disrupting the progress of therapy.

MAKE THE COVERT, OVERT

Making the covert dynamics of a situation overt to the clients is one of the most powerful strategic interventions any therapist can employ. (So much of the power of a maladaptive recursive cycle hinges upon the fact that it is steeped in covert dynamics. Becomming cognitively aware of the mechanisms keeping these maladaptive recursive cycles running does much to reduce their power.) What you don't know can hurt you much more than what you do know! In fact, so powerful is this single intervention that, in my role as a therapist educator, I have labeled it as my number one rule of therapy: "When in doubt—shout it out!"

I tell my students that, when they are stuck in therapy and nothing is going the way they want it to go, they should recognize their feelings (most likely frustration and incompetence), tell the clients their feelings, and simply say they are confused as to what to do next: "When in doubt—shout it out!"

The majority of young therapists are most frightened that they will get stuck in the therapy process, they will feel and look incompetent, and the client will leave in disgust. Therefore, in fear of that moment, the student therapist becomes anxious and tries to obsessively control the therapy process. Paradoxically, the more they obsess and try to control, the worse it gets. It becomes a self-fulfilling prophecy. Therefore, I designed a simple rule for the student to blurt out when they are stuck and the anxiety starts to build.

This intervention works for many strategic reasons. First, and foremost, it makes the covert dynamics fueling the maladaptive recursive cycle overt to both the client family and to the therapist. It puts them on the table, "front and center." It creates a demand for the dynamics that are causing the therapy to be "stuck" to be discussed here and now (a very "immediate" situation). The professional, with all his or her knowledge and training, takes a one-down position and admits to being frustrated or feeling incompetent and to being confused as to what is going on. Typical clients would not expect the "expert" to admit he or she doesn't know the answer. This violates some of the hidden assumptions about therapy upon which the maladaptive recursive cycle is built and forces the clients to reconstruct their ideas about therapy. It gives them a share of the expert role. The therapist models honest and open feelings in the here and now. When I did my "When in doubt—shout it out" with a farm couple, the husband turned to the wife and said, "Shit! Finally someone who is willing to be honest with us!" This rule also sets the groundwork for bringing in a supervisor or a consultant to help with the process if necessary. In my 34 years of training therapists, it is amazing how many of my students have sought refuge in that phrase when they got stuck in therapy: When in doubt—shout it out!

Making the covert overt is especially important for suicidal adolescents and their families. Adolescents are trying to create their own independent ego identity. Therefore, autonomy and control over their environment is a very important issue (Jurich, 1987). Control over one's life is a crucial issue among those individuals who are considering suicide as an option in their lives (Jurich, 2002a). Therefore, control over his or her life is a very important element in the suicidal adolescent's life. This is why a maladaptive recursive cycle, fueled by covert dynamics, pushing the suicidal adolescent to the edge of the cliff, is such a powerful force. It is also why exposing the covert elements of this cycle is a very powerful intervention for the suicidal adolescent.

The utility of making the covert overt is so pervasive in treating suicidal adolescents that the previous pages of this book are filled with examples. In Chapter 8, I cited a case in which a seventeen-year-old sexual abuse victim used her suicidal actions to expose her father's sexual abuse of her. In this case the seventeen-year-old made the family's covert secret (Dad's sexual abuse) overt by taking an overdose of sleeping pills in the girls' bathroom during school hours. As her mother and father chose to keep Dad's sexual abuse covert and secret, the daughter made it very overt with a very public suicide attempt. Sometimes it is up to the therapist to make the covert overt. Again, in Chapter 8, I gave the case example of the family who had threatened their children that the gypsies would come and get them if they did not behave. As silly as this childhood myth may have been, it still held a great deal of power in the lives of the children, even when they became adolescents. A large portion of the power of this threat was that it lived on through subtle and covert means (e.g., humming "Green Tambourine"). When the therapist explored this covert threat, much of the power of the old myth evaporated. In this way, "making the covert overt" deflates the power of the more covert aspects of the maladaptive recursive cycle, allowing it to be examined in therapy and better understood by the client. Beneath each rock are creepy, crawly creatures who can't stand the light of day. Once they are exposed to the sun, they shrivel up and blow away.

REDIRECTING THE FLOW OF ENERGY

In every system, there is a flow of energy. In a biological system, such as a human body, there is an influx of energy through inhaling, eating, and drinking. There is an egress of energy through exhaling, urination, and excretion. Likewise, in a human system there is an energy flow through the transfer of information from the speaker to the listener and a feedback loop of information from the listener back to the speaker (Watzlawick et al., 1967). This is elementary Systems Theory. Likewise, in therapy there is a flow of energy, via communications, among the family members, including the client, and between family members and the therapist. When therapy is going smoothly, this energy flow represents a collaborative process in which exchanges of energy ebb and flow, according to the needs and abilities of the clients and the skill of the therapist. To use a baseball metaphor, the therapist and clients are "in a zone." In this state, therapy can proceed along a steady course with few interruptions.

Although the strategic therapist revels in these periods of "in the zone" therapy, he or she does not expect them to last. As the process of therapy moves forward, the suicidal adolescent may become frightened of the changes that therapy is instigating. This does not mean that the suicidal adolescent lacks courage or fortitude. It means that the adolescent's journey to a healthier method of functioning contains a lot of unknowns. It is the fear of those unknowns and the changes they may bring in his or her life that create resistance to change in the adolescent. Similar fears of the unknown can create resistance in the suicidal adolescent's other family members.

In order to cope with this increased resistance to change, the clients shift their framework from the image of collaborative team members accomplishing a mutual goal to a vision of a group of anxious soldiers (the clients) being led into battle by a "gung-ho" commander (the therapist) to fight a battle whose outcome the soldiers doubt. This is quite a different image than the collaborative team working together towards a common goal. Instead of harmony and unity of purpose, the clients restructure the energy flow of the therapy into adversarial roles with the therapist on the opposing side. This typically takes the form of "therapist and the family vs. the suicidal adolescent." It is at this point that more direct interventions (such as many of these which were suggested in the previous two chapters) start to break down and the therapeutic process becomes "stuck." Regardless of the best intentions and skills of the therapist, suicidal adolescents, with or without family, will begin to treat the therapist as an adversary and begin to defend themselves against a person whom they now believe is dangerous to the safety of the future. As long as the suicidal adolescent and/or his or her family define the therapist in this way, therapeutic progress will grind to a halt.

If the therapist attempts to be truly client-centered (Rogers, 1951) and work at the client's own pace, the client may lead the therapy into many detours or dead-ends before getting back on track in therapy. This may frustrate the rest of the suicidal adolescent's family who see no progress being made. It will send insurance companies and HMOs through the roof, causing them to limit or cut off the client's reimbursement for services. In addition, a suicidal client who achieves some degree of success in therapy, only to have therapy subsequently become frozen by the chill of resistance, may blame himself or herself for the "failure" in therapy. This could lead to depression, further feelings of loss of control, and another suicidal episode. Therefore, giving in to the resistance would be contraindicated.

A therapist could try to push the suicidal adolescent and his or her family through the resistance—in essence, trying to force them to change. This is problematic for several reasons. First, the therapist is accepting the role of the adversary, which the client or clients have given him or her. An old adage with a second verse added by Kansan farmers is appropriate here:

> You can lead a horse to water,
> But you can't make him drink.
> If you do try to make him drink,
> He will either kick you in the groin,
> Or run away.

If the client feels attacked by an adversary, he or she will either fight or flee. If the suicidal adolescent decides to fight, he or she can lash out at the therapist in defense of his or her "attacked" identity, something that the adolescent is still trying to develop. Because adolescents are especially sensitive to accomplishing their primary developmental task, developing their own independent ego identity is extremely important for their perceived survival. Because adolescents are in their molten stage of identity development, they feel very vulnerable to attacks on their identities from others. Their reactions to such perceived threats may be forceful and extreme. Many adolescents could attempt to commit suicide as an aggressive attempt to exact revenge on a therapist who pushed them too hard and too fast.

When a therapist tries to push the suicidal adolescent through his or her resistance, the therapist assumes the "expert role" and asks or demands the adolescent to follow. The power lies with the therapist, instead of its being shared with the suicidal adolescent. This may reawaken and perpetuate the feelings of helplessness that so often accompany suicidal clients. Once again, this may push the suicidal adolescents back into another suicidal episode. If the suicidal adolescent decides not to fight back, he or she may choose to flee the confrontive therapist by either quitting therapy or reapproaching suicide as an escape from life. Neither of these is an acceptable solution to the problem. Therefore, pushing the suicidal adolescent and his or her family is also contraindicated. So if the therapist can't give in to the client's resistance and can't fight through the resistance, what is a therapist to do?

It is at times like these when the techniques of strategic therapy are very useful. Rather than trying to go along with the energy flow of the resistance or trying to confront it, the therapist can redirect the flow of energy. Instead of trying to "create energy" by externally persuading the suicidal adolescent to change, the strategic therapist attempts to "redirect the flow of energy" so that the suicidal adolescent will see the motivation to change as stemming from the set of circumstances that led to his or her suicidal thoughts, feelings, or actions. At first, that source of motivation to change may be anything other than the therapist's wishes or desires. The motivation may be attributable to the family's wishes or desires, peer pressure, or societal expectations for an adolescent of his or her age. Instead of using the therapist as a target of the suicidal adolescent's resistance to change, the therapist redirects the object of the resistance to another entity.

For example, in a court-ordered case where the adolescent was ordered to go to therapy, it is easy for the adolescent client to transfer all of these negative feelings from the police officer who arrested him or her, from the judge who handed down the sentence, and from his or her parents who were judgmental and scolding in their attitude to the therapist who must carry out the court order to do therapy. All of the anger towards those other people, the fear of the unknown, and self-doubts as to whether the adolescent can progress in therapy are all projected upon the therapist. This is a set of dynamics more suited to adversarial competition rather than mutual respect and collaboration. However, if the therapist can redirect the flow of energy, the client can be able to transfer this resistance to some other entity (for example, the courts) and, thereby, can free the therapist to at least comment on the situation from a more neutral vantage point. Eventually, the therapist might be able to convince the client that the therapist is on his or her side, setting up a collaboration between them. Using the example of the court-ordered therapy, the therapist might tell the client that the goal of therapy doesn't have to be to change to meet some idealistic image imposed by the society. The goal of court-appointed therapy is to do the things that will lead the therapist to write the client a good letter to the court, so that the client can stop coming to therapy. The therapist can explain that the court wants to hear three things in the letter to the court:

1. The client has shown up for appointments.
2. The client has worked hard in therapy.
3. The client has made some progress on the presenting problem.

The therapist needs to establish "out front" that he or she will not lie in the letter. However, the therapist can then offer the client his or her help in collaborating together in the task of being able to write a good but honest letter to the court to get the client out of any further trouble with the law and eventually finish with court-ordered therapy. In this case, the therapist has joined with the client to cope with the task imposed by the court system. Any client resistance is directed towards the courts and not the therapist, (who is faced to collaborate together with the client).

Once the object of the resistance has been transferred to another entity, like the court system, the therapist can begin to work with the client to realize that the motivation for change is not really tied to an outside entity but rests within the client. To use the above example, the therapist can tell the client that writing a good letter to the courts is a good goal to have but that the client also would benefit by some internal motivation to change so that he or she never gets into this type of trouble with the law again. Once a client accepts some internal motivation for wanting to change, he or she will become a much better participant in therapy and more can be accomplished in the therapeutic process. This reestablishes a collaboration relationship between the client and the therapist. In family therapy, this collaboration process would also include family members as crucial elements of successful therapy. Everybody can help motivate the client to change but therapy works best when the client is self-motivated to change in therapy. This is a primary goal of Strategic Therapy. For suicidal adolescents, for whom control is such an issue, centering the motivation for change squarely on their shoulders is not only useful for the therapy process but it also validates the suicidal adolescent as an individual who is able to take responsibility and control over his or her life. Therapy with the suicidal adolescent can now get back on track.

FOCUSING ON DISCREPANCIES

Suicidal adolescents who build a wall of resistance to block the therapeutic process attempt to present a web of solid, logical arguments as to why therapeutic change should be avoided. It is upon this logic that the adolescent grounds his or her resistance. If the therapist can find some discrepancy in the structure of logic, the resistance will crumble from lack of support. These discrepancies may be one of three types: (1) intrapersonal, (2) interpersonal, or (3) objective. Each will be addressed with a case study example.

Intrapersonal Discrepancies

One of the most efficient strategic tactics to reduce resistance is for the therapist to look for discrepancies between what the suicidal adolescent says at one time and what he or she says at a later time that contradicted the first statement. Sometimes, these discrepancies will be simple contradictions of what has already been said. In Chapter 8, I presented a case of a reluctant beauty queen who was relieved when she was not accepted as a contestant for a beauty pageant but her mother was devastated that her daughter did not gain acceptance. The eighteen-year-old daughter felt guilty that she had so disappointed her mother that she began having suicidal ideation. Her mother was shocked that her daughter would have suicidal thoughts over a beauty pageant. This case was fraught with intrapersonal incongruities. As the therapist, I pointed out to the suicidal eighteen-year-old that she had given her mother two contradicting messages. When her mother first prompted her to enter the beauty pageant, she enthusiastically agreed to do so. She explained that she was trying to please her mom and believed that her mother would, in time, forget about the contest. Later, when she did not qualify for the event, the daughter told her mother that she felt relieved. A large part of that was the truth but she was also trying to spare her mother's feelings by minimizing her loss. When she was confronted with her mother's disappointment, she was convinced that she did some horrible thing to her mom. She became trapped in a maladaptive recursive cycle in which she was to blame for her mother's misery. I told this young woman that, although her logic made those two messages very understandable, she did not present her logic to her mother. Therefore, all Mom heard her daughter say was that she "really wanted" to be in the show and she was really glad she wasn't in the show. These two contradictory remarks added confusion to the mother's perception of the situation. Therefore, some of her mother's disappointment reaction was fueled by Mom's misunderstanding of the true nature of the daughter's feelings that she really felt out of place as a contestant and was genuinely relieved not to get in. The mother said that she would have been less disappointed if she would have known her daughter's true feelings. Pointing out this discrepancy eased back the adolescent from her suicidal thoughts. She felt less trapped in her maladaptive recursive cycle.

Some intrapersonal discrepancies are more complicated. On the surface, the two contradictory statements may appear to be compatible. It is only after further examination of the consequences of these statements that the logical conclusions are contradictory. A fifteen-year-old female had suicidal ideation and some cutting behavior in response to her failing grades at school. On one hand, she described herself as being "a total and absolute failure." However, she also said that she "deserved more than what the teachers gave" her. On the surface, these two remarks do not seem to be incompatible. It seems possible that a person could fail and still deserve more from her teachers. However, three weeks into therapy, the client became resistant to direct approaches to challenging her thinking or behaviors. She appeared to be frightened that, if she changed as a result of therapy, she would be forced to become more responsible at school, a task for which she lacked confidence. Therefore, her resistance to therapy grew. In order to break this maladaptive recursive cycle, I asked the client if she felt like a "little failure" or a "total failure"? Sensing that I was going to try to block her resistance, she gave me the more extreme answer, "total failure." I reminded her that she had said, in the past, that she had deserved more than she had gotten from her teacher. She agreed. I then asked her how she could hold two such contradictory statements? She looked puzzled. I explained:

> Your two statements contradict themselves. If you are truly a "total failure," why would you deserve to have anyone "do better by me"? Likewise, if you deserved more effort from your teacher to help you, you are not a "total failure." Can you help me understand how you can be a total failure and deserve more help at the same time?

As long as the young woman could hold both those thoughts at the same time, she could feel sorry for herself and also feel self-righteously indignant about not receiving help from her teacher. For this client, this was a comfortable place to be. Consequently, her motivation for encouraging change in therapy was severely diminished and resistance rose. By taking a "one-down position" in asking her to help me understand how she resolves this discrepancy, I strategically forced her to surrender one or both of her beliefs that formed the foundation for her comfortable position. This disrupted her maladaptive recursive cycle. I told her that I agreed with her that she deserved more from her teacher than what she had gotten, but I said that the consequence of believing that was to admit to herself that she was not a "total failure." Therefore, she was not helpless and, in fact, with the proper help, could take an active role in raising her grades. This was not the conclusion the suicidal adolescent wanted to draw. In fact, it was the one she was resisting. However, it was better than the cognitive dissonance I caused her by pointing out the discrepancy in her logic, using the logical conclusions, based on her own words.

Interpersonal Discrepancies

Discrepancies between or among people are often evident when conducting family therapy. There are many occasions where one family member makes a statement that is later brought into dispute by a statement by another family member. In the above-mentioned case of the reluctant beauty queen, the suicidal adolescent woman began having suicidal thoughts when she thought that her mother was "devastated" at her not being accepted as a contestant for the beauty pageant. When her mother was shocked at her daughter's suicidal ideation over not being a contestant, the daughter was confused. She told her mother:

> Mom, the reason why I felt so bad is that I thought that I had let you down. You said you felt devastated! Now you're making it sound like you thought it was no big deal!

Her mother responded:

> I wasn't devastated! I was disappointed for you but I wasn't devastated! Dear, you overreacted. That's why you're in therapy and we're all here to help you with your problem.

Everyone in the family sat in silence. Instead of validating the "family nature" of the concern, the mother had extracted herself from any contribution to the daughter's suicidal ideation. To gain allies among the other family members, she added the fact that as this was obviously the daughter's overreaction, the rest of the family, including her, were there to help the daughter with the daughter's problem—her suicidal ideation. This left the daughter feeling blindsided and off-balance. The daughter felt as if she had lost touch with reality. Perhaps she really was crazy.

At the time the mother did this, I was setting the stage where the family could gain insight into the relative importance of beauty pageants in the "grand scheme of things" in an attempt to have both the daughter and the mother change their cognitions by gaining some perspective on the event. I had hypothesized that the mother was more "grounded in reality" because of their relative ages and the wisdom that would come through the mother's experience in living. The mother's response about not being devastated fit that tentative hypothesis. However, the mother's denial about being devastated was too absolute. If the mother had said that she was upset but that her daughter had overinterpreted her feelings as being more extreme than they actually were, I would have considered that to be in the realm of possibility. We could have proceeded to work on the perspective that was needed about the beauty pageant for the daughter, primarily (having a teenager's perspective about the disappointment of life), and, secondarily, for the mother who had expressed her disappointment in her own right. This did not happen. The mother said that the only reason why she "felt bad" was because her daughter was so disappointed. That logic made it her daughter's problem only. It redefined therapy as individual therapy, rather than family therapy. Furthermore, it directly contradicted the daughter's report of the family dynamics.

As I could no longer pursue a course of cognitive therapy, I initiated strategic therapy. I pointed out the contradiction between the daughter's version of the story and the mother's. This was recognizing the proverbial "elephant in the room." It made the covert overt. The tension in the room rose substantially, although no one uttered a word. I broke the silence by asking if anyone in the family had videotaped Mom's response? There were a few smiles at the absurdity of the question, followed by more silence. I then said the following:

> Well guys, I'm stuck! I'm at a crossroads and I don't know which way to turn. If [the daughter's] version of Mom's reaction is correct, we have some work to do as a family. If Mom's version is correct, I will have to do some individual work with [the daughter] to test her perceptions of reality before we can move onto family matters. "Whose view is correct?" is a very important question and a lot rides on the answer to that question.

One of the younger siblings said:

Mom went ballistic. We all heard it!

Although Mom protested vigorously, gradually every family member eventually confirmed the young child's statement. One of the major maladaptive recursive cycles in this family was the myth that Mom was too fragile to be confronted. Nobody in the family would contradict the mother, even if he or she knew Mom was wrong. Therefore, the mother had started to alter reality whenever it relieved her of responsibility when something went wrong. Working with such a handicap when problem-solving, few issues were resolved very well in family discussions. The family was trapped in this maladaptive recursive cycle. This fueled the daughter's not wanting to disappoint her mother and accelerated into suicidal ideation. However, the daughter's suicidal ideation so scared the other family members that they saw the daughter as more fragile than the mother and unveiled the maladaptive recursive cycle.

Subsequently, I normalized the mother's wanting to minimize her contribution to her daughter's suicidal ideation and asked her to heroically accept her responsibility in this matter. Using the scheme presented in Chapter 5, I "hooked" both the mother and daughter into the intervention by giving both versions of the story equal weight and not judging which version I believed to be correct. My "slam" was setting the situation in motion for the family to unveil what had actually happened and to expose the maladaptive recursive cycle to everybody's scrutiny. I then rejoined with the whole family, especially Mom. We could then commence with family therapy.

Objective Discrepancies

Sometimes a client will make a statement that simply does not fit with reality. If a client is offering resistance to therapeutic change by referencing a heart condition that the rest of the family can demonstrate doesn't exist (through previously done medical tests), the therapist can pin the client's story on reality. This will reduce the resistance that was built upon the story that was discrepant with reality, as it is in most cases.

However, caution must be exercised, especially when dealing with suicidal adolescents. If a suicidal adolescent is desperate enough, he or she may have constructed a rigid "reality" to provide safety for him or her, even though that alternative reality may have a little or no resemblance to any objective reality. To the suicidal adolescent, there may be no back-up plan to an alternative reality. Objective reality may simply be too painful to confront. Therefore, without their alternative reality, there is nothing. The denial of an objective reality may be the last action of a desperate person. If it is taken away from him or her, there may be nothing left but oblivion. In this case, suicide could be the likely outcome of taking away the adolescent's view of the situation, even though it may have little basis in reality.

In some cases, the therapist can keep the suicidal adolescent's construction of reality as a temporary device until the adolescent can better join with the therapist and gain a degree of safety in the therapy room. Eventually, this rigid view can be gently examined by the therapist and the client to tease away where this rigid viewpoint is in conflict with a more objective reality. This is a delicate and arduous process in which the suicidal adolescent must be kept safe from self-harm. Because of this, this type of therapy is best done in an in-patient unit with access to medication. It can be done in out-patient therapy but there are enough dangers possible that the therapist should be encouraged to select in-patient therapy as the treatment of choice in most cases.

Focusing on a client's discrepancies can reduce the logic upon which his or her resistance is built. In this task, the therapist must be reactive to the discrepancies presented by the suicidal adolescents, their family, or some objective criteria. The therapist needs to be patient for these discrepancies to present themselves and to redirect the systemic energy flow to advocate for change in therapy. In pointing out these discrepancies, the therapist needs to be direct and overt but also nurture the suicidal adolescent and his or her family members so that they do not feel criticized and abandoned by the therapist. After the hook and slam disrupts the client's logic, the therapist must rejoin with the suicidal adolescent and the rest of the family to keep them together as a team, striving for a goal: therapeutic change.

REFRAMING

There are times where the clients do not express any discrepancies. There are also cases in which, given a long enough length of time, the clients would demonstrate discrepancies, but there is a time pressure to disrupt the maladaptive recursive cycle sooner rather than later. This latter situation is often the case in doing therapy with a suicidal adolescent, where the possibility of active suicidal behavior necessitates a quick response to disrupt the maladaptive recursive cycle that fuels the resistance to more direct forms of therapy. One way to accomplish this is through the use of "reframes." "Reframing" is the taking of the suicidal adolescent's or the family's description or logic of an event and relabeling it in a way that would be more conducive to bringing about change. For example, an adolescent male who says that he can't talk to a girl he likes is expressing his feelings of helplessness at broaching a conversation with the young woman. This definition of his problem is problematic for several reasons. It gives the adolescent no information as to why he will not approach the young woman. Therefore, it offers the adolescent no added perspective that could help him do things differently. The word "can't" implies an external locus of control in which the young man is not able to approach the young woman. If he is unable to approach her, he is certainly unable to change his thoughts, feelings, or behaviors in order to obtain a more desired outcome. Therefore, such a sentence creates, for this young man, a maladaptive recursive cycle in which he is stuck.

However, if the therapist were to "reframe" that sentence to "Because I feel self-conscious, I choose not to approach this young woman," the dynamics of the situation dramatically shift. The verb shifts from "can't" to "choose not to." Whereas the former implies helplessness and an external locus of control, the latter implies choice and an internal locus of control. Therapy with a person who has choice in his decision-making consists of exploring different courses of action and using problem-solving techniques to choose the best alternative. This is quite different from doing therapy with a young man who "can't approach a girl." If he truly cannot take action, he can't choose a new course of behavior. Therefore, therapy is important to bring about any changes on his behalf. Furthermore, in the reframe of the young man's message, there is some speculative information about the young man's motivation for not approaching the young woman. This gives the therapist and the young man something to discuss concerning the ways to alter that motivation in a way that might bring about a change of behavior. The reframe of the client's definition will be more conducive to bringing about therapeutic change than the client's original depiction of the event.

Reframes may be of two types. One reframe may redefine an act or situation in a less acceptable way than the client had defined it. Once this is done, the client has received a definition of his or her actions which prompts him or her not to continue that action, lest he or she be defined in an unfavorable way (Haley, 1984). For example, I had a seventeen-year-old male client with a lot of suicidal ideation. When he spoke about his suicidal thoughts in therapy, he always referred to suicide as being a noble sacrifice for others. As long as he held onto that framework of suicide's being noble, suicide would be an attractive alternative for him. I noticed that whenever he referred to suicide as being noble, both the mother and the father winced noticeably. I pointed that out to the entire family and asked them how they felt about suicide's being noble. They both said that they disagreed that suicide was noble. I asked them, "Well, if it isn't noble, what is it?" They had no answer. I asked the parents if they viewed suicide as "a coward's way out." At first, they thought that my reframe was rather harsh. I proceeded to describe suicide as "a way to avoid talking responsibility because it was too scary to do so." Although they hesitated at first, both parents agreed with my reframe of suicide as a cowardly, rather than a noble action. Needless to say, the suicidal adolescent did not like this reframe. It took away the nobility of suicide and redefined it in a way that subverted its positive appeal. It broke him out of his maladaptive recursive cycle.

Another type of reframe could take a negative definition of an action or a situation and turn it to connote a positive meaning. I had a case of a suicidal fifteen-year-old female who described herself as a "loser" all of her life. When I asked her what "loser" meant, she explained that she was a "below-average student" with below-average looks, and a shyness which kept her from being very sociable. She described herself as being "a person with few friends and few prospects." Her parents were in the middle of a bloody divorce. They complained that their daughter did not help them out and, in fact, made matters worse. This made the fifteen-year-old feel even worse and she began to feel suicidal. One night, after a particularly venomous argument between the mother and the father, the fifteen-year-old took an overdose of pills. Mom and Dad rushed her to the emergency room. Upon release from the hospital, the parents took her to see me for therapy.

When I said that I wanted to see the entire family, they equivocated at first, and then agreed to come in as a triad (mother, father, daughter). The father described the daughter's suicide attempt as "stupid." He said that, "It was another example of his daughter making things harder for herself and them." He was especially perturbed by the timing of the suicide attempt: right in the middle of the "bloody divorce." I asked both the daughter and her parents to consider that the fifteen-year-old's suicide attempt may have had a different motivation. Because of her parents' contentious divorce, the fifteen-year-old had two of the most important people in her life seeming to hate each other, they were breaking up their marriage, and there was not a damn thing that she could do about it. I posed to all three of them that:

> On some level, [the daughter] engaged in a behavior that got Mom and Dad to stop fighting, to work as a team to get her to the hospital, and to set aside, at least for a few hours, their bickering and fighting. I think that [the daughter] was playing the role of "white knight," trying to bring you parents back together.

This reframe floored the parents and even puzzled the fifteen-year-old. They struggled with this concept for a while but eventually embraced the idea. What this reframe accomplished was to positively connote a motivation to the adolescent which would break up the maladaptive recursive cycle in which the daughter was a loser who was causing more problems than she was worth. That maladaptive recursive cycle looked like a recipe for the suicide of the adolescent. Therefore, the positive reframe I placed upon her behavior labeled her as a competent, caring, adult, who was overtaking responsibility for her parents but who was doing so for the right reasons, mainly trying to help her parents in their difficult times. The fifteen-year-old daughter felt competent. Her parents recognized the daughter's good intentions and started to see their daughter as more competent than they had believed she was. From that moment, the daughter also saw herself as more competent than she had believed she could be. This attitude was much better in promoting positive therapeutic change. The parents lessened their propensity for triangulating their daughter into their squabbles and began to view her as a competent adult, rather than a misfit child. The parents also toned-down the volume of their arguments, which led to a better divorce process for them. They still got divorced, but they told their daughter that they would take care of their problems without her help. I worked with the daughter to recognize that, while well intentioned, using her own suicide to help her parents had a flaw in logic. We considered alternative courses of action, such as encouraging her parents to seek divorce counseling. The daughter's suicidal feeling diminished significantly and eventually disappeared.

BIFURCATING THE CLIENT

There are cases in which the suicidal adolescent will present a resistant front that offers no discrepancies and that may be difficult to reframe. The strategic therapist needs to have some energy to redirect him or her. The resistant client, who is entrenched in a rigid defensive position, may appear to have no energy to redirect. All of his or her energy is aimed at combating the therapist's efforts to bring about change. At this point, the therapy is "stuck." The therapist can create a flow of energy by bifurcating the client. This process consists of suggesting to the client the possibility that the client, in reality, is not so sure of his or her position and, instead, is really ambivalent about his or her situation.

Contrary to the popular meanings attributed to "ambivalence," the meaning of the word does not mean that a person feels nothing. Conversely, ambivalence means that a person feels two equal but opposite ways about the same thing. Consequently, an ambivalent person may feel very strongly about a situation. However, that person feels two opposing ways about it, each very strongly. As these feelings are polar opposites, the person is often "stuck" between these two strong but opposing feelings. This may make the person feel debilitated, unable to form a course of action that will resolve the ambivalence. This is not a pleasant position for a client, especially a suicidal adolescent. As this adolescent needs to feel a sense of control over his or her life, feeling the impotence of ambivalence is highly disturbing.

The therapist can create dynamic tension within the client by dividing the client into two people, each feeling very strongly but quite opposite from the other. Because the strategic therapist is very aware of the paradoxical nature of much of life, he or she can take the client's entrenched resistant position and create an opposing position that also may have some attractions for the client. Rather than accepting the client's definition of the situation as a "contest of wills" between the therapist and the client, the therapist redefines and restructures the definition of the situation as an internal battle between two parts of the client's own person. It is not interpersonal war but an intrapersonal war. The therapist can tell the client that he or she cannot imagine that it is very pleasant being in a situation where the client feels this internal tension within himself or herself and also feels powerless to stop it. In this way, the therapist has taken a "stuck" therapeutic situation and transformed it into a struggle internal to the client. The therapist can then offer to assist the client in resolving this internal battle by helping him or her to change, thereby empowering himself or herself.

If a suicidal adolescent male tells the therapist that he is more comfortable feeling suicidal than embracing therapeutic change, the therapist can probably speculate that the adolescent is motivated by fear of what might happen if he did change. The old motto of "'Tis better the devil you know, than the devil you don't" fits well to express this client's feelings. The therapist can approach the client in the following way:

> I know that it is scary to consider the possibility of changing. You don't know what will happen. In some ways, it seems easier and safer to do nothing and "stonewall" therapy. Inside part of you is a scared little boy who is afraid to take that chance and change. But there is also a young man inside of you who wants to protect that little boy. He's sick of watching that young boy feel pain and feeling helpless to do anything about it. He wants to embrace therapy and the potential positive changes it can bring. But the little boy is too afraid to take that chance. [Client's name], do you think that

I could join with that young man to make it safer for the little boy? Maybe, if we work together, we can convince him that he is stronger than he thinks he is, and the three of us can find a way out of being stuck with suicide as the only answer.

In this example, there are several elements operating at once. The therapist is bifurcating the suicidal adolescent into two separate persons, one of whom is a scared little boy and one of whom is a competent young man who will embrace therapy. For the typical adolescent male, these two parts of him are typically recognized as being present in his personality structure. However, the competent young man is much more socially acceptable to the adolescent than is the scared little boy. Furthermore, aligning with the young man holds the promise of giving the suicidal adolescent a greater sense of social acceptance and control over his environment. Lastly, since the young man persona recognizes the importance of change in therapy, the therapist can readily form an alliance with the young man to "help" the little boy participate in therapy under the watchful eyes of the young man and the therapist. The fear and ambivalence become the enemies to fight, not the therapist and therapy.

The technique of presenting the adolescent with the cognitive options of being a victim or a survivor can be looked upon as a cognitive approach, as was presented in Chapter 9. However, it can also be looked upon as a bifurcation of the person into two warring parts of a person: the victim versus the survivor. In the case example presented in Chapter 9, the therapist bifurcated the young woman into two separate people: a victim and a survivor. The therapist asked the sexual abuse victim to recognize both parts of herself: the victim and the survivor. The therapist joined with the survivor to make things safer for the little girl inside the suicidal teenager to embrace change. That change was defined as moving herself from more victim behaviors to more survivor behaviors. Although this was a cognitive intervention, the strategic blueprint of bifurcating the young woman into two parts (victim and survivor) laid the foundation for the cognitive intervention. Resistance was replaced by collaboration.

METAPHORS

There are times when the suicidal adolescent takes a rigid position of resistance and will not entertain any further discussion of his or her position. Although family members may also act in this manner, this type of position is often assumed by an adolescent who is too frightened to take into consideration any direct challenge of his or her position. The suicidal adolescent is in such fear of losing control over his or her life that "listening to an adult tell me I'm wrong" may seem like an alternative worse than the prospect of suicide. Even helpful suggestions may be looked upon as losing some sense of control over a life that already feels like it's spinning out of control. When there is perceived danger all around, sometimes it seems like the best thing to do is to "lay low and do nothing." When confronted with two choices, each of which could lead to his death, Yosarian (the main character in Joseph Heller's Catch-22 (1961)) is afraid to do anything. As any action could get him killed, he resorts to inaction. He tries to do nothing and slow time down to a crawl. He reasons that as time seems to crawl by when a person is bored, he tries to think of the most boring thing he can think about—Kewpie dolls—to slow time down so that he will not have to make a decision. To a suicidal adolescent using this coping strategy, the thought of active participation in bringing about therapeutic change is more than disturbing. It may be terrifying. Consequently, the therapist needs to create a therapeutic strategy that will allow a discussion to be initiated without spooking the adolescent into a rigidly held "shutdown."

Metaphors are excellent tools for introducing the possibility of therapeutic change indirectly (at least at first) and opening up a discussion of alternatives to the maladaptive recursive cycle that has entrenched the suicidal adolescent in resistance. In Chapter 8, I presented a case example of a young fourteen-year-old female who had been brought up in a home where sarcasm was a protection from becoming too intimate with loved ones. She was chastised by her boyfriend for being sarcastic when he wanted to get close. This made her question whether she was loved by her parents, who were always sarcastic to her. All of these self-doubts triggered some suicidal feelings in her, and her parents brought her into therapy. As she was filled with self-doubt about her lovability, she was afraid to say anything in therapy for fear that she would receive feedback from her family or me (as the therapist) that she was, in fact, unlovable. She was afraid that her vulnerability would be met with sarcastic "wisecracks." As a defense, she refused to discuss her feelings, and any attempt to open a discussion with her was met with either sarcasm or anger. I decided to employ a metaphor. I asked the suicidal adolescent, "Would you rather hug a teddy bear or a porcupine?" She responded:

That's stupid! A teddy bear, of course. Everybody knows that!

I asked the rest of the family if they agreed. After some initial puzzlement, they all agreed that it would, indeed, be better to hug a teddy bear than a porcupine. I then asked everybody, "Why?" The suicidal adolescent refused to answer. So I asked the rest of the family, "Why?" Between the suicidal adolescent's siblings and parents, they decided that teddy bears were "cuter and cuddlier." They said that porcupines have quills and "could stick you." As one kid brother put it, "Who would be crazy enough to hug a porcupine?" I asked the suicidal young woman if she agreed and she sarcastically snipped back, "of course!" I then told her the following:

> Then I'm puzzled. You said you wanted your boyfriend to like you but you were sarcastic when he got close. You said that you weren't sure that your family loves you but you push them away by being "snippy." I would guess that you would like me to help you in therapy but you give me "attitude" when I try to do so. It seems like you want to get hugged but you act more like a porcupine than a teddy bear.

She responded:

> Yeah, but it's safer when you're a porcupine. Nobody messes with you.

I replied:

> I agree! It's safer! But you don't get hugged.

The suicidal young woman said that she had to think about that for a while. While she was ruminating on this, I asked the rest of the family to tell me how they would act if the suicidal young woman did act more like a teddy bear. Would they be uncomfortable and resort back to sarcasm? Could they show her that it was safe to be a teddy bear? This stopped the joking around and I told them that that was a good start, as the suicidal adolescent was talking about ending her life and that was no joking matter. I turned to the suicidal adolescent and invited her to be a teddy bear. With just a little prodding from her family and me, she did take that chance. At the end of the session, after she began some self-disclosure, I asked her what the moral of the teddy bear–porcupine story was. She said, "If you really want hugs, you have to be a teddy bear."

Utilizing principles of strategic therapy, let us analyze what went on. The young woman was stuck in a maladaptive recursive cycle which she learned from her family of origin. The family rule was:

> If you feel close or intimate with someone, you become vulnerable to being hurt. Therefore, the way you protect yourself is to distance yourself by being sarcastic. This creates a "safe distance."

This is the way her parents managed intimacy and distance in their relationship. The fourteen-year-old had this rule modeled for her on countless occasions. Consequently, she assumed that this was the rule she needed to follow in her intimate relationships. This worked well in the family of origin relationships with her parents and her siblings. However, in a relationship with her first boyfriend, this rule posed problems as her boyfriend had no such rule in his family of origin. He took her sarcasm as an attack. Therefore, he withdrew. This posed some major problems for the young woman. She lost the affection and affirmation of her boyfriend. Her intimacy needs, which we later found out were greater than those of her parents (at least during her teenage years), were unfulfilled if she used this sarcasm-to-regulate-distance mechanism in her relationships outside the family. She began to doubt her family's love of her, as they needed to distance her so much with sarcasm. Consequently, she felt unlovable and began to have suicidal feelings and thoughts. She was too afraid to engage in therapy for fear that she might discover that she actually was unlovable. Therefore, she demonstrated a maladaptive recursive cycle of resistance to direct methods of therapy.

Taking a less direct, strategic approach to therapy, I stopped talking about her in therapy and began to ask questions about teddy bears and porcupines. This was my "hook." The client felt that she could talk about such frivolous topics because, crazy though they may be, they were safe. Surely commenting on whether it made more sense to hug a teddy bear or a porcupine would not demonstrate to her that she was unlovable. The "slam" in the strategic intervention was being puzzled by the young woman's inability to apply that simple logical conclusion to her own life. If she wanted to be hugged (the metaphor for loved), why did she act like a porcupine?

Once the young woman understood the moral of the metaphor, I asked her why that was such a hard message for her whole family to understand. The fourteen-year-old found it much easier to talk about her family's problems with intimacy and sarcasm, rather than talking about her own problems with those same matters. It was less "immediate" for her and, therefore, safer to discuss. This "family discussion" allowed us to discuss the dynamics of the sarcasm—an intimacy maladaptive recursive cycle—without singling out the suicidal adolescent as the only one having a problem. We defined it as a family problem, as opposed to an individual problem. In doing so, it was much easier to work with the problem directly through cognitive therapy. Eventually, we redefined the problem again as an intergenerational problem with intimacy in both extended families. As the therapist, I asked the family to take a heroic stand to change the rules that had been passed on through the generations. I told them that it would take courage and a heroic effort to do so. We reconstructed the family dynamics to be more open about intimacy and the fears that surround intimacy. Each family member, including the suicidal young woman, began to see sarcasm as an intimacy-reducing mechanism that could be used for fun or for protection. Once we worked together to overtly voice their need for safety and developed mechanisms for protection that were overt, all the family members felt not only safer but also more loved and validated. For the suicidal fourteen-year-old girl, all thoughts of suicide faded away.

RITUALS

Rituals play an extremely important role in our lives. Some rituals, like anniversaries and birthdays, demarcate the passage of time in our lives. They are badges of accomplishment. "We have survived for another year" or "our marriage has grown with another year's experience." Other rituals, like weddings and graduations, denote a nodal point in our lives, such as moving from one status to another. These rituals symbolize our achievement of a new status and create a structure by which others can share in our accomplishments and help us celebrate. There are also rituals that help us to cope through rough times. Rituals like funerals provide a structure to guide our journey through a crisis. A ritual provides a familiar, structured environment with proscripted courses of action to assist us in coping with stressors that would overwhelm us without the support of our resources. This type of ritual is very much like a cast on a broken arm. Although the cast contains no medication to assist the bone in healing, it does create a stable environment in which the bone can heal itself. This third type of ritual provides us stability and structure, in which we can best heal ourselves. A funeral provides a familiar structure around which our friends and family can gather to comfort and support us. The ritual of the funeral (the wake, the memorial services, the eulogy, the graveside service) provides us with a sequence of events that we can follow. The ritual provides us with a "known" in a time of "unknown." Most funerals also invoke the recognition of a "higher power." For deists, this would be God, in His/Her/Its many forms. For atheists and agnostics the "higher power" could be "humankind" or "the greater good." It connects us with a reason for an event that often seems to have no meaning or purpose (like the death of a loved one). If used properly, rituals have the power to greatly enhance our ability to cope.

Any of these types of rituals may be useful in therapy. Rituals that demarcate the passage of time can be reframed as celebrations within therapy of another year of improving oneself and one's relationships.

Rituals to celebrate passages help promote a feeling of accomplishment and validation. Rituals to celebrate transitions in therapy validate both the clients and the therapy process. When the presenting problem is a suicidal adolescent, coping rituals are likely to be of greatest benefit to both the adolescent and his or her family. In fact, a number of rituals have already been discussed previously in this book. For example, many of the behavioral interventions in Chapter 10 are very ritualistic. Behavioral contracts, if done correctly, establish a ritualistic pattern of rewards and punishments to accomplish a goal. They combine Strategic Therapy with Behavioral Therapy (Duncan & Parks, 1988). Behavioral interventions such as saying goodbye to a dead child's picture or setting an alarm to give the client time to mourn are very ritualistic. They furnish the client with a prescribed set of behaviors to help them cope with a difficult situation.

Rituals may also be used to overcome a maladaptive recursive cycle of resistance to therapeutic change. Some suicidal clients feel that they are walking a tightrope. Any slight misstep could plunge them into suicide. Consequently, they feel "stuck" in their present situation. They are afraid that therapy could bring about changes over which they have even less control than they do over their present lives. They are very resistant to any therapeutic change. If a therapist could construct a ritual that would provide a familiar structure to help guide the suicidal client during therapy, the client may be able to feel safe enough to explore other alternatives and embrace therapeutic change.

In Chapter 8, I described a case in which a young man was disturbed by his emerging sexual identity. Although he tried to act and feel as a heterosexual, his feelings of attraction were only centered around other males. Knowing of our society's stigma placed upon homosexuals, he tried to work at being heterosexual. No matter how hard he tried, his feelings were still homosexual. He felt trapped between what he knew would be an easier life and what his sexual feelings were. He felt so strongly about these equal but opposite feelings that he felt trapped in his ambivalence. This ambiguity caused him to consider suicide as a way out of what he identified as a hopeless dilemma. He felt so "balanced on the head of a pin" that he was afraid to embrace therapy for fear that he would escalate his suicidal feelings. He felt trapped by his sexual ambiguity, by his ambivalence between his choices, and by the fear that any changes would push him into suicide. Needless to say, he felt helpless.

As his therapist, I attempted to engage this suicidal young man in a ritual that might help him out of his ambivalent maladaptive recursive cycle. I approached him in the following way:

You know, I've been doing marriage and family therapy for a lot of years. As I speak with married clients and ask them to think back to how certain they felt about getting married to their fiancé, I get a lot of interesting answers. The most interesting answers came from the clients who say that they never had any doubts about marrying their boyfriend or girlfriend but they had a lot of doubts about doing something (marriage), which would close them off from possibly marrying someone else in the future. Choosing marriage wasn't a problem nor was choosing the partner they married. What worried them most was having to "shut the door" on other relationships. It wasn't opening the door to marriage that gave them "cold feet." It was closing the door to other potential relationships that gave them second thoughts.

While I was saying this the suicidal young man seemed anxious at first but then relaxed as he followed my account of the phenomenon of "cold feet" before the wedding. His response was:

That's interesting but what does that have to do with me? I'm not planning on getting married anytime soon.

He ended his remarks with a small smile. My "hook" was to talk about something which, at least on the surface, appeared to be unrelated to the suicidal young man and his ambivalence about his sexual identity, as, on the surface, my remarks were perceived to be irrelevant to him and, therefore, were less "immediate" to his predicament. Consequently, this resistant young man felt "safe" to engage me in a discussion.

Once the suicidal young man became relaxed and "at ease," I made the connection between my experiences with "cold feet" and his own presenting problem. I continued:

In many ways, you seem to be in the same predicament as those couples about to be married. You feel like you're faced with a big decision that will alter your life forever: Are you straight or gay? Focusing on which sexual identity to choose has become a burden for you. Maybe we can learn something from those people who experienced "cold feet"? What if we looked at what you would give up if you chose to live a straight or gay lifestyle?

The young man's countenance went from nervous surprise to intrigue. He asked, "How could we do that?" My "slam" was to take our conversation into a direction towards which he hadn't expected the conversation to go. Although he felt some uneasiness at this sudden turn of events, he was also interested in considering a possible way of looking at his problem that he had not heretofore considered. I interpreted his question. "How could we do that?" to really mean, "How could we safely do that?"

To make this journey safest for my young client, I created a ritual to give structure to this process. I said the following:

> You know, I bet there are a lot of ways to accomplish this. Perhaps this might be a good idea. We would be talking about the death of one of those lifestyles if the other one were chosen. In our society, when we experience the death of a loved one, we hold a funeral service. We ask loved ones to join us, we give a eulogy to the deceased in which we talk about the good things he or she did in life, we say some prayers, and we bury our dead. What if we arranged to have two funeral services? One would be for the homosexual lifestyle, assuming that you chose a heterosexual lifestyle. The second funeral would be for the heterosexual lifestyle, assuming that you would choose a homosexual lifestyle.

The young man seemed intrigued with this notion of two funerals. He asked me to elaborate how this could be done.

I explained that the first task was to decide which loved ones should attend the funeral. He listed off a few friends, and said that he supposed that his family should also be invited. Next, I explained, we would have to come up with a good eulogy for each lifestyle. I would assign the suicidal adolescent to write a eulogy that would sing the praises of the lifestyle we were burying that day. I asked him if he thought that he could do that. He responded, "Yes." I told him that I would come up with some funeral prayers and preside over each ceremony if he wished. He answered affirmatively. For his homework that week he was assigned three things:

1. Finalize your guest list.
2. Decide which funeral to have first.
3. Write a preliminary draft of your first eulogy.

He agreed to do these tasks.

When he showed up for therapy the next week, the young man seemed energized. He had completed his three assignments and even went beyond the assignment by arranging for funeral announcements to be printed and mailed out when we could decide on the date. He decided to do homosexuality's death first. We decided that we would work on the eulogy for that session, he would rewrite it, and we would "fine-tune it" the week after that. Therefore, the "funeral for homosexuality" would take place in three weeks.

The suicidal adolescent, who was so stuck in his ambivalence, was now thinking about the situation with great enthusiasm. My ritual allowed him to process his thoughts and feelings through the structured tasks of creating a eulogy. The ritual gave him the "cast" with which to surround his broken identity. Three weeks later, with his family and his select friends witnessing his ceremony, he read his eulogy to his homosexuality, describing the benefits of being gay and how much he would miss being gay. I said the funeral prayers from a Catholic service. Instead of burying the homosexuality, we decided to cremate it. I had asked the young man to pick something symbolic that would represent his homosexuality. He chose a picture of a homosexual entertainer who had "come out of the closet" years before. We asked the "loved ones" to give remembrances about the good things about this adolescent's homosexuality. When we had exhausted the remembrances, we took out a small pail, placed the picture in the pail, and set it on fire. I finished the ceremony by reading a graveside prayer.

We repeated this ritual for the adolescent's heterosexuality four weeks later. By using these two rituals, the suicidal adolescent was able to overcome his resistance to therapy, share his feelings in therapy with the therapist, and talk about them with his loved ones. The ritual gave him a blueprint to follow in deciding which aspect of himself, his heterosexuality or his homosexuality, he would miss more. After his two funerals he decided that losing his heterosexuality was less costly to whom he is than losing his homosexuality. This decision helped him eliminate most of his ambiguity and ambivalence, thereby greatly reducing the amount of anxiety that was previously generated by indecision. In this way, the use of a funeral ritual provided enough structure and safety to allow the adolescent to explore his sexual identity and come to a conclusion about who he really is.

PARADOXICAL INTERVENTIONS

When a suicidal adolescent enters into a therapeutic process, he or she is declaring to the therapist an intention to change something in his or her life so that suicide will no longer be considered a viable alternative to life. This has a great deal of appeal to the suicidal adolescent because he or she is taking control over an aspect of his or her life, and this self-empowerment holds the promise of relief from his or her pain as a result of therapy. Therefore, two of the most problematic aspects of feeling suicidal—feeling pain and feeling powerless—may be ameliorated by embracing the pursuit of therapeutic change. However, change is scary for most people, especially adolescents who do not have adequate experience with therapeutic change to feel comfortable with it. Therefore, the adolescent may become resistant to therapy. This creates a paradox. On an overt, intellectual level, the client would like to change in order to feel more control over life and less pain. However, on an emotional, covert level, the same client may be very bound to the same behavioral and emotional patterns because of a fear of change. This puts suicidal adolescents into a paradoxical double bind. If they embrace therapy, they will have to face their fears. However, if they do not embrace therapy, the suicidal ideation and behavior still exists and may get worse. The way that the client escapes from this paradoxical situation is to pay lip service to being invested in the therapy, while creating barriers so that therapy will fail. This is the essence of resistance in therapy. Over time, such a pattern becomes a maladaptive recursive cycle.

If the therapist tries to intervene directly, it may play into the hands of the resistance, which is designed to counter direct interventions. Consequently, if the therapist attempts a more indirect form of intervention, it may have a greater chance at success. Many of the techniques described above (e.g., reframing) are attempts at intervening in an indirect way to achieve therapeutic change. Another method may be through the use of a paradoxical intervention. As the adolescent is familiar with the paradoxical situation in which he or she exists, a "counter-paradox" (a paradox to rebut the existing paradox) (Selvini, Palazzoli, Boscolo, Lecchin, & Prata, 1978) is sometimes a useful tool.

Many of the interventions discussed in the previous two chapters have drawn upon the idea of looking for or creating a counter-paradox to overcome resistance. For example, looking for discrepancies within the suicidal adolescent's or the family's logic and pointing them out to the family is a form of counter-paradox. Either the adolescent or the family will manifest logical discrepancies that create natural paradoxes within their lives. As much as we would like to think that our lives fall into logical patterns, life contains many naturally occurring paradoxes. I would hypothesize that when we are under stress our lives become filled with more paradoxes because our emotions take over. Our fears guide actions and behaviors that begin to surface and that would normally be foreign to our behavioral repertoire. We cope with these "out of character" behaviors by either rationalizing their existence or ignoring the existence of any inconsistency. Either of these techniques pushes the logic discrepancy into a more covert plane of existence. The paradox exists but, because of the person's or family's fear that exposing this discrepancy will result in increased anxiety, there is a negative injunction to not recognize the existence of this paradox. The therapist makes the covert paradox overt to the awareness of the individual or the family.

This situation now has all of the elements of the classic "double bind" (Bateson, Jackson, Haley, & Weakland, 1950). There are two or more people in an important relationship. In family therapy, we have the adolescent and his or her family. In individual therapy, we have the adolescent and the therapist. Because the paradox and its defense become a maladaptive recursive cycle, it is repeated. There is a primary negative injunction, together with a secondary injunction that counters or contradicts the first injunction. For example, the adolescent comes to therapy to reduce the pain and gain more control over his or her life. This is the primary injunction. However, the fear and anxiety of changing present a countervailing injunction not to change. The ambivalence the suicidal adolescent feels "traps" the suicidal adolescent, causing inertia or resistance to any therapeutic movement. The adolescent has been conditioned by this sequence to believe that this is the way the world is and there is nothing that he or she can do about it. Therefore, the resistance to therapy seems to be the natural method of survival. When the therapist makes the covert overt, he or she creates cognitive dissonance within the adolescent. As the feelings of cognitive dissonance are very unpleasant for the adolescent, the therapist has created a "demand" for the adolescent to respond to the original paradox, rather than being confronted with the new paradox of knowing that the original paradox exists but doing nothing about it. Thus the new paradox, making the covert original paradox overt, fueled by the adolescent's cognitive dissonance, forms a double-bind to unbalance the suicidal adolescent's resistance to therapy. It is a counter-paradox.

Any of the cognitive interventions, elaborated upon in Chapter 9, follow this pattern of counter-paradox. For example, creating a "win–win" situation for suicidal adolescents by giving them insight into the world of adolescence or family dynamics creates a counter-paradox to the previously held belief that the world had to consist of only "win–lose" situations. When facing the resistance to therapy of a suicidal adolescent and his or her family, the therapist may be able to point out discrepancies in the logic of their inertia, creating cognitive dissonance to act as a counter-paradox to the already existing paradoxes that underlie the client's resistance. The adolescent is placed in a therapeutic double-bind to reconsider his or her assumption that therapy will bring about changes that will be frightening. Instead, therapeutic change is presented as a way to reduce cognitive dissonance, relieve the pain triggering the suicidal ideation, and restore a greater sense of control in the adolescent's life.

In most cases in which an adolescent is suicidal, there exists a paradox, as explained above, underlying his or her resistance to therapeutic change. However, there are cases in which this paradox is not present. Most often these are cases in which the suicidal adolescent is resistant to therapy because he or she has already given up on life. For this individual, the process of therapy is more painful than the promise of the nothingness of death. He or she does not want to change in therapy because death is easier. For some teenagers, the certainty of suicide outweighs the uncertainty of life. In both of these cases, the adolescent is not willing to admit that he or she is ambivalent about the choice of death. Therefore, there is no natural basis for an underlying paradox. Even if the adolescent is really ambivalent, his or her unwillingness to admit to that fact makes it difficult to point to a paradox that he or she will not admit exists. Often, these suicidal adolescents do not wish to be in therapy and have been pushed to attend therapy by their parents. The advantage to doing family therapy with these adolescents is that this dynamic tension between the family, who wants to come to therapy, and the suicidal adolescent, who is resistant to therapy, can be discussed as a topic for therapy. A family who wants the adolescent to go to therapy but will not attend therapy themselves sends the dangerous message to the suicidal adolescent that he or she is not worth the family's time and energy to work in therapy. However, a family who is willing to attend therapy and work with their suicidal adolescent sends a powerful message of support and hope to the troubled adolescent. Although there may be a discrepancy between the adolescent's motivation and his or her family's willingness to explore change, and it may produce a family paradox that may be exposed, it may not provide the internal motivation for the adolescent to embrace therapeutic change.

When an individual has no discrepancies or paradoxes that can be double-bound, the therapist may choose to create a paradoxical intervention. In this situation, the therapist has to create a paradox that will bind an adolescent from considering suicide to be an option. The therapist may employ several methods covered previously in this chapter. If the therapist can reframe the adolescent's motivation or employ a metaphor that will double-bind the adolescent, he or she can create a counter-paradoxical strategy to disrupt the resistance.

One of the most common paradoxical interventions is to employ a therapeutic paradox. For Jay Haley (1984), the purpose of a therapeutic paradox is to finesse a client into changing his or her behavior by taking a stand against the therapist and owning his or her behavior. The therapist takes a stand with the expectation of the client's rebelling against the therapist's proscription. These paradoxical directives often encourage, rather than attack, problematic behavior (Selvini Palazzali et al., 1978). Haley (1963) gives an example of Milton Erickson's asking a family who was reluctant to open up in therapy to refrain from revealing everything in the first session. In this way, Erickson set up a command that went with the flow of the family's resistance to open up in therapy. His expectation was to have the family rebel against his directive and open up to demonstrate to the therapist that he could not control them. Haley (1963) refers to this as "prescribing the symptom." He gives an example of one of his own cases in which he told an insomniac client to get up and clean his house when he could not sleep. His rationale to the client was that if he couldn't sleep, at least he could get some housework done. His therapeutic rationale was that since everybody hates to do housework, his directive would be so unpleasant as to invite the client's rebellion against it, which the client would do by sleeping. In this way, the therapist creates a paradoxical intervention by prescribing the symptoms.

When dealing with suicidal clients, especially adolescents, great caution must be used when using this technique. As I explained in Chapter 6 on crisis intervention, the therapist cannot prescribe suicide for a suicidal client. Although in the folklore of therapy, many therapists have claimed to have done this and gotten great therapeutic gains from employing this technique, the stakes are too high. The suicidal adolescent may take such a prescription of the symptom and treat it as the therapist's permission to go ahead and kill himself or herself. The costs are just too high to risk. Therefore, any paradoxical directive must make it clear that, although a paradox is being set up, it specifically does not give permission or encouragement to the adolescent to commit suicide. This is indeed a delicate balance.

I had a case in which a seventeen-year-old male had unsuccessfully tried to commit suicide by taking an overdose of sedatives. His family (mother, father, ten-year-old sister, and nineteen-year-old sister) came into therapy with him. When they tried to explain to him that they loved him and were afraid of his suicidal ideas and actions, he responded to them by asking, "Why should you care?" This suicidal young man explained that "it is my life, so it isn't anybody's business if I want to end my life." He seemed to be especially angry at his 10-year-old sister, whom he labeled as "spoiled" because she was the baby of the family. I asked the adolescent if he felt that his younger sister should have the same privileges as he does, considering that she is seven years younger than he is. With a loud voice, he answered defiantly:

Strategic Interventions • 233

Hell no! She can't be trusted with the stuff I have to do. She couldn't handle my curfew without getting into a ton of trouble. That little turd is just a kid!

I responded:

So you think that the life of a seventeen-year-old is so tough that a ten-year-old just couldn't cut it? She'd fail and wind up in a lot of trouble?

He said, "Yea!" I continued:

So if I turn your logic around, you think that it takes a lot of experience, skill, and guts to be able to make it as a seventeen-year-old teenager in our culture. If a kid— let's say your younger sister— doesn't have the experience, skills, and guts to hack it, she needs a set of rules and restrictions to save her from making a fool of herself or worse. Is that what you mean?

He responded:

Yea! She just couldn't hack it as a seventeen-year-old! If she tried, she'd look dumb. She might even get hurt. I guess someone needs to look out for her butt. She needs rules to help protect her.

I replied:

I agree with you but I'm confused about what that means for you if you're feeling suicidal. What kind of rules should there be for you to protect you from looking foolish or getting hurt?

The look on his face told me that my question took him by surprise and threw him off balance. I continued:

If rules need to be given to young people to protect them, I guess you would agree that rules need to be put on you to protect you. In every aspect of your life you've got it all over [his youngest sister]. You're bigger and stronger. You've got more experience. But in one area, the guts to face life and spit in its eye, she's got it all over you. She's never mentioned suicide. Your parents feel comfortable leaving her at home alone for the evening without worrying about her killing herself. They can't say the same for you. You're much more competent and able to take care of yourself than she is. But in the area of stayin' alive, she's got it all over you. So, using your logic, you should have an earlier curfew than [your younger sister].

He yelled:

> Are you nuts? She's seven years younger than me! Why should she get to stay out later?

I answered:

> She's not a threat to kill herself. You are! I can't tell you to stop thinking about suicide. Nobody can! Only you have the power to tone down the thoughts of killing yourself. If your sister decided she wanted to drive the car at age 10, nobody could stop her from thinking about it. But we wouldn't let her drive the car. Parents (and therapists) can't stop you from thinking about suicide but we can try to keep you from doing it, just like we would stop your sister from driving. She doesn't know how and she doesn't have the experience. She might think she can but we know she can't. She's too young to make the kind of choices you have to make when you drive. You're old enough to make these decisions. She's not.

He replied:

> Of course not! She's just a kid. Who in their right mind would let her drive?

I replied:

> Nobody, I hope! The problem is that you're in the same situation. You think that you're old enough to take your own life and want to be given the right to do so. Just as your sister thinks she can drive a car at age 10, you think you can commit suicide at age seventeen. You're both wrong! You don't have the skills or experience to make that kind of "life-or-death" choice for yourself.

The suicidal adolescent fell silent. He was still angry but he exhibited the look of a young man who was deflated. I continued:

> I would make the following proposition to you (the 17-year-old) and your family. As we can't control your thoughts anyway, I propose that we let you think about suicide whenever you want to do so. However, when you do want to think about suicide, you need to tell your mom and dad or me, so that we can protect you from your suicidal actions. To accomplish that, I propose that, for the time that you feel suicidal, you be restricted to the rules and restrictions of a *nine*-year-old.

He countered:

> But I'm not nine! I'm seventeen! Why should I follow the rules of a nine-year-old?

I responded:

> Because the rules of a nine-year-old will keep you alive! If you choose to kill yourself, you'll never have another choice to make. You'll be dead. If we can keep you alive right now, you will have the opportunity to make other choices after that, perhaps even make the choice of life or death when you've got more experience and more life skills. So I'm suggesting that you should think about suicide but, if you do, you need to do it under the rules of a nine-year-old. Because thinking about suicide may help you understand it better, I'd encourage you to think about killing yourself.

He responded:

> Yea, but I'd have to have the rules of a nine-year-old when I'm thinking about it. For God's sake, it would mean my little sister would have more freedom than me!

I answered:

> I know! But thinking about suicide would help you understand why it takes guts to face life's challenges. It's like a comic book hero. He's got to face danger and go someplace dangerous in order to learn about himself. This makes him strong enough to fight the villains. Maybe your "dangerous place" is thinking about killing yourself. You need to go there to learn about yourself. That way you can grow so that you can meet life's challenges as an adult. I don't know. Maybe you've already gone through all of that when you took your overdose of pills. I don't think so because, if you had, you wouldn't still be considering suicide. What do you think?

The adolescent answered, with a bewildered look on his face:

> I don't know. I think I need some time to think about what I think. Can we talk about it?

The paradoxical directive was constructed to put the suicidal adolescent into a therapeutic double-bind. I used his feelings of jealously toward his younger sister to fuel this paradox. I began by, at least in his eyes, changing the topic of therapy from him and his suicidal ideation and behaviors to his sister and her lack of competence to live the life of a seventeen-year-old. *That was my hook.* As I seemed to agree with his view of his sister and as the conversation did not center on him, he agreed to engage in the conversation. I described the corollary of his criticism of his sister, namely that, if she did not have the skills to be seventeen, she had to have restricted rules to protect her from her own incompetence. The seventeen-year-old liked that even more, because he thought that a differential set of rules, based on age, would allow him much more privilege than his sister. *The hook is set deeper.*

Then I took a one-down position and said I was confused. I asked him that, if we used the same logic (his logic), what are the rules we should apply to him if we were to keep him safe. *There is the slam.* This created a paradox. On one hand, I complimented him on being competent enough to live the difficult life of a seventeen-year-old. On the other hand, I defined his suicidal behavior as being something from which we must protect him, just like we would protect a ten-year-old from trying to be seventeen. One message was that he was competent and should have more privilege. The competing message was that his suicidal behavior was a sign of incompetence, and he needed to have restricted rules to protect him. As I based these two competing messages upon his own logic, he was forced into an imperative in which he had to follow his own logic for himself or admit that his sister was more competent than he was, because she was not suicidal. For him this was a horrible double-bind that threw him off balance (as a good slam should) and increased his cognitive dissonance and, therefore, his anxiety. This pressed him to have to do something about his cognitive dissonance and, consequently, made him more amenable to therapeutic change.

I restricted his response by continuing to press the idea that, although he was more competent than his sister, in the area of staying alive, she was more competent than he was. I knew this would upset him and that would create energy I could rechannel. *This was a juice.* I even threw in an incentive which would tweak his macho image of himself. I told him that his ten-year-old kid sister was better at facing life and spitting in its eye than he was. *This was another juice.* It got the response I wanted. He yelled and questioned the logic of my statements that his sister was more competent than he was.

At that point I stayed calm and gave him an escape hatch. I closed the door but opened a little window. I separated out his suicidal sequence into two components: thoughts and actions. I told him that he had a right to his suicidal ideation but we needed to protect him from his suicidal behavior. I used an example of his sister's trying to drive a car to fuel his emotions, keeping him motivated to engage me. I reengaged him in the logic of protection from harm and used his sister's desire to drive a car—but her incompetence to do so—as a metaphor for his thoughts of committing suicide but his incompetence to make such a global and final choice. *This was another hook, slam, and juice.*

I then gave him a paradoxical directive. I prescribed the symptom of suicidal ideation by asking him to think about committing suicide.

I even gave him the logic about how that would help him to understand himself better. The competing directive was that, when he thought about suicide, he had to adhere to the rules appropriate for a nine-year-old. It is important to note that I did not prescribe the symptom of suicidal behavior. That would have been irresponsible and dangerous. By prescribing the symptom of suicidal ideation and countering it with having to be treated like a nine-year-old (even a year younger than his annoying kid sister), I constructed a paradoxical directive which was safe but against which he could rebel.

I then gave him an extra motivation by tying him into the path of the epic hero, which I described in Chapter 9. I knew from previous sessions that, as a younger child, he had been into superhero comic books (e.g., Superman, Batman, Spiderman). Using the myth of the epic hero, I linked his struggle with suicide to the struggles of his comic heroes when they fought the villains of evil. This metaphorically connected his struggle with suicide similar to his heroes' struggles with the villains of evil. It made him a hero and labeled suicide as a villain with whom he had to struggle. This objectified the problem (suicide) into a villain, whom the hero (the suicidal adolescent) had to vanquish. This draws from Narrative Therapy (White and Epston, 1990), but serves the strategic purpose of giving the suicidal adolescent a new role, that of hero combating evil. I gave him one last "escape hatch" by suggesting that he may have already gone through his ordeal when he took his overdose of pills. However, I created one last paradox by defining that he would know that his heroic journey had come to an end when he stopped needing to think about suicide. I gave him a benchmark that he had not already achieved but that he *could* achieve by rebelling against my paradoxical directive. I pointed out a path, labeled him a hero, defined a goal, and told him that I did not think he was there yet. Under those circumstances, it was little wonder that he was confused. The purpose was to challenge his resistance and invite him into the therapeutic process. That purpose was achieved.

From here on, the suicidal adolescent began to participate in therapy. He had a hard time giving up the sense of power he felt (having everyone focused on him as a potential risk for suicide). It gave him a feeling of control over his life. However, he was not going to be able to feel that sense of control if he was restricted to the rules of a nine-year-old. In addition, as he gave up his suicidal ideations, his family did not desert him in therapy. They stayed with him to work on his problems and the family's issues. This validated him as a person and helped him to have a greater feeling of predictability in his life. Therefore, he felt that he had more control over his immediate environment and his life in general.

This gave him the confidence to develop coping skills to deal with his problems and reduce his pain. Therapy lasted about six months. He still contacts me on occasion, at first by letter and now by email. His life has gone well. He recently emailed me:

> Things are going well ... I can't believe that I was so screwed up, once upon a time, that I thought suicide was the answer to my problems. Thanks for straightening me out.

My man, you are very welcome.

Strategic Therapy often places the therapist in an expert role and is often seen as manipulative of the clients. This seems to be contraindicated in the case of a suicidal adolescent who is struggling with issues of power and control over his or her life. Part of the paradoxical aspects of life is that I have found this type of therapy to work well with suicidal adolescents. In my role as the "expert of the process," I aim to empower the adolescent to be responsible for himself or herself and make his or her own decisions. My therapeutic manipulations are constructed not to meet my needs but to meet the needs of my clients. They are my tools to bring about change that will back the suicidal adolescent away from the precipice of suicide to live a life of less pain and hopelessness and more wisdom and control.

EPILOGUE

Our journey now draws to a close. I have presented a framework for family therapy as it applies to suicidal adolescents. This is, if you will, my magic sword for taming the beast of suicide. However, like any tool or weapon, it must be used with skill and commitment. I present this model of therapy not as a "cookbook" but as a "springboard." It is not a recipe for therapy which, if followed precisely, will guarantee success. It is, instead, a system of theory, research, ideas, and suggestions which a therapist can integrate with his or her therapeutic style to create a hybrid mode of intervention to help suicidal adolescents. This mode of therapy is a hybrid not only of therapeutic frameworks, but also a hybrid of the science of theory and the art of therapeutic practice. This process cannot separate the model of therapy from the person of the therapist who utilizes that model. The person of the therapist is integral in the use of this process.

The practice of theory with suicidal adolescents is a very personal process. The therapist cannot insulate himself or herself from that process. As I edited this manuscript, I often found myself reliving some of the cases I used as examples, often with a few tears and a great deal of emotion. These clients still have the power to tug at my heartstrings. While in the process of editing this manuscript, I ran into a young man with whom I had done therapy for suicidal ideation when he was a high school senior. I asked him how he was doing? He responded that he was doing much better than he did when we worked together in therapy. I asked him a question I often ask former clients when I meet them later in life. I asked him if therapy had helped him and, if it did, what was it that made the most difference in therapy. He answered, "You were you. No B.S. You weren't a suit but a real person. Not many adults were real to me in those days. You were. So I listened to you." This confirmed for me the importance of the person of the therapist.

I can follow my therapeutic model because it is wedded with my style. The reader is encouraged to take from this volume what he or she feels will be useful. Make it your own. Don't follow the model as a recipe. Use it as a springboard to achieve new therapeutic heights. It must be bonded to who you are as a therapist and who you are as a person. The tool is only as effective as the one who uses it. A sword, even a magic sword, is useless unless wielded by a hero. Only a hero can tame the beast within. There are far too many adolescents who need such a hero.

REFERENCES

American Psychiatric Association (1994). *Diagnostic and statistical manual of mental disorders* (4th ed.). Washington, DC: American Psychiatric Association.

Allberg, W.R. & Chu, L. (1990). Understanding adolescent suicide: Correlates in a developmental perspective. *The School Counselor, 37,* 343–350.

Anderson, H. & Goolishian, H. (1988). Human Systems as linguistic systems: Preliminary and evolving ideas about the implications for clinical theory. *Family Process, 27,* 371–394.

Arensoman, E. & Kerkhof, A.D. (1996). Classification of attempted suicide: A review of empirical studies, 1963–1993. *Suicide and Life-Threatening Behavior, 26,* 46–67.

Asarnow, J.R. (1992). Suicidal ideation and attempts during middle childhood: Association with perceived family stress and depression among child psychiatric inpatients. *Journal of Clinical Child Psychology, 21,* 35–40.

Andriolo, K.R. (1998). Gender and the cultural construction of good and bad suicides. *Suicide and Life Threatening Behavior, 28,* 37–49.

Bandler, R. & Grinder, J. (1975). *The structure of magic: A book about language and therapy.* Palo Alto, CA: Behavior Books.

Bateson, G., Jackson, D.D., Haley, J., & Weakland, J. (1950). Toward a theory of schizophrenia. *Behavioral Science, 1,* 251–264.

Bard, M. (1972). Training police as specialists in family crisis intervention. In L.J. Sager & H.S. Kaplan (Eds.), *Progress in group and family therapy.* New York: Brunner/Mazel.

Beautrais, A.L., Joyce, P.R., & Mulder, R.T. (1999). Personality traits and cognitive styles as risk factors for the serious suicide attempts among young people. *Suicide and Life Threatening Behavior, 29,* 37–47.

Beck, A.T. (1976). *Cognitive therapy and emotional disorders.* New York: International Universities Press.

Beck, A.T., Brown, G.K., Steer, R.A., Dahlagaard, K.K., & Grisham, J.R. (1999). Suicide ideation at its worst point: A predictor of eventual suicide in psychiatric outpatients. *Suicide and Life Threatening Behavior, 29,* 1–9.

Beck, A.T., Kovacs, M., & Weissman, A. (1979). Assessment of suicidal ideation. *Journal of Consulting and Clinical Psychology, 47,* 343–352.

Beck, A.T. & Steer, R.A. (1989). Clinical predictors of eventual suicide: A 5 to 10 year prospective study of suicide attempts. *Journal of Affective Disorders, 17,* 203–209.

Beck, A.T., Steer, R.A., & Brown, G. (1993). Dysfunctional attitudes and suicidal ideation in psychiatric outpatients. *Suicide and Life Threatening Behavior, 23,* 11–20.

Beck, A.T., Steer, R., & Brown, G. (1996), *Beck depression inventory* (2nd ed.). San Antonio, TX: Psychological Corp.

Beck, A.T., Brown, G., Berchick, R.J., Stewart, B.L., & Steer, R.A. (1990). Relationship between hopelessness and ultimate suicide: A replication with psychiatric outpatients. *American Journal of Psychiatry, 147,* 190–195.

Beck, A.T., Steer, R.A., Kovacs, M., & Garrison, B. (1985). Hopelessness and eventual suicide: A 10-year prospective study of patients hospitalized with suicidal ideation. *American Journal of Psychiatry, 142,* 559–563.

Beck, A.T. Steer, R., & Ranieri, W. (1988). Scale for suicidal ideation: Psychometric properties of a self-report version. *Journal of Clinical Psychology, 44,* 499–505.

Beck, A.T., Weissman, A., Lester, D., & Trexler, L. (1974). The measurement of pessimism: The hopelessness scale. *Journal of Consulting and Clinical Psychology, 42,* 861–865.

Beevers, C.G. & Miller, I.W. (2005). Unlinking negative cognition and symptoms of depression: Evidence of a specific treatment effect for cognitive therapy. *Journal of Consulting and Clinical Psychology, 73,* 68–77.

Berlin, I.N. (1987). Suicide among American Indian adolescents: An overview. *Suicide and Life Threatening Behavior, 17,* 218–232.

Berman, A.L. (1985). The teenager at risk for suicide. *Medical Aspects of Human Sexuality, 19,* 123–124.

Berman, A.L. & Jobes, D. (1991). *Adolescent suicide: Assessment and intervention.* Washington, DC: American Psychological Association.

Blake, W. (1956). A poison tree, In H.F. Lowry & W. Thorp (Eds.), *An Oxford anthology of English poetry* (p. 538). New York: Oxford University Press.

Blenkiron, P., House, A., & Milnes, D. (2000). The timing of deliberate acts of self-harm: Is there any relation with suicidal intent, mental disorder, or psychiatric management. *Journal of Psychosomatic Research, 49,* 3–6.

Blumenthal, S. & Kupfer, D. (1986). Generalizable treatment strategies for suicidal behavior. In J. Mann & M. Stanley (Eds.), *Annals of The New York Academy of Science, 487,* 327–340.

Blumenthal, S. (1990). Youth suicide: Risk factors, assessment, and treatment of adolescent and young adult suicidal patients. *Psychiatric Clinics of North America, 13*, 511–556.

Boszormenyi-Nagy, I. & Spark, G.L. (1973). *Invisible loyalties: Reciprocity in intergenerational family therapy.* New York: Harper & Row.

Bowen, M. (1975). Family therapy after twenty years. In S. Aricti (Eds.), *The American handbook of psychiatry* (Vol. 5). New York: Basic Books.

Bowen, M. (1976). Theory in the practice of psychotherapy, In. P.J. Guerim (Ed.), *Family therapy: Theory and practice.* New York: Garner Press.

Boyd, J.H. & Moscicki, E.K. (1986). Firearms and youth suicide. *American Journal of Public Health, 76,* 1240–1242.

Breuk, R.E., Sexton, T.L., Van-Dam, A., Disse, C., Doreleijers, T.A., Slot, W.N., & Rowland, M.K. (2006). The implementation and the cultural adjustment of functional family therapy in a Dutch psychiatric day treatment center. *Journal of Marriage and Family Therapy, 32,* 515–529.

Broderick, C.B. (1993). *Understanding family process: Basics of family systems theory.* Newbury Park, CA: Sage.

Broderick, C.B. & Schrader, S.S. (1991). The history of professional marriage and family therapy. In A.S. Gurman & D.P. Kniskern (Eds.), *Handbook of family therapy* (Vol. 2). New York: Brunner/Mazel.

Brent, D.A., Crumrine, P.K., Varma, R.R., Allan, M., & Allman, C. (1987). Phenobarbital treatment and major depressive disorder in children with epilepsy. *Pediatrics, 89,* 909–917.

Brent, D.A., Perper, J., Moritz, G., Baugher, M., & Allman, C. (1993). Suicide in adolescents with no apparent psychopathology. *Journal of the American Academy of Child and Adolescent Psychiatry, 32,* 494–500.

Bronfenbrenner, U. (1986). Ecology of the family as a context for human development: Research perspectives. *Developmental Psychology, 22,* 723–742.

Bronfenbrenner, U. (1970). *The ecology of human development: Experiments by nature and design.* Cambridge, MA: Harvard University Press.

Buehler, C. & Gerard, J.M. (2002). Marital conflict, ineffective parenting, and children's and adolescent's maladjustment. *Journal of Marriage and Family Therapy, 64,* 78–92.

Burr, W.R., Klein, S.R., Burr, R.G., Doxey, C., Harker, B., Holman, T.B., Martin, P.H., McClure, R.L., Parrish, S.W., Stuart, D.A., Taylor, A.C., & White, M.S. (1994). *Reexamining family stress: New theory and research.* Thousand Oaks, CA: Sage.

Callahan, J. (1998). Crisis in theory and crisis intervention in emergencies. In P.M. Kleespies (Ed.), *Emergencies in mental health practice.* New York: Guilford.

Campbell, J. (1956). The hero with a thousand faces. Cleveland, OH: Meridian Books.

Camus, A. (1961). *Resistance, rebellion, and death.* New York: Random House.

Canetto, S.S. & Lester, D. (1999). Motives for suicide in suicide notes from women and men. *Psychological Reports, 85,* 471–472.

Canetto, S.S. & Sakinofsky, I. (1998). The gender paradox in suicide. *Suicide and Life Threatening Behavior, 28,* 1–23.

Carr, A. (2000). Evidence-based practice in family therapy and systemic consultation. I: Child-focused problems. *Journal of Family Therapy, 22,* 29–60.

Cassidy, C., O'Connor, R.C., Howe, C., & Warden, D. (2004). Perceived discrimination and psychological distress: The role of personal and ethnic self-esteem. *Journal of Counseling Psychology, 51,* 329–339.

Centers for Disease Control (1991). *Morbidity and Mortality Weekly Report, 37*(Suppl. 5–6), 1–12.

Centers for Disease Control (1996). *Violence Surveillance Summary Series No. 2.* Washington, DC: United States Government Printing Office.

Centers for Disease Control and Prevention. Web-based Injury Statistics Query and Reporting System (WISQARS) [online]. (2002). National Center for Injury Prevention and Control, Centers for Disease Control and Prevention (producer). Available from www.cdc.gov/ncipc/wisqars [2003, March 27].

Chance, S., Kaslow, N., & Baldwin, K. (1994). Anxiety and other predictors of severity of suicidal intention in urban psychiatric inpatients. *Hospital and Community Psychiatry, 45,* 716–718.

Cole, D.A. (1988). Hopelessness, social desirability, depression, and parasuicide in two college student samples. *Journal of Consulting and Clinical Psychology, 56,* 131–136.

Collins, O.P. (1990). *Individual and family factors influencing probability for suicide in adolescents.* Unpublished doctoral dissertation, Kansas State University, Manhattan, KS.

Compton, S.N., March, J.S., Brent, D., Albano, A.M., Weersing, V.R., & Curry, J. (2004). Cognitive-behavioral psychotherapy for anxiety and depressive disorders in children and adolescents: An evidence-based medicine review. *Journal of the American Academy of Child and Adolescent Psychiatry, 43,* 930–959.

Cotton, C.R., Peters, D.K., & Range, L.M. (1995). Psychometric properties of the suicidal behaviors questionnaire. *Death Studies, 19,* 391–397.

Cotton, C.R. & Range, L.M. (1996). Suicidality, hopelessness, and attitudes toward life and death in clinical and nonclinical adolescents. *Death Studies, 20,* 601–610.

Crocker, J. & Park, L.E. (2004). The costly pursuit of self esteem. *Psychological Bulletin, 130,* 392–414.

Crockett, L.J., Randall, B.A., Shen, Y., Russell, S.J., & Driscoll, A.K. (2005). Measurement equivalence of the center for epidemiological studies depression scale for Latin and Anglo adolescents: A national study. *Journal of Consulting and Clinical Psychology, 73,* 47–58.

Corder, B.F., Page, P.V., & Corder, R.F. (1974). Parental history, family communication and interaction patterns in adolescent suicide. *Family Therapy, 1,* 285–290.

Crosby, A.E., Cheltenham, M.P., & Sacks, J.J. (1999). Incidence of suicidal ideation and behavior in the United States, 1994. *Suicide and Life Threatening Behavior, 29,* 131–140.

Davidson, L.E. (1989). Suicide clusters and youth. In C.R. Pfeffer (Ed.), *Suicide among youth: Perspectives on risk and prevention* (pp. 83–89). Washington, DC: American Psychiatric Press.

Deci, E.L. & Ryan, R.M. (2000). The "what" and "why" of goal pursuits: Human needs and the self-determination of behavior. *Psychological Inquiry, 11,* 227–268.

Delise, J.R. (1986). Death with honors: Suicide among gifted adolescents. *Journal of Counseling and Development, 64,* 558–560.

Denton, W.H., Walsh, S.R., & Daniel, S.S. (2002). Evidence based practice in family therapy: Adolescent depression as an example. *Journal of Marriage and Family Therapy, 28,* 39–45.

DeRisi, W.J. & Butz, G. (1975). *Writing behavioral contracts.* Champaign, IL: Research Press.

de Shazer, S. (1985). *Keys to solutions in brief therapy.* New York: Norton.

de Shazer, S. (1988). *Clues: Investigating solutions in brief therapy.* New York: Norton.

de Wilde, E.J., Kienhorst, I.C., Diokstra, R.F., & Wolters, W.H. (1993). The specificity of psychological characteristics of adolescent suicide attempts. *Journal of American Academy of Child and Adolescent Psychiatry, 32,* 51–59.

Dorn, F.J. (1983). Assessing primary representational systems (PRS) preference for neurolinguistic programming (NLP) using three methods. *Counselor Education and Supervision, 23,* 149–156.

Dowling, F. (2005). The child and adolescent services program of the world trade center healing services, St. Vincent Catholic Medical Centers, New York. *Psychiatric Services, 56,* 1309–1312.

Duberstein, P.R. & Conwell, Y. (1997). Personality disorders and completed suicide: A methodological and conceptual review. *Clinical Psychology, 4,* 359–376.

Duncan, B.L., Hubble, M.A., & Miller, S.D. (1997). *Psychotherapy with "impossible" cases.* New York: Norton.

Duncan, B.L. & Parks, M.B. (1988). Integrating individual and systems approaches: Strategic-behavioral therapy. *Journal of Marriage and Family Therapy, 14,* 151–161.

Durkheim, E. (1951). Suicide: *A study in sociology.* (J.A. Spaulding & G. Simpson, Trans.). Glencoe, IL: Free Press.

Eisenberg, N. & Morris, A. (2004). Moral cognitions and prosocial *responding* in adolescence. In R. Learner & L. Steinberg (Eds.). *Handbook of adolescent psychology* (pp. 155–180). New Jersey: John Wiley & Sons.

Ellis, A. (1962). *Reason and emotion in psychotherapy.* New York: Lyle Stuart.

Erikson, E.H. (1968). *Identity, youth, and crisis.* New York: W.W. Norton & Co.

Eugenides, J. (1993). *The virgin suicides.* New York: Warner Books.

Festinger, L. (1957). *A theory of cognitive dissonance.* Evanston, IL: Row, Peterson.

Fischer, E.P., Comstock, G.W., Monk, M.A., & Sencer, D.J. (1993). Characteristics of completed suicides: Implication of differences among methods. *Suicide and Life Threatening Behavior, 23,* 91–100.

Fitts, W.H. (1965). *Tennessee self-concept scale.* Nashville, TN: Counselor Recording and Tests.

Flisher, A.J. (1999). Mood disorder in suicidal children and adolescents: Recent developments. *Journal of Child Psychology and Psychiatry and Allied Disciplines, 40,* 315–324.

Forehand, R., Jones, D.H., Brody, G.H., & Armistead, L. (2002). African American children's adjustment: The roles of maternal and teacher depressive symptoms. *Journal of Marriage and Family, 64,* 1012–1023.

Forrest, S. (1988). Suicide and the rural adolescent. *Adolescence, 90,* 341–347.

Freud, S. (1955). *The standard edition of the complete works of Sigmund Freud.* London: The Hogarth press.

Gallup, G. (1991). *The Gallup survey on teenage suicide.* Princeton, NJ: The George H. Gallup International Institute.

Garland, A.F. & Zigler, E. (1993). Adolescent suicide prevention. *American Psychologist, 48,* 169–182.

Gelman, D. & Gangelhoff, B.K. (1983, August 15). Teenage suicide in the sun belt. *Newsweek, 102,* pp. 71–72, 74.

Geller, B. & Luby, J. (1997). Child and adolescent bipolar disorder: A review of the past 10 years. *Journal of the American Academy of Child and Adolescent Psychiatry, 36,* 1168–1176.

Gould, M.S. (1990). Suicide clusters and media exposure. In Menthal & D.J. Kupfer (Eds.), *Suicide over the life cycle: Assessment and treatment of suicidal patients.* (pp. 517–532). Washington, DC: American Psychiatric Press.

Gould, M.S., Petric, K., Kleinman, M., & Wallenstein, S. (1994). Clustering of attempted suicide: New Zealand national data. *International Journal of Epidemiology, 23,* 1185–1189.

Graunke, B. & Roberts, T.K. (1985). Neurolinguistic programming: The impact of imagery tasks on sensory predicate usage. *Journal of Counseling Psychology, 32,* 525–530.

Guerney, B.G. Jr. (1969). *Psychotherapeutic agents: New roles for nonprofessionals, parents, and teachers.* New York: Holt, Rinehart, and Winston.

Guerney, B.G. Jr. (1977). Relationship enhancement: Skill-training programs for therapy, problem prevention, and enrichment. San Francisco, CA: Jossey-Bass.

Haley, J. (1963). *Strategies of psychotherapy.* New York: Grune & Stratton.

Haley, J. (1976). *Problem-solving therapy.* San Francisco, CA: Jossey-Bass.

Haley, J. (1984). *Ordeal therapy.* San Francisco, CA: Jossey-Bass.

Hamilton, E. (1940). *Mythology.* Boston, MA: Little, Brown & Company.

Hammer, C., Shih, J.H., & Brennan, P.A. (2004). Intergenerational transmission of depression: Test of an interpersonal stress model in a community sample. *Journal of Consulting and Clinical Psychology, 72,* 511–522.

Handy, B. (1994, April 18). Never mind. *Time: The Weekly Newsmagazine, 143,* 70–72.

Harrell, J.A. & Guerney, B.G. (1976). Training married couples in conflict negotiation skills. In D.H. Olson (Ed.), *Treating relationahips.* Mills, IA: Graphic Publishing.

Harris, G. (2004). Antidepressants seen as effective in the treatment of adolescents. *New York Times,* June 2, 2004.

Hawton, K. (1986). *Suicide and attempted suicide among children and adolescents.* Beverly Hills, CA: Sage.

Hawton, K., Kingsbury, S., Steinhardt, K., James, A., & Fagg, J. (1999). Repetition of deliberate self-harm by adolescents: The role of psychological factors. *Journal of Adolescents, 22,* 369–378.

Heller, J. (1961). *Catch-22.* New York: Random House.

Hendin, H., Brent, D.A., Cornelius, J.R., Coyne-Beasley, T., Greenberg, T., Gould, M., Hass, A. P., Harkavy-Friedman, J., Harrington, R., Henriques, G., Jacohs, D.G., Kalafat, J., Kerr, M.M., King, C.A., Ramsay, R., Shaffer, D., Spirito, A., Sudak, H., & Thompson, E.A (2005). Youth suicide. In D.C. Evans, E.B. Foa, R.E. Gar, H. Hendin, C.P. O'Brien, M.E.P. Seligman, & B.T. Walsh (Eds.). *Treating and preventing adolescent mental health disorders.* New York: Oxford.

Henry, C.S., Stephenson, A.C., Hanson, M.F., & Hargott, W. (1993). Adolescent suicide and families: An Ecological approach. *Adolescence, 28,* 291–308.

Hill, R. (1949). *Families under stress.* Westport, CT: Greenwood.

Hill, M.N. (1970). Suicidal behavior in adolescents and its relationship to the lack of parental empathy. *Dissertation Abstracts International, 31*(a–A), 472.

Holinger, P.C. & Offer, D. (1981). Perspectives on suicide in adolescents. In R.G. Simmons (Ed.), *Research in community mental health* (Vol. 2, pp. 139–157). Greenwich, CT: JAI Press.

Hogue, A., Dauber, S., Samuolis, J., & Liddle, H.A. (2006). Treatment techniques and outcomes in multidimensional family therapy for adolescent behavior problems. *Journal of Family Psychology, 20,* 535–543.

Hurrelmann, K. (Ed.). (1994). *International handbook of adolescents.* Westport, CT: Greenwood Press.

Irish, D.P., Lundquist, K.F., & Nelsen, V.J. (Eds.). (1993). *Ethnic variations in dying, death, and grief: Diversity in universality.* Washington, DC: Taylor & Francis.

Ivanoff, A. Jang, S.J., Smyth, N.J., & Linehan, M.M. (1994). Fewer reasons for staying alive when you are thinking of killing yourself: The brief reasons for living inventory. *Journal of Psychopathology and Behavioral Assessment, 16,* 1–13.

Jackson, D.D. & Weakland, J.H. (1971). Conjoint family therapy: Some considerations on theory, technique, and results. In J. Haley (Ed.), *Changing families: A family therapy reader.* New York: Grune & Stratton.

Jacobs, D.G., Brewer, M., & Klein-Benham, M. (1999). Suicide assessment: An overview and recommended protocol. In D.G. Jacobs (Ed.). *The Harvard Medical School guide to assessment and intervention* (pp. 3–39). San Francisco, CA: Jossey-Bass.

Johnson, W.B., Lall, R., Bongar, B., & Nordlund, M.D. (1999). The role of objective personality inventories in suicide risk assessment: An evaluation and proposal. *Suicide and Life Threatening Behavior, 29,* 165–185.

Jourad, S.M. (1964). *The transparent self.* Princeton, NJ: Van Nostrand.

Jurich, A.P. (1979a). The challenge of adolescence for youth and parents. *Family Perspectives, 13,* 93–99.

Jurich, A.P. (1979b). Parenting adolescents. *Family Perspective, 13,* 137–149.

Jurich, A.P. (1983a). Family therapy and suicidal crisis: An empirical analysis. In D.A. Bagarozzi, A.P. Jurich, & R.W. Jackson (Eds.), *Marital and family therapy: New perspectives in theory, research and practice* (pp. 191–205). New York: Human Sciences Press.

Jurich, A.P. (1983b). The Saigon of the family's mind: Family therapy with families of Vietnam Veterans. *Journal of Marriage and Family Therapy, 9,* 355–364.

Jurich, A.P. (1987). Adolescents and family dynamics. In H.G. Lingren, L. Kimmons, P. Lee, G. Rowe, L. Rottmann, L. Schuab, and L. Williams, (Eds.), *Family strengths 8–9: Pathways to wellbeing.* Lincoln, NE: University of Nebraska Press.

Jurich, A.P. (1990). The jujitsu approach. *Family Therapy Networker, 14*(4), 42–47, 64.

Jurich A.P. (2001). Suicidal ideation and behavior, *Clinical Update, 3*(6), Washington, DC: The American Association for Marriage and Family Therapy.

Jurich, A.P. (2002a). The journey to and from the brink of suicide. A paper presented at the National Council on Family Relations Annual Conference in Houston, TX on November 11, 2002.

Jurich, A.P. (2002b). You might get what you wish for. In D.A. Baptiste Jr. (Ed.), *Clinical epiphanies in marital and family therapy.* New York: Haworth.

Jurich, A.P., Bollman, S.R., & Schumm, W.R. (1984). Intrafamily concordance on aspects of quality of life in metropolitan and nonmetropolitan communities, *A North Central Regional Publication,* #295 and *Research Bulletin* #646, Manhattan, KS: Kansas Agricultural Experiment Station, Kansas State University.

Jurich, A.P. & Collins, O.P. (1996). Adolescents, suicide, and death. In C.A. Corr & D.E. Balk (Eds.), *Handbook of adolescent death and bereavement* (pp. 65–84). New York: Springer.

Jurich, A.P. & Johnson, L.N. (1999). The process of family therapy: Defining family as a collaborative enterprise. In B.H. Settles, S.K. Steinmetz, G.W. Peterson, & M.B. Sussman (Eds.), *Concepts and definitions of family for the 21st century.* New York: Haworth.

Jurich, A.P. & Jones, W.C. (1986). The worst of times: The effects of divorce upon adolescence. In G. Peterson & J. Leigh (Eds.), *The adolescent and his family.* Cincinnati: South-Western.

Jurich, A.P. & Jurich, J.A. (1974). Correlations among nonverbal expressions of anxiety. *Psychological Reports, 34,* 199–204.

Jurich, A.P. & Jurich, J.A. (1978). Factor analysis of expressions of anxiety. *Psychological Reports, 42,* 1203–1210.

Jurich, A.P. & Polson, C.P. (1984). Reasons for drug use: Comparison of drug users and abusers. *Psychological Reports, 55,* 371–378.

Jurich, A.P., Polson, C.J., Jurich, J.A., & Bates, R.A. (1985). Family factors in the lives of drug users and abusers. *Adolescence, 20,* 143–159.

Jurich, A.P. & Wearing, S. (2004). Predictors of adolescent suicidal ideations in junior high school students. (Unpublished Manuscript).

Kalafat, J. & Lester, D. (2000). Shame and suicide: A case study. *Death Studies, 24,* 157–162.

Kaufman, N.K., Rohde, P., Seeley, J.R., Clarke, G.N., & Stice, E. (2005). Potential mediators for cognitive-behavioral therapy for adolescents with comorbid major depression and conduct disorder. *Journal of Consulting and Clinical Psychology, 73,* 38–46.

Kehrer, C.A. & Lineham, M.M. (1996). Interpersonal and emotional problem solving skills and parasuicide among women with borderline personality disorder. *Journal of Personality Disorders, 10,* 153–162.

Kidd, S.A. (2004). "The walls were closing and we were trapped": A qualitative analysis of street youth suicide. *Youth & Society, 36,* 30–55.

Kirk, W.G. (1993). *Adolescent suicide: A school based approach to assessment and intervention.* Champaign, IL: Research Press.

Klein, D.N., Santiago, N.J., Vivian, D., Arnow, B.A., Blalock, J.A., Dunner, D.L., Kocsis, J.H., Markowitz, J. C., Manber, R., McCullough Jr., J.P., Rothbaum, B., Rush, A.J., Trivedi, M.H., Thase, M.E., Borian, F.E., Keitner, G.I., Miller, I.W., & Keller, M.B. (2004). Cognitive-Behavioral analysis system of psychotherapy as a maintenance treatment for chronic depression. *Journal of Consulting and Clinical Psychology, 72,* 681–688.

Klomek, A.B. & Mufson, L. (2006). Interpersonal psychotherapy for depressed adolescents. *Child and Adolescent Psychiatric Clinics of North America, 15,* 959–975.

Kochanek, K.D. & Hudson, B.L. (1994). Advance report of final mortality statistics, 1992. *Monthly Vital Statistics Report, 43*(6), (Suppl.).

Kohlberg, L. (1969). Stage and sequence: The cognitive developmental approach to socialization. In Goslin, D.A. (Ed.). *Handbook of socialization theory and research.* Chicago, IL: Rand McNally.

Kreitman, N. & Casey, P. (1988). Repetition of parasuicide: An epidemiological and clinical study. *British Journal of Psychiatry, 153,* 792–800.

Kullgren, G., Tengstroem, A., & Grann, M. (1998). Suicide among personality-disordered offenders: A follow-up study of 1943 male criminal offenders. *Social Psychiatry and Psychiatric Epidemiology, 33*(Suppl. 1), S102–S106.

Ladame, F. (1992). Suicide prevention in adolescence: An overview of current trends. *Journal of Adolescent Health, 13,* 406–408.

Lattanzi-Licht, M. (1996). Helping families with adolescents cope with loss. In C.A. Corr & D.E. Balk (Eds.), *Handbook of adolescent death and bereavement.* New York: Springer.

Leigh, G.K. (1986). Adolescent involvement in family systems. In G.K. Leigh & G.W. Peterson (Eds.). *Adolescents in families* (pp. 38–72). Cincinnati: South-Western.

Lester, D. (1996). On the relationship between fatal and non-fatal suicide behavior. *Homeostasis in Health and Disease, 37,* 122–128.

Lester, D. (1988). *The biochemical basis of suicide.* New York: Thomas.

Linehan, M. (1987). Dialectical behavioral therapy: A cognitive-behavioral approach to parasuicide. *Journal of Personality Disorders, 1,* 328–333.

Linehan, M., Armstrong, H., Suarez, A., Allmon, D., & Heard, H. (1991). Cognitive-behavioral treatment of chronically parasuicidal borderline patients. *Archives of General Psychiatry, 48,* 1060–1064.

Linehan, M., Goodstein, J., Neilsen, S., & Chiles, J. (1983). Reasons for staying alive when you are thinking of killing yourself: The reasons for living inventory. *Journal of Consulting and Clinical Psychology, 51,* 276–286.

Litt, F., Cuskey, W.R., & Rudd, S. (1983). Emergency room evaluation of the adolescent who attempts suicide: Compliance with follow up. *Journal of Adolescent Health Care, 4,* 106–108.

Madaness, C. (1981). *Strategic family therapy.* San Francisco, CA: Jossey-Bass.

Malouf, R.E. & Alexander, J.F. (1974). Family crisis intervention. In R.E. Hardy & J.G. Cull (Eds.), *Techniques and approaches in marital family counseling.* Springfield, Ill: Charles C. Thomas.

Manor, I., Vincent, M., & Tyano, S. (2004). The wish to die and the wish to commit suicide in the adolescent: Two different matters? *Adolescence, 39,* 279–293.

Mann, J.J., DeMeo, M.D., Keilp, J.G., & McBride, P.A. (1989). Biological correlates of suicidal behavior in youth. In C.R. Pfeffer (Ed.), *Suicide among youth: Perspectives on risk and prevention* (pp. 185–202). Washington, DC: American Psychiatric Press.

Marcia, J.E. (1980). Identity in adolescence. In J. Adelson (Ed.), *Handbook of adolescent psychology.* New York: John Wiley & Sons.

Marzuk, P.M., Tierney, M., Tardiff, K., Gross, E.M., Morgan, E.B., Hsu, M., & Mann, J.J. (1988). Increased risk of suicide in persons with AIDS. *Journal of the American Medical Association, 259,* 1333–1337.

Mattejat, F. (2005). Evidenzbasierte prinzipien und grundkomponenten familientherapeutischer interventionen bei psychischen storungen von kindern und jugendlichen/Evidence-based family therapy. Which family-based interventions are empirically supported? *Kindheit und Entwicklung*, 14, 3–11.

McCauly, B. (1998). *Small mercies*. Santa Fe: Sherman Asher Publishing.

McGovern, M.P., Fox, T.S., Xie, H., & Drake, R.E. (2004). A survey of clinical practices and readiness to adopt evidence-based practices: Dissemination research in an addiction treatment system. *Journal of Substance Abuse Treatment*, 26, 305–312.

McCubbin, H.I. & Patterson, J.M. (1982). Family adaptation to crisis. In McCubbin, H.I. (Ed.), *Family stress, coping, and social support* (pp. 26–47). Springfield, IL: Charles C Thomas.

McHolm, A., MacMillan, H., & Jamieson, E. (2003). The relationship between childhood physical abuse and suicidality among depressed women: Results from a community sample. *American Journal of Psychiatry, 160*, 933–938.

McKenry, P.C. & Price, S.J. (1994). Families coping with problems and change: A conceptual overview. In P.C. McKenry & S.J. Price (Eds.), *Families and change: Coping with stressful events* (pp. 1–18). Thousand Oaks, CA: Sage.

Meichenbaum, D.H. (1977). *Cognitive-behavior modification: An integrative approach*. New York: Plenum.

Minuchin, S. (1974). *Families and family therapy*. Cambridge, MA: Harvard University Press.

Menninger, K.A., Mayman, M., & Pruyser, P. (1963). *The vital balance: The life process in mental health and illness*. New York: Viking.

Miller, K.E., King, C.A., Shain, B.N., & Naylor, M.W. (1992). Suicidal adolescents' perceptions of their family environment. *Suicide and Life Threatening Behavior, 22*, 226–239.

Minuchin, S. & Barcai, A. (1972). Therapeutically induced family crisis. In C.J. Sager & H.S. Kaplan (Eds.). *Progress in group and family therapy*. New York: Brunner/Mazel.

Morano, C.D., Cisler, R.A., & Lemerond, J. (1993). Risk factors for adolescent suicidal behavior: Loss, insufficient family support, and hopelessness. *Adolescence, 28,* 851–865.

Mundy, C. (1994). The lost boy. *Rolling Stone*, pp. 51–53.

Murry, V.M. & Bell-Scott, P. (1994). Dealing with adolescent children. In P.C. McKenry & S.J. Prince (Eds.), *Families and change: Coping with stressful events* (pp. 88–110). Thousand Oaks, CA: Sage.

Murray, H.A. (1943). *Thematic perception test manual*. Cambridge, MA: Harvard University Press.

National Institute of Mental Health (2001). *Bipolar disorder*. NIH Publication No. 02-3679. Washington, DC: U.S. Government Printing Office.

National Institute of Mental Health (2004). Antidepressant medications for children: Information for parents and caregivers. A statement issued on April 23, 2004 and reprinted on the NIMH website (www.nih.gov/press/stmtantidepmeds.cfm).

Neuringer, C. (1974). Attitudes toward self in suicidal individuals. *Life Threatening Behavior, 41,* 96–106.

O'Connor, R.C. & Sheehy, N.P. (2001). Suicidal behavior. *Psychologist, 14,* 20–24.

Olson, D.H., Sprenkle, D.H., & Russel, C.S. (1979). Circumplex model of marital and family systems: 1. Cohesion and adaptability dimensions, family types, and clinical applications. *Family Process, 18,* 3–28.

Orbach, I. (1988). *Children who don't want to live.* San Francisco, CA: Jossey-Bass.

Orbach, I., Feshbach, S., Carlson, G., & Ellenberg, L. (1984). Attitudes toward life and death in suicidal, normal, and chronically ill children: An extended replication. *Journal of Consulting and Clinical Psychology, 52,* 1020–1027.

Orbach, I., Feshbach, S., Carlson, G., Glaubman, H., & Gross, Y. (1983). Attraction and repulsion by life and death in suicidal and normal children. *Journal of Consulting and Clinical Psychology, 51,* 661–670.

Paykel, E.S., Prusoff, B.A., & Meyers, J.K. (1975). Suicide attempts and recent life events: A control and comparison. *Archives of General Psychiatry, 32,* 327–333.

Peck, M. (1982). Youth suicide. *Death and Education, 6,* 29–47.

Patterson, G.R. (1971). *Families: Application of social learning theory to family life.* Champaign, IL: Research Press.

Pfeffer, C.R. (1986). *The suicidal child.* New York: Guilford.

Phillips, D.P., Carstensen, L.L., & Paight, D.J. (1989). Effects of mass media news stories on suicide, with new evidence on the role of story content. In C.R. Pfeffer (Ed.), *Suicide among youth: Perspectives on risk and prevention* (pp. 101–116). Washington, DC: American Psychiatric Press.

Piaget, J. (1954). *The construction of reality in the child.* New York: Basic Books.

Powers, P.S. & Santana, C.A. (2002). Childhood and adolescent anorexia nervosa. *Child and Adolescent Psychiatric Clinics of North America, 11,* 219–235.

Puryear, R.A. (1979). *Helping people in crisis.* San Francisco, CA: Jossey-Bass.

Reekers, G.A. & Jurich, A.P. (1983). Development of problems of puberty and sex roles in adolescence. In C.E. Walker & M.C. Roberts (Eds.), *Handbook of clinical child psychology.* New York: John Wiley and Sons.

Reich, J.H., Yates, W., & Nduagbe, M. (1989). Prevalence of DSM III personality disorders in the community. *Social Psychiatry and Psychiatric Epidemiology, 24,* 12–16.

Richman, J. (1979). Family therapy of attempted suicide, *Family Process, 18,* 131–142.

Rogers, C.R. (1951). *Client-centered therapy: Its current practice, implications and theory.* Boston, MA: Houghton Mifflin.

Rogers, C.R. (1957). The necessary and sufficient conditions of therapeutic personality change. *Journal of Consulting Psychology, 21,* 95–103.

Roy, A. (1986). Genetic factors in suicide. *Psychopharmacology Bulletin, 22,* 666–668.

Rubenstein, J.L., Heeren, T., Housman, D., Rubin, C., & Stechler, G. (1989). Suicidal behavior in "normal" adolescents: Risk and protective factors. *American Journal of Orthopsychiatry, 59,* 59–71.

Rutter, P.A. & Behrendt, A.E. (2004). Adolescent suicide risk: Four psychosocial factors. *Adolescence, 39,* 295–302.

Ryan, N.D., Puig-Antich, J., Rabinovitch, H., Ambrosini, P., Robinson, D., Nelson, B., & Novacenko, H. (1988). Growth hormone response to desmethylimipramine in depressed and suicidal adolescents. *Journal of Affective Disorders, 15,* 323–337.

Ryland, D.H. & Kruesi, M.J. (1992). Suicide among adolescents. *International Review of Psychiatry, 4,* 185–195.

Sands, R.G. & Dixon, S.L. (1986). Adolescent crisis and suicidal behavior: Dynamics and treatment. *Child and Adolescent Social Work, 3,* 109–122.

Selekman, M.D. (2002). *Living on the razor's edge.* New York: Norton.

Selekman, M.D. (2005). *Pathways to change: Brief therapy with different adolescents* (2nd ed.). New York: Guilford.

Selvini, M. (Ed.)(1988). *The work of Mara Selvini Palazzoli.* Northvale, NJ: Jason Aronson.

Selvini Palazzoli, M., Boscolo, L., Cecchin, G., & Prata, G. (1978). *Paradox and counter paradox.* New York: Jason Aronson.

Sheehy, G. (1974). *Passages.* New York: Dutton.

Shaffer, D. (1988). The epidemiology of teen suicide: An examination of risk factors. *Journal of Clinical Psychiatry, 49,* 36–41.

Shafii, M., Carrigan, S., Whittinghill, J.R., & Derrick, A. (1985). Psychological autopsy of completed suicide in children and adolescents. *American Journal of Psychiatry, 142,* 1061–1064.

Shaughnessy, M.F. & Nystul, M.S. (1985). Preventing the greatest loss- suicide. *Creative Child and Adult Quarterly, 10,* 164–169.

Shreve, B.W. & Kunkel, M.A. (1991). Self-psychology, shame, and adolescent suicide: Theoretical and practical considerations. *Journal of Counseling and Development, 89,* 305–311.

Slaby, A.E. & McGuire, P.L. (1989). Residential management off suicidal adolescents. *Residential Treatment for Children and Youth, 7,* 23–43.

Smith, K. & Crawford, S. (1986). Suicidal behavior among "normal" high school students. *Suicide and Life Threatening Behavior, 16,* 313–325.

Smith, M.B. (1969). *Social psychology and human values.* Chicago, IL: Aldine.

Sneidman, E.S. (1998). The suicidal mind. Oxford: Oxford University Press.

Sneidman, E.S. (Ed.) (1999). *Comprehending suicide: Landmarks in 20th century suicidology*. Washington, DC: American Psychological Association.

Strauss, N. (1994, June 2). The downward spiral. *Rolling Stone*, pp. 35–43.

Stuart, R.B. & Lott, L.A. (1972). Behavioral contracting with delinquents: A cautionary note. *Journal of Behavior Therapy and Experimental Psychiatry, 3*, 161–169.

Triolo, S.J., McKenry, P.C., Tishler, C.L., & Blyth, D.A. (1984). Social and psychological discriminants of adolescent suicide: Age and sex differences. *Journal of Early Adolescence, 4*, 239–251.

Twain, M. (1876). *The adventures of Tom Sawyer*. Hartford: American Publishing.

Videon, T.M. (2002). The effects of parent-adolescent relationships and parental separation on adolescent well-being. *Journal of Marriage and Family, 64*, 489–503.

Waizenhofer, R.N., Buchanan, C.M., & Jackson-Newman, J. (2004). Mothers' and fathers' knowledge of adolescents' daily activities: Its sources and its links with adolescent adjustment. *Journal of Family Psychology, 2*, 348–360.

Watzlawick, P.A., Beavin, J.H., & Jackson, D.D. (1967). *Pragmatics of human communication*. New York: Norton.

Weiner, M. & Mehrabian, A. (1968). *Language within language: Immediacy, a channel in verbal communication*. New York: Appleton-Century-Crofts.

Wekstein, L. (1979). *Handbook of suicidology: Principles, problems, and practice*. New York: Brunner/Mazel.

Wenz, F.V. (1979). Self-injury behavior, economic status, and family anomie syndrome among adolescents. *Adolescence, 14*, 387–398.

Westefeld, J.S., Range, L.M., Rogers, J.R., Maples, M.R., Bromley, J.L., & Alcorn, J. (2000). Suicide: An overview. *The Counseling Psychologist, 28*, 445–510.

Whitaker, C.A. & Bumberry, W.M. (1988). *Dancing with the family: A symbolis experemental* approach. New York: Bruner/Mazel.

White, M. & Epston, D. (1990). *Narrative means to a therapeutic end*. New York: Norton.

Wilburn, V.R. & Smith, D.E. (2005). Stress, self-esteem, and suicidal ideation in late adolescents. *Adolescence, 40*, 33–45.

Wodarski, J.S. & Harris, P. (1987). Adolescent suicide: A review of influences and the means for prevention. *Social Work, 32*, 477–484.

Wolpe, J. (1973). *The practice of behavioral therapy* (2nd ed.). New York: Pergamon Press.

Young, T.J. (1985). The clinical manifestation of alienation. *High School Journal, 69*, 55–60.

INDEX